# Class against class

## The miners' strike 1984-5

Edited by Sean Matgamna

# Class against class
# The miners' strike 1984-5

Edited by Sean Matgamna

Second edition
Published December 2015 by Phoenix Press
20E Tower Workshops
Riley Road
London SE1 3DG

www.workersliberty.org
awl@workersliberty.org

Printed by Imprint Digital, Exeter EX5 5HY

"The April sun was now well up in the sky, shedding its glorious warming rays on the teeming earth. Life was springing from her fertile womb, buds were bursting into leaf and the fields were quickening with fresh green grass. Everywhere the seeds were swelling and lengthening, cracking open the plain in their upward thrust for warmth and light. The sap was rising in abundance with whispering voices, the germs of life were opening with a kiss.

"On and on, ever more insistently, his comrades were tapping, tapping, as though they too were rising through the ground. On this youthful morning, in the fiery rays of the sun, the whole country was alive with this sound. Men were springing up, a black avenging host was slowly germinating in the furrows, thrusting upwards for the harvests of future ages. And very soon their germination would crack the earth asunder."

The last paragraphs of Emile Zola's great novel *Germinal,* describing the defeat of a miners' strike in northern France in the 1860s.

This book is a reprint of a pamphlet, *Magnificent Miners*, published in March 1985, to which a few pieces have been added.

Some of the assessments and judgements in it, for example, on the Labour Party and on nuclear power, are dated, but the reader will easily see what is dated and what is not. Our intention on this 30th anniversary is to make available to new working-class generations the story of the greatest class struggle in Britain for many decades.

The 1985 pamphlet did not include individual by-lines on the various sections. The named authors were: John Bloxam, Judith Bonner, Clive Bradley, Robert Fine, Jean Lane, Sean Matgamna (John O'Mahony), John McIlroy, Martin Thomas, and Paul Whetton. To this edition we have added a review by the late Rob Dawber.

The pamphlet was originally published as a special double issue of the weekly paper *Socialist Organiser*.

# Contents

**Issues and experiences**



**Lessons of the strike**



**Afterwords**

# The year of the great fightback

Between March 1984 and March 1985, British miners fought one of the great epics of working-class history. In scope, intensity and duration their strike is unique in the history of the British labour movement.

At issue in that strike was the fate of the "social democratic" welfare-state "compromise" between the ruling class and the working class that had held since the Second World War. When the Tories launched their offensive, the miners responded with a head-on challenge to Thatcher and Thatcherism. Implicitly, they challenged capitalism itself.

The miners' rallying cry, "no economic pit closures", was the demand for a radically different society. It implied a society whose mainspring is not profit but need. It implied socialism.

The miners fought for the whole working class; the tragedy was that the working class movement did not rally to ensure the victory of the embattled miners.

For decades the labour movement had been strong enough to inhibit what the ruling class could do, but politically too weak to overthrow capitalism. Now the Tories were going all out to break the power of the working-class movement.

The miners fought in very unfavourable conditions, under flawed leaders. Laws forbidding solidarity strikes by workers in one industry for workers in another industry, or in a different firm, were already in place. At the end of 1983, in a fierce dispute during which the union's funds were seized, those laws had been used to break the strength of the print union, the National Graphical Association.

There was mass unemployment. The industrial slump that had coincided with the Tories' assumption of power in May 1979 had undermined the industrial militancy of the 1970s. There had been no all-out resistance to the class-war Tory onslaught. The trade unions had suffered a number of defeats, mainly defeats with little battle.

The Labour local government left had taken power in a number of cities, including London, at the beginning of the 1980s, but it had failed to be the rallying centre of resistance to the Tories which its leaders had loudly promised it would be.

The miners' strike came very late in the Thatcherite day. The miners faced a government that was militant, class-war-making, relentless, intent on using the state to break the working class and, immediately, the National Union of Mineworkers. In the general election of June 1983, the Tories had won a triumphant victory over the Labour Party.

The miners were divided: striking miners had to appeal for solidarity from other workers while they were denied solidarity by strike-breaking "working miners", mainly in Nottinghamshire. The "good reason" the scab miners gave for scabbing was that there had not been a proper NUM strike ballot. The "real reason" was that they thought that their jobs were secure in the modernised, high-productivity Notts coalfield.

The ruling class had spent years planning and preparing this class war. They were united behind the Tory government. They were using the state power against the miners with little restraint or inhibition.

That government waged a coordinated and long-planned class war on the three decisive fronts of the struggle: in industry, in the politics that was so central an aspect of the strike, and in the crucial propaganda war against the miners.

When NUM leader Arthur Scargill told the truth about the Tories' intention to close many coal mines, the Tories denied it, and their press echoed and reinforced their lies.

The striking miners and their families were the victims of police violence, but the press, the Tory politicians, and — too often — Labour politicians, succeeded in making miners' violence on picket lines a major propaganda weapon against the miners.

Press and television echoed and augmented denunciations of miners' picket-line violence made by a government that was itself using massive and sometimes extra-legal violence against miners, and, in the "occupied" villages, against their families.

Police "occupied" many pit villages. Like an invading army in a foreign country, they coerced, regimented and forcibly controlled the movements of the people who lived there.

They stopped striking miners moving freely from one area to another. They used as much force as they needed to physically beat down the picketing miners. Crying for "law and order", the government and its police ignored and broke the law with impunity. The "order" they imposed was based on brute police force.

Thatcher reorganised the police forces to fight the civil war — low-level, limited, civil war, but civil war nonetheless — that the Tory government knew itself to be fighting. Appealing to British patriotism, she infamously diabolised the miners as "the enemy within". The striking miners, Thatcher's "enemy within", saw Thatcher and the Tories as the enemy in power, using the state as a bludgeon against the working class.

Miners and police fought pitched battles, as at Orgreave in June 1984. A number of miners died on picket lines. Many were injured in clashes with the body-armoured and shield-and-baton-wielding police.

One of the often repeated tragedies of the strike was that we were unable to muster and concentrate sufficient force to do to the police what they re-

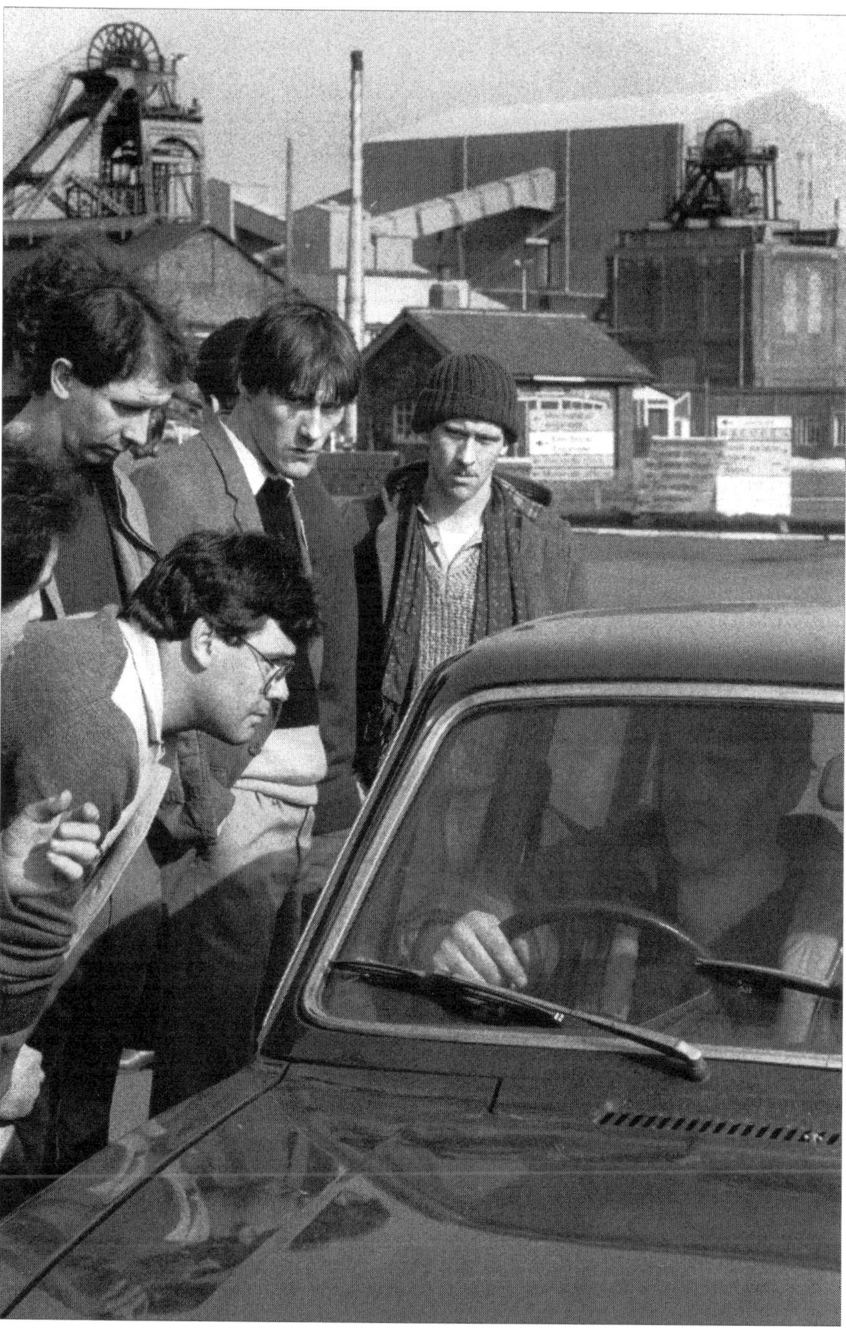

Flying pickets persuading other miners to come out on strike, first day, Thurcroft, Yorkshire.
John Harris/reportdigital.co.uk

peatedly did to us — overwhelm by force.

Seven years after the end of the miners' strike the courts ruled that the police had acted illegally in the Battle of Orgreave. By then there had been many pit closures; the mining communities had been gutted along with the industry. There are no replays in the class struggle!

To go through the pages of *Socialist Organiser, Socialist Worker* and *Militant* for the year of the miners' strike is to go in a time machine to a different world, and to relive in concentrated form the history of the labour movement.

In and around the miners' strike sprang to life a tremendous renaissance of bedrock labour movement culture, attitudes, enlightenment, political and social education. The idea of class allegiance and class solidarity was sharpened for those who already had it, or a half-petrified residue of it; and it shone like a searchlight into the activities, the purposes, the understanding, and the lives of new thousands and tens of thousands.

The mining communities were shaken to their foundations — and, indeed, their foundations, the mining industry, were being torn up. Thousands of miners threw themselves into mass picketing, which routinely included fighting the police.

Whole layers of the working class felt themselves profoundly alienated from the way the British economy and British politics were organised. The women of the mining communities were roused to action and self-assertion as never before. Many hundreds of them joined picket lines and moved around the country, alerting the working class to what was happening to the miners, and what was in store for other workers if the miners lost.

The lives of thousands of "miners' wives" were transformed, opened out, greatly enlarged in the course of a year of heroic endeavour. So were the lives of many miners.

Around the embattled miners, many groups and individuals rallied and clustered, mobilised and threw what they could into the struggle. Such endeavours as "Lesbians and Gays Support the Miners" helped broaden the outlook of striking miners and miners' wives.

The political contradictions and unevenness of the labour movement were also raised to a new pitch of urgency in the course of the strike. Political Stalinism was a powerful force during the strike. Arthur Scargill was in politics a Stalinist, though of a somewhat untypical sort.

The Stalinist dictators of Poland seized the commercial opening offered by the strike to triple their exports of coal to Britain, thus helping Thatcher break the strike. Scargill criticised them. But far too inhibitedly; and after the strike, in September 1985, he helped set up an International Miners' Organisation whose main component would be the police-state fake "unions", the fascist-labour-front-style stooge "unions", of the Stalinist states, including Poland. (The IMO still exists, renamed IEMO, as a shadowy group, with Scargill, aged 76, still president.)

The renaissance of working-class culture; the sense of reliving in concentrated form the history of the labour movement and its battles against unequal odds; the experience of being ranged against the whole phalanx of the "Establishment" while being misrepresented and demonised by most of the organs of official society; the upsurge of working-class self-realisation and class awareness; the rise of sharp and clear working-class perception of the fundamental nature of the class society in which workers live and work (so long as by working they produced profits considered big enough) — all that was a tremendously positive experience, although an experience paid for by the suffering of miners and their families.

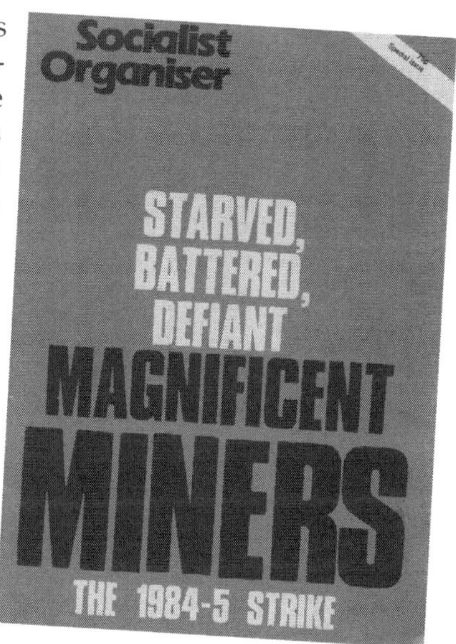

**This book is a reprint of this pamphlet published in March 1985.**

In the history of the British labour movement that re-living and recapitulation turned out to be not a rebirth but an Indian summer. The miners were defeated. After the defeat the working-class movement would experience decades of destruction and decline.

Yet there was nothing impossible about a miners' victory in the strike; nothing that made it pointless bravado. It was a battle against the odds, against great odds; but the heroic mineworkers who took on Thatcher and her semi-militarised police storm-troopers knew from the start that that was what it would be.

With broader active working-class support the miners could have defeated the government, as they had defeated Tory governments in 1972 and 1974.

In its first few years, the Tory government of 1979-97 had been unpopular and fragile. The miners' leaders, knowing that Thatcher planned to run down the industry and break their union, tried to hasten a decisive conflict; Thatcher and the Tories were still unready, their plans to take on the miners still incomplete. In 1981 they conceded on the immediate issues and the battle was postponed. Thus the strike happened only after the Tories had won their first victories against other groups of workers (steelworkers in particular), and had been re-elected in 1983 on the back of the Falklands War.

Even in 1984, so we now know from cabinet papers of the time, the Tories were often nervous. At times they feared defeat. During the year of the miners' strike, dockers struck twice; the pit deputies [overseers], who could have closed down every pit in the country, came very close to striking alongside the miners; a national rail strike, which would have halted the substantial movement of scab coal to power stations, was avoided by the Tories conceding their wage demands; the Liverpool labour movement came close to confronting the government over the cuts, but (under the leadership of Militant, forerunner of the Socialist Party and Socialist Appeal) chose to make a rotten short-term deal instead.

At a number of points, the temporary near-conjunction of other working-class mobilisations threatened to spread the miners' fire to other layers of the working class, and offered the likelihood of victory. That did not happen. The miners were left to a long agony of state-organised grinding-down, and, finally, after a year, defeated. Other workers, too, would pay the price of that defeat for decades in the future.

The least that can be said for the miners, and for Arthur Scargill, is that they saved the honour of the old labour movement. They ensured that when it went down to radical defeat, it did so with a fight — and what a fight!

Rosa Luxemburg long ago pointed out that it is in the logic of working-class life that most of the great class confrontations before the socialist revolution itself — as distinct from the piecemeal, important though frail, victories won in times of relative capitalist quiet — end in defeat. The socialist revolution, she wrote, "is the only form of 'war' — and this is another peculiar law of history — in which the ultimate victory can be prepared only by a series of 'defeats'.

> "What does the entire history of socialism and of all modern revolutions show us? The first spark of class struggle in Europe, the revolt of the silk weavers in Lyon in 1831, ended with a heavy defeat; the Chartist movement in Britain ended in defeat; the uprising of the Parisian proletariat in the June days of 1848 ended with a crushing defeat; and the Paris commune ended with a terrible defeat. The whole road of socialism — so far as revolutionary struggles are concerned — is paved with nothing but thunderous defeats. Yet, at the same time, history marches inexorably, step by step, toward final victory!
>
> "Where would we be today without those 'defeats,' from which we draw historical experience, understanding, power and idealism? We stand on the foundation of those very defeats, because each one contributes to our strength and understanding."

Neo-liberalism is now the typical regime in a world where capitalism has spread everywhere; where almost every state is integrated into world markets; where global production chains and global competition are much more developed; where global finance circulates faster and more; and where capitalist states orient to making their national terrains good perches for mobile global capital, rather than to creating integrated national industrial complexes.

That regime was only fumbling into life in 1984-5. But from that point profit rates picked up and capital become more confident. US capitalism gathered new momentum after the "Volcker shock". In 1984 China opened up 14 coastal cities to foreign investment, a major step in the huge conversion of China to world market capitalism in the last 30 years. In 1989-91, the old Stalinist regimes in Eastern Europe and the USSR, and their imitators elsewhere, except Cuba and North Korea, collapsed, and those countries slid into world-market capitalism.

In 1985, though we didn't know it then, a dramatic era of capitalist expansion and more-rapid-than-ever industrial restructuring was just starting. So far, that global restructuring has largely been nimble enough to keep labour movements in defensive, catch-up mode; and to enable capital to enlarge inequality, to privatise, to contract out, and to emaciate welfare, across the world.

Those who fought and led the miners' strike will yet be recognised in working-class history as the labour movement champions and heroes they were and remain. Those who led that strike, the glaring political faults of Arthur Scargill — a good man fallen among Stalinists — and the NUM leaders notwithstanding, will be recognised as the farsighted and principled labour movement leaders they surely were. The strike will be the greatest of the sources from which the British working class draws "historical experience, understanding, power and idealism".

*John Bloxam, Sean Matgamna, Martin Thomas*
*March 2014*

# Chronicle of the great confrontation

**1 March 1984.** The National Coal Board (NCB) announces the closure of Cortonwood Colliery in Yorkshire and a cutback of 4 million tonnes of coal in the forthcoming year, with a loss of 20,000 jobs. South Yorkshire miners go on unofficial strike.

**6 March.** Scottish and Yorkshire Areas of the NUM call official strike action. Polmaise pit in Scotland has been out against closure for three weeks.

**8 March.** The NUM executive endorses Scottish and Yorkshire action and endorses in advance the decision any other area might take for strike action.

**9 March.** Durham and Kent Areas call strikes. South Wales Area delegate conference recommends strike but over the weekend 10-11 March pits in the area decide by two to one not to strike.

Notts delegate conference declines to take action before area ballot. Northumberland and Leicestershire leaderships vote against a strike.

**12 March.** Half of the miners on strike nationally. Flying pickets go into action to make it a national strike and enforce the area strike decisions. South Wales, despite vote, comes out immediately.

**14 March**. The NCB admits that 132 out of 174 pits have been shut.

The National Reporting Centre (police co-ordinating office based at Scotland Yard) at the request of the Nottingham Police drafts 8,000 police officers into the county from half of the 43 forces in Britain.

Court rules that Yorkshire NUM must withdraw flying pickets.

**15 March.** David Jones, miner aged 23, is killed whilst picketing in Ollerton, Notts. Notts leaders call an area strike (but the strike is called off after an area vote and delegate conference).

**15-16 March.** Ballots held in many areas. Northumberland votes for strike. Cumberland, Midlands, South Derbyshire, North Derbyshire, Lancashire, Notts and North Wales vote not to strike.

**18 March.** Kent miners stopped by police and turned back at the Dartford Tunnel. Police are barracked in army camps in Nottinghamshire.

**19 March.** Yorkshire NUM found in contempt of court (the case is postponed indefinitely). NUM members picket 27 Notts pits and peacefully persuade their colleagues to join the strike action. Police decide to blockade the county of Nottinghamshire.

**21 March 1984.** Power unions (including the GMB) advise their members to cross picket lines. Steelworkers will also cross picket lines.

**Third week in March.** Women in Barnsley, having formed Women Against Pit Closures, hold first activity, a picket of the NCB local offices. Other women's groups spring up. Initially, they are involved in organising food collections and distribution and fund raising. Soon they are organising pickets, rallies, demonstrations and public speaking.

**26 March.** Lancashire NUM joins the strike. The strike support has reached a steady level which will increase only slightly (after the NUM conference on 19 April).

**28 March.** Yorkshire miners block a section of the Ml motorway.

**29 March.** Transport unions impose a ban on the movement of coal and this is partially successfully. Nurses join the picket lines in South Wales.

By late March it was clear that this miners' strike would be a long and grim affair.

**3-9 April.** Food kitchens are opened in every coalfield.

**12 April.** NUM Executive faces down right-wing calls for a national ballot and right wing Notts area president Ray Chadburn emerges from the meeting to tell his members: "get off your knees and support the strike."

**14 April.** 7,000 miners and their supporters marched in Nottingham to demand "Police out of the coalfields."

**16 April.** Notts rank and file strike committee formed.

**16 April.** Notts railworkers begin to stop coal trains.

**19 April.** NUM Special Conference ratifies strike action in the areas and calls on all miners to rally to the defence of their industry.

**20 April.** Notts and Midlands NUM decide to join strike. However, a majority of Notts miners continue to scab.

**25 April.** The Labour Party national executive votes to support the strike and to ask every Party member to donate 50p a week.

**26 April.** The High Court says "No" to NUM policy on investment of pension funds in Britain.

**30 April.** 150-strong women's picket at Thoresby colliery, Notts. They broke through the police lines twice.

**End of April.** Support committees begin to be set up.

**Beginning of May.** Series of mass pickets in Notts coalfield. On 2 May police estimate 10,000 at Haworth and on 3 May almost as many at Cotgrave.

**2 May.** Central Electricity Generating Board figures show more oil being used to counterbalance coal shortage.

**4 May.** West Thurrock, Didcot and Aberthaw power stations shut down.

From May to August the strike was at its peak. About 80% of miners were out. There was some drift back, especially in those areas where the strike was weaker: Notts and Staffordshire.

**9 May.** Scottish TUC day of action.

**12 May.** Barnsley women's demonstration.

**14 May.** 40,000 march in Mansfield. The strike is now at its peak.

**17 May.** Leon Brittan admits in Parliament that plain clothes police are operating in the Notts coalfield.

**23 May.** National Coal Board walks out of talks with NUM and demands pledge of union co-operation in the closing of "uneconomic pits".

**25 May.** Full-scale picketing at the Orgreave coke works begins. Nottinghamshire scab miners obtain a court order which allows them to continue working, but which declares that those on strike were striking officially.

**29 May-18 June.** Thousands of pickets and police fight battles outside Orgreave coking plant, near Sheffield. Coke runs from Orgreave were suspended on 18 June.

**30 May.** Major confrontations at Orgreave. 82 arrests including Arthur Scargill, 62 injured.

**31 May.** 3,200 police in riot gear at Orgreave confront unarmed strikers.

**7 June.** Transport unions agree not only to boycott coal and coke, but also to block substitute oil movements. By 13 July only 10 coal trains are running daily in Britain out of a normal 356. House of Commons debate on the miners' strike. Thousands march to lobby Parliament. 100 arrests.

**15 June.** Joe Green, miner, is crushed to death on picket duty at Ferry Bridge.

**18 June.** The battle of Orgreave. Police run amok. 93 arrests and many injuries.

**25 June.** Railworkers stop iron ore supplies to Llanwern steel works in South Wales, on 28 June to Ravenscraig.

**1 July.** Leon Brittan endorses the use of Criminal Law rather than Civil Law against the miners.

**5 July.** National Coal Board and NUM talks.

**6 July.** Management visits NUM members at home encouraging them back to work.

**8 July.** High Court declares NUM Annual Conference unlawful.
First national dock strike called against the movement of coal.

**13 July.** Government withholds tax refunds to striking miners.

**19 July.** NUM/NCB talks last three days. Despite NUM willingness to negotiate, the NCB are ordered to stand firm by the government. Some of the NCB officials wanted to settle. They were later sacked or resigned. First dock strike collapses.

**31 July.** South Wales NUM fined £50,000 and the High Court seizes South Wales NUM funds. The union had defied an injunction against picketing granted to two haulage firms. The Tories are beginning to up the stakes.

**Beginning August.** After South Wales NUM is fined £50,000 the NUM calls on the TUC and the rest of the trade union movement for solidarity action. Nothing happens. The movement begins to go into retreat, although the miners would remain, fundamentally, solid until November, and other possibilities for widening the front against the Tories would emerge.

**8 August.** 50p a week trade union levy in support of NUM introduced. MacGregor writes to all striking workers urging a return to work.

**16 August.** South Wales NUM found in contempt of court for refusing to pay fine. £770,000 of their funds seized.

**24 August-18 September.** Second docks strike; it begins after unloading of coal at Hunterstone.

**Late August.** National Working Miners' Committee set up by David Hart. A few scabs appear in South Yorkshire. Mass picketing resumes to stop scabbing. Police occupy the pit villages to "protect" working miners and barricade pits so that a few men can go in.

**3 September.** TUC pledges support for the NUM

**12 September.** TUC attempts to organise talks between the NUM and the NCB. NACODS ballot to strike over instructions to cross picket lines.

**18 September.** Three-week dock strike called off.

**26 September.** National Coal Board offers pit deputies, NACODS, a compromise package.

**28 September.** High Court rules NUM strike was "unlawful" because there has been no national ballot. The action has been brought by two scab miners. The legal action parallels the new Tory anti-union laws which has come into force in the course of the strike, requiring ballots for all strikes, but that law is not actually used. The court took it upon itself to interpret the NUM's rule book, and declared the strike unlawful. NACODS ballot result announced, an 82.5% majority for strike.

**29 September.** NCB/NUM agree to hold separate exploratory talks.

**1 October.** Overwhelming support for the NUM at the Labour Party Conference, whilst NUM/NACODS meet NCB. NUM President served with a High Court writ while sitting in the NUM delegation. The National Executive of the NUM reaffirms that the strike action is official despite the court decision.

**2 October.** Rail workers are sent home for refusing to move coal.

**4 October.** The High Court gives NUM five days to obey the interlocutory injunction and to call the strike off. On 10 October the court fines the NUM £200,000.

**8 October.** The NUM and the National Coal Board agree to meet at ACAS under an independent Chair on 11 October.

**10 October.** The NUM fined £200,000 and found in contempt of a High Court ruling which states the strike is unlawful because of the lack of a national ballot.

**12 October.** Restrictive bail conditions on striking members are upheld in the Divisional Courts.

**15 October.** NCB walk out of ACAS talks.

**25 October.** ACAS prepare a formula which both NACODS and NUM accept and which includes provision for an independent review procedure. The NCB continue their demands on NUM. Despite TUC advice NACODS call off strike. Courts attempt to seize £200,000 NUM funds.

**26 October.** The NUM reject the NCB demands. High Court orders total sequestration of NUM funds.

**28 October.** Court moves to makes 24 members of the NUM executive liable for the £200,000 contempt fine.

**1 November.** Ian MacGregor says, "There is no basis for further talks with the NUM".

**2 November.** The NCB offers miners a back to work cash bonus.

**17 November.** Coal Board refuses to negotiate unless NUM agrees to close pits.

**21 November.** Government increases deduction of benefits to £16 per week for strikers' families.

**28 November.** TUC General Council seeks talks with Government.

**30 November.** A receiver is appointed to control NUM assets and funds.

**5 December.** Ian MacGregor comes clean and announces plans to privatise pits.

**9 December.** Receiver and sequestrator unsuccessfully try to seize £4.6 million of NUM funds from Luxemburg.

**December.** NUM leaders' speaking tour of villages. Back to work drive tapers off, and collections increase as Christmas comes nearer.

**January 1985.** The steady dribble back to work can be measured in hundreds per day. Neil Kinnock, now the strike looks to be failing, manages to visit a picket line (by a chauffeur-driven car). Nonetheless, something like 130,000 miners remain on strike.

**12 January 1985.** Henry Richardson, pro-strike leader of Notts NUM, is suspended.

**22 January.** A challenge to the government's deduction of £16 from benefits to striking miners fails in the High Court.

**23 January.** Peter Walker, the Secretary of State for Energy, refuses to hold an independent inquiry into the future of the coal industry. NUM General Secretary, Peter Heathfield, meets with NCB Director for informal discussions, but MacGregor intervenes to prevent negotiations.

**6 February.** As the dribble back to work increases, South Wales NUM official Kim Howells floats the idea of a collective return to work without an agreement. The union executive does not even discuss the idea, and Howells is removed from his post as an area NUM spokesperson.

**19 February.** Seven TUC leaders visit Downing Street and take a message from there to the NUM demanding surrender. The NUM rejects the demand, and the TUC lets it be known that it is washing its hands of the strike. Arthur Scargill now says he would accept the NACODS compromise package (from September), but the government withdraws it.

**3 March.** NUM conference meets and votes 98 to 91 in favour of a South Wales proposal to return to work without an agreement. Most pits return to work on Tuesday 5 March; the Kent area, and a few pits elsewhere, stay out a week longer.

## THE STORY OF THE STRIKE

# Thatcher's assault

In the small hours of Monday 12 March 1984, hundreds of Yorkshire miners moved across the border from Yorkshire into Nottinghamshire. Their destination was Harworth pit, and by the evening shift they had picketed it out.

Over the next few days, hundreds of Yorkshire pickets came down over the border again and spread out across the Notts coalfield. Their mission was to persuade Nottinghamshire's miners to join them in a strike to stop the pit closures announced by the National Coal Board chief, Ian MacGregor. Their tactic was to picket Notts to a standstill.

In the great miners' strikes of 1972 and 1974, miners had picketed coke depots and power stations. In 1984, for reasons which we examine, it had to be miners picketing out miners. That fact dominated and shaped the course of the strike.

Within hours, 1000 extra police had been thrown into Nottinghamshire against the picketing miners. Within days there would be 8000 extra police — highly mobile, centrally-controlled, semi-militarised police — moving around the coalfields of Nottinghamshire.

The state had spent a dozen years preparing for this strike and everything had been made ready. Plans to beat mass picketing had been refined; police had been trained; special equipment had been assembled; and a national police nerve centre had been prepared and readied for action.

The Tory government had manoeuvred for years to avoid a premature battle with the miners. In 1981 sweeping pit closures were announced, and then withdrawn when a wave of strikes swept the coalfields. The Tories were determined that the battle would come when the government was ready and thought the time right. In 1981 they weren't ready. The labour movement had not been softened up enough. So Thatcher backed off from

### Time to organise!

Every local Labour Party, every union branch, every stewards' committee must, in the next few days, put the miners' strike at the centre of all their activities. Victory to the miners! Intensify the picketing! Boycott all coal movement! Bring out the power stations! TUC: call a 24 hour general strike! Organise for an all-out general strike!

*Socialist Organiser* Industrial Special, 4 April 1984

a showdown with the NUM.

In 1984 they were ready. Now they would provoke the miners to fight back by giving them the alternative of surrendering and letting the NCB do as it liked with the industry.

After years of slump and mass unemployment the labour movement was in a weakened condition. Its morale was low, its combativity declining, its leaders more concerned to undercut, and sabotage militancy than to fight the Tories. The NUM had been weakened too.

Between the miners' bloodless victory over Thatcher in 1981 and March 1984, 40 pits had been closed or merged. Morale had been eroded. The closures of Kinneil (December 1982) and Lewis Merthyr (March 1983) provoked only limited local struggles.

Arthur Scargill was elected NUM president in December 1981 with 70 per cent of the vote; but in January 1982 miners rejected a leadership proposal to strike over pay by 55%. In October 1982 61% of miners voted not to strike over pay and pit closures — despite a campaign by Arthur Scargill for strike action. In March 1983, when the strike over Lewis Merthyr began to spread from South Wales, the National Executive Committee called for a national miners' strike, but 61% of miners rejected the proposal.

Arthur Scargill repeatedly warned miners that the NCB had a secret "hit-list" of 70 or so pits marked down for closure, but either he lacked credibility with them or the miners no longer had the stomach to defend themselves.

That's how the Tories read it. So they decided that the time had come for a showdown with the miners.

In September 1983 Ian MacGregor became chair of the NCB. MacGregor had carved up the steel industry for the Tories. In America in the 1970s he had masterminded the employers' campaign in one of the most brutal labour wars of recent American history — the successful war to break the miners' union in Harlan County. MacGregor was to be the Tories' pit-butcher and union-buster. His appointment was undisguised preparation, if not an outright declaration, of war.

But was the NUM ready for war? The election for NUM secretary in January 1984 showed only a small margin in favour of the victorious left-wing candidate, Peter Heathfield, over his right wing opponent John Walsh. The miners still seemed in the mood to retreat; the militant leaders of the NUM increasingly out of line with their movement.

So the Tories attacked.

On 1 March, when local management announced the closure of Cortonwood colliery in Yorkshire, South Yorkshire miners immediately went on unofficial strike. On 5 March, with half the Yorkshire miners already out, the Yorkshire area council called an official strike from 9 March.

But South Wales miners had come out over the closure of Lewis Merthyr — and Lewis Merthyr had nevertheless closed. More than local action was needed. Miners had been this far towards confrontation before without an all-out fight.

On 6 March the Scottish area council called on Scottish miners to strike from 9 March. Polmaise pit had already been out for three weeks against closure.

Now Ian MacGregor took a hand, pouring petrol on the fire. On 6 March he told the NUM that 20 pits would close in 1984, that 20,000 jobs would be cut, and that there might be compulsory redundancies.

MacGregor was telling the NUM either to back off, or to try to stop him closing down 20 pits. The Tories, not the miners, chose this fight. But — after the rejection of their proposal for a national strike over Lewis Merthyr exactly a year before — did the NUM national executive have any alternative but to back off and let the Tory juggernaut roll unopposed over the "uneconomic" pits and coalfields? To their eternal glory they thought they did have an alternative.

On 8 March the executive endorsed the decision of the Yorkshire and Scottish areas to strike, and they endorsed in advance the decision any other area might take for strike action.

## Standard bearers of the working class

The miners' strike is a tremendously important mobilisation, the most important working class battle for many years (...)

Once again, the miners — despite their divisions — are the shock troops and standard bearers of the working class. Once more the miners are telling a foul anti-working class Tory government that they can't run things exactly as they like and that the miners are calling them to account. It is the most vital and direct interest of every worker in Britain to stand on the line with the miners and help them win.

*Socialist Organiser* Industrial Special, 4 April 1984

# Picket or ballot?

Should they have a national ballot? The executive was in the business of mobilising the miners to resist MacGregor's attack, not out to demobilise those who had decided to act. So the executive voted 21 to 3 against a ballot.

They were 100 per cent right to refuse to go to a ballot at that point. It was the responsibility and the duty of the executive to respond to MacGregor's attack and to give a fighting lead — not to paralyse the NUM in the face of the challenge thrown down by the Tory hit-man MacGregor.

If Britain were engaged in a conventional war, having to respond to an attack, and with battles raging over a wide front, then the Tories, and the Denis Healeys and Neil Kinnocks, would reject with indignation and scorn the idea that a national plebiscite should be held to determine whether the people wanted to fight or not.

They would say that anyone who wanted such a plebiscite intended that the country, and in the first place its "leadership", the government, should be paralysed, and was, therefore, deliberately or unknowingly, helping the enemy. They would be dead right about that, from their point of view.

The advocates that the NUM should have held a plebiscite instead of immediate action when the Tories unleashed the war they had spent many years preparing against the NUM either wanted the NUM to be paralysed or didn't care whether it was or not. None of them demanded of MacGregor and the Tories that there should be a ballot to see how many miners voted for pit closures. Neither the establishment politicians, nor the press, expressed indignation in 1977-8 against the introduction of area incentive schemes, despite a national ballot vote against such incentives. They were keen to take advantage of a division among miners which, in part, resulted from those schemes. In the case of Notts, this was a major factor in the strike.

The miners' NEC refused to let themselves be paralysed. And now that the lines were drawn, the miners responded magnificently. Encouraged by the executive, the strike spread. On 9 March Durham and Kent called area strikes. A South Wales delegate conference recommended that South Wales should strike, but over the weekend of 10th-11th pits in the area decided by about two to one not to strike.

A MORI opinion poll showed 62% of miners wanting a strike.

The Notts delegate conference declined to take action before an area ballot, and the Northumberland and Leicestershire leaderships voted against a strike.

That was the situation on Monday 12 March as flying pickets went into action to make it a national strike and to enforce the area strike decisions. Despite their branch votes, most of South Wales came out immediately. The

South Wales miners would prove to be obdurate, solid and immovable throughout the long year of hardship and deprivation that was to follow.

By Wednesday 14 March the NCB admitted that 132 out of 174 pits had been shut. But Notts was the major problem. The Yorkshire flying pickets had some initial successes. When Yorkshire miner Davy Jones was killed picketing at Ollerton, on Thursday 15 March, the Notts leaders called an area strike — until the following Sunday.

By Friday 16 March only 11 collieries were working normally, according to the NCB itself.

On Thursday 15 March and Friday 16 March ballots were held in many areas. Northumberland voted for a strike. Right-wing Cumberland, Midlands, South Derbyshire, Lancashire, Notts and North Wales voted not to strike. So, narrowly, did North Derbyshire. On Sunday 18th a Notts delegate conference decided to go back. On 20 March the result of a ballot showed 90% against a strike in Leicestershire.

The miners were split, without a common line. What happened next would be determined by the strength of the picketing by striking miners and their supporters, and by how the miners in areas which voted not to strike would respond when confronted by pickets from the striking areas. The press and politicians set up a tremendous din, telling the miners that they should not strike without a national ballot. The ballot was democracy, and anything else was not democratic.

Newly elected Peter Heathfield put the issue squarely when he said this about the demand for a national ballot: "Can miners in successful areas have the right to vote miners in less successful areas out of a job?" To make a national ballot the essence of "democracy" here was to make democracy into tyranny, and to deny the right of a minority — if miners who wanted to strike were in fact the minority: an opinion poll said that 62% wanted to strike — to defend itself.

The Tories tried to use the framework of the NUM as a straitjacket to imprison miners whose jobs were threatened. They could only fight, these strange democrats said — and not only the Tories, but Kinnock and Hattersley too — if they could get a national majority in the federal union to agree to fight. If they could not, they should lie down and let the Tories walk all over them, smash up their communities and devastate whole areas like Kent and South Wales.

The call for a national ballot was never a democratic demand, but a demand to repress and straitjacket the militants. (Tactical considerations about the ballot are a separate matter.)

The provisions about balloting in the new Tory trade union laws are designed precisely to make the unions into machines for repressing militancy. The pseudo-democrats in the Labour Party leadership who joined in the propaganda against the NUM leadership over the ballot stood throughout the miners' strike — and stand now — on the ground and within the framework of the Tory anti-union legislation.

Once the militants had struck they had every right to appeal for basic working-class solidarity to other workers — and in the first place to miners. South Wales, which voted not to strike, showed what was possible here.

Or didn't they have that right? If not, why not? Those who say they didn't stand yet again on the ground of the new Tory legislation, which forbids "secondary" picketing.

Of course a united NUM would have been better by far. The fundamental thing about the NUM in March 1984 was that it was not united, and nevertheless its leaders and militants had to fight back against the well-timed Tory offensive.

## Leicestershire's "Dirty Thirty"

We are a small band of striking miners in Leicestershire given the name of "The Dirty Thirty" by the 2,000 who are still working. The name was meant to be a derisory title but we are proud to be so named because it identifies us from the rest who are prepared to see their pits close and the future of their families in jeopardy by not supporting the strike and NUM policy.

We say: no surrender. The strike goes on till we achieve victory on our terms.

Statement by Leicestershire striking miners to NUM delegate conference carried in *Socialist Organiser*, 16 August 1984

# The miners divided

The first part of the miners' tragedy — and that tragedy would unfold inexorably for a full year until the last moving scenes in March 1985, when singing miners, escorted by their families and by bands, marched back to work — lay in this: that, the NUM being divided, the militant, fighting part of the NUM had to appeal for basic working-class solidarity in defence of their jobs and their communities first to other miners, to members of their own union — and that solidarity was refused them.

Scab miners crossed picket lines, sheltered behind the police, played the media's game against the strikers, and used the bosses' courts against their own union and its embattled members and leaders.

The second part of the tragedy was that most of the labour movement did pretty much the same thing as the NUM's scabs.

Both the broad labour movement and the miners had had some of the fight knocked out of them by the slump and mass unemployment. But more than that was involved in the heartland of scabbing, Notts, where it was claimed they scabbed because they were refused a national ballot.

Most of the Notts scabs did not scab because of the ballot, or because of violence by pickets. That was the "good reason", not the real one. It keyed the Notts working miners into the Tory propaganda offensive against the strikers, and it allowed the scabs to think of themselves as peaceful democrats and not as scabs. The real reason was that they were scared by the daunting battle ahead, they didn't feel their jobs were threatened, and they had been doing well under the area incentives scheme.

They made a religion of the national ballot because they needed a respect-worthy excuse for refusing to help the threatened miners to defend their jobs and communities.

A majority of both South Wales and Notts voted against the strike. That's what they had in common in March 1984, though their motives were most likely very different. The magnificent one-year stand that the miners of South Wales can look back on in March 1985 pinpoints where the difference between them lay — in the absence of gut class loyalty among the majority of prosperous, unthreatened Notts miners. Only a minority of Notts miners had the self-respect to stand with their class.

The scabbing in Notts shaped the strike. As well as supplying coal throughout the strike, the "working miners" gave the NCB a powerful hard core of scabs to build on. Without Notts the Leicestershire and other scabs would not have counted for much. When Notts went back to work on Monday March 19, after one day out, the NCB could claim that 42 pits were working normally.

With the miners split, the fate of the strike would be determined by the outcome of battles on two fronts — the battle of the pickets against the centrally-controlled semi-militarised police, who turned some coalfields into something like police states; and the political battle in the labour movement for solidarity from non-miners. In the battle for solidarity the propaganda front was the decisive one.

Never in the living memory of the labour movement had the police behaved as they did in the miners' strike. They concentrated in large masses, deployed and controlled from a centre at Scotland Yard. They set up roadblocks to stop Yorkshire miners moving into Notts and Kent miners into the Midlands. They stopped, searched, and arrested at will. They used thuggery and violence on a scale not known in any modern labour dispute in Britain — not even the Grunwick strike of 1977. They behaved as wreckers and bully-boys in certain pit villages as if they were understudying the British army in the Catholic parts of Northern Ireland.

And something else was new — organised scab-herding, on a vast scale backed up by a very loud barrage of propaganda.

Many railworkers and dockers refused to move scab coal. On 29 March the transport workers' leaders recommended a total blockade of all coal. But decisive solidarity lay in the hands of the power workers and steel workers to give or withhold — and they withheld it. On 21 March the power unions (including the GMBU) advised their members to cross miners' pickets. Steelworkers, fearful for their industry and bruised and battered from their own 1980 strike, crossed miners' picket lines.

The propaganda war against the miners was waged fiercely so as to limit and to try to stop workers supporting the miners. Picketing miners who were at the receiving end of the violence that police officials had spent years preparing for were pilloried and denounced as purveyors of mindless and gratuitous violence. Miners fighting for their jobs were denounced as undemocratic because they were on strike without sanction of a national ballot — and those who denounced them were industrial autocrats and dictators who were using massed armies of police to try to force the miners to accept the ruin of some of their communities!

Though the Labour Party gave its support to the miners, the high-profile leaders of the Party hemmed and hawed, joined in the calls for a national ballot — the cutting edge of the propaganda war — and denounced violence, meaning pickets who stood up to the police.

By Monday 26 March, when the NCB claimed that 38 pits were working normally, the strike had reached a steady level. The strike would strengthen slightly after the NUM conference on 19 April, but the contours of the battlefield were already visible, the areas of strength and weakness of either side known, the balance of forces stabilised. An unbudgeable minority of miners — the NUM said about 25,000 — refused to strike. Scabbing miners, picket-crossing power and steel workers, and far too limited general solidarity, forced the miners to dig in for a war of attrition. They knew it would take time. They could not have guessed just how long their war of attrition with the Thatcher government would be.

The 1974 miners' strike lasted just over a month — from 9 February to 11 March. Just over a month after the start of the 1972 strike, Saltley coke depot was closed by mass pickets and the government was on the run. (It appointed the Wilberforce inquiry, which finally brought about a settlement, on 28 February. The strike had started on 9 January.)

By late March it was already clear that 1984 would be a much longer and more grim affair. Miners talked about "staying out until Christmas". The *Times* reported (18 April): "Mrs Margaret Thatcher is willing to spend any amount of money to ensure that the Government is not again defeated by the miners' union". Chancellor Nigel Lawson would later publicly explain that the money spent on beating the miners was a "worthwhile investment". They would spend over £2 billion on it directly, with indirect losses of perhaps another £3 billion [equivalent, as shares of national income and government budget, to about £8 billion and £12 billion today].

But the miners were as determined as the government. Kent area NUM executive member John Moyle voiced their determination:

"No one should be in any doubt about what is at stake in this dispute. We are up against the most basic facts of this government's philosophy — they care about profits, not people...

"The rank and file will fight on under any circumstances, and they will win. The only question is how long it takes. We are not looking for a victory for the miners, but for the whole working class" (*Socialist Organiser* 174).

Arthur Scargill appealed to other workers: "Stop merely saying you support us. Come out and join us. We are facing a fundamental challenge to the whole working class, not merely miners. We are facing the organised might of the state machine" (Nottingham, April 14: *SO* 175).

A Kent miner told *SO* in mid-March: "Once we've got our own people out solid, we'll go to the rest of the movement and say: 'give us your support. Let's have you all out and deal with this government'.

"A general strike?

"Yes, if that's what you want to call it" (*SO* 171).

The pickets never did get the whole coalfield out solid. The scabbing in Notts would be a terrible drag on their efforts to get solidarity from other trade unionists.

But the energy of the strike was still expanding, and it became stronger. On 12 April, the executive faced down right-wing calls for a national ballot, and the right wing Notts area president, Ray Chadburn, emerged from the meeting to tell his members: "Get off your knees and support the strike!"

On April 14 7000 miners and supporters marched in Nottingham to demand "Police out of the coalfields". On 16 April a Notts rank and file strike committee was formed. If the scabs in Notts disgraced themselves and the labour movement, the Notts strikers summed up everything alive and good in the labour movement. Led by Paul Whetton and others, they kept the flag of militant labour flying in the Notts coalfield. Intimidated, assaulted, deprived, the hard core never let themselves or the NUM down.

## The Coalville railworkers

Out of it have come good things and bad things.

On the bad side you've got train crews in the East Midlands, not at Coalville, who are moving coal trains. They are breaking every condition of service.

But it won't deflect us from what we are doing. Because it is more than compensated for by good.

We've made friendships with other railway depots, particularly in London. We've forged an alliance with the 30 striking miners in Leicestershire: we even share the same office. That's a strong alliance and that will remain even when the dispute finishes.

These friendships will stand us in good stead when the miners' strike is over and if the railway unions get involved in their own dispute.

Railwaymen's wives have become friends with striking miners' wives. So you've got these marvellous bonds and these marvellous friendships which more than outweigh the bad.

The miners' strike is not just about pit closures. It's become a question of solidarity, a question of loyalty, it's become a question of trade unionism and standing up for what you believe in.

Roy Butlin, secretary of Coalville NUR.
*Socialist Organiser*, 28 November 1984

# April-May: the strike gets stronger

To stop miners striking the bosses relied, as we have seen, on a vicious caterwauling of propaganda about democracy in general and about a national ballot in particular. The rank and file of the NUM had the chance to reject their NEC's policy at the NUM special conference which met on 19 April — the first of eight to be held during the strike — lobbied by tens of thousands of chanting, singing, cheering miners. In fact the special conference called on every area to join the strike.

It boosted the strike. Midlands and Notts NUM leaders then declared the strike official in their areas, and more miners stopped work, though in Notts a majority or something near that continued to scab.

There was now a surge of solidarity. The rail and transport unions had promised to boycott scab coal. Railworkers in Coalville, Leicestershire, enforced this boycott throughout the strike, in the midst of the most solidly scabbing coalfield in the country (30 strikers out of 2000 miners). Notts railworkers began stopping coal trains on 16 April.

The Labour Party national executive voted on 25 April to support the strike and to ask every Party member to donate 50p a week.

By the end of March, steel production at Scunthorpe had been cut by half, and by early May three major power stations had been taken off the grid — West Thurrock, Aberthaw and Didcot. By massive use of oil, nuclear power, and imported coal, the Central Electricity Generating Board was in fact able to last out the entire strike without crippling power cuts: but that was not at all clear at the time. The strike was making progress, albeit slowly.

From May to August the strike was at its peak. About 80% of miners were out. There was some drift-back in this period (the strike was already a long one by usual standards): but it was marginal. Notts suffered a drift back after the High Court, on 25 May, ruled the strike unofficial in the county: by late August only 20% of Notts miners were out, as against maybe 40 or 50% at the peak. In Staffordshire the strike was fraying at the end of May, and over 50% were scabbing at every pit except Wolstanton by early August. Lancashire weakened.

In the vast majority of pit communities, however, the strike was solid, and becoming more determined and confident.

This was a strike in which something in excess of a hundred thousand workers and their families found themselves up against a pitiless, relentless, determined government which had all the advantages on its side; entrenched power and wealth; the police; the deprivation and sometimes hunger that gripped miners and their families a few weeks into the strike. To stay in the fight the miners and their families had to find in themselves reserves of strength, determination, fortitude, and creativity. The mining communities had to rouse themselves completely and throw everything they had into the class war. The strike had to become more than a mere strike. And it did.

The outstanding new thing in the miners' strike was the involvement of the women of the mining communities.

By early May the pit villages were full of militant women's groups.

The women's groups ran communal kitchens or food-parcel centres — and many of them went out on the picket line: that hadn't happened before. On 30 April there was a 150-strong women's picket at Thoresby colliery, Notts. They broke through police lines twice, and a local miner commented: "If the women had been there from the beginning, the strike would have been won by now" (*SO* 177).

Women's pickets were a regular feature of the strike, and on 12 May the streets of Barnsley were swamped by an exuberant women's demonstration.

Repeatedly the pit women would cite the women's peace camp at Greenham Common as an inspiration. Direct links were made between the normally somewhat isolated, conservative, male-dominated pit villages, and feminists who might never before have seen class struggle as anything central to politics.

For a lot of people, the strike shook up their ideas in a way that normally

## Women invade Barnsley

On Wednesday 12 May Barnsley was invaded by some 10,000 miners' wives, marching to oppose pit closures. It was very much a women's march, not just in its constitution but in its atmosphere.

Women from all over the country — Yorkshire, Derbyshire, Staffordshire, Northumberland and South Wales — came together to give a very lively and resounding No to MacGregor's closure plans.

Not your boring run of the mill trudge, this... chants of "the miners united will never be defeated" and "I'd rather be a picket than a scab" continued throughout the march. Drum majorettes provided more noise and colour. And I don't think anyone in Barnsley centre escaped without getting a 'coal not dole' sticker plonked on some part of their anatomy.

*Socialist Organiser*, 17 May 1984

happens only in great semi-revolutionary struggles like a general strike. Opposed to the Tory class-warriors, the police chiefs, the Fleet Street editorialists eulogising the heroic scabs, here at last was something more than the quibbling, middle-of-the-road, trimming whines of Michael Foot and Neil Kinnock. The miners were a pole of opposition, and inevitably they became a magnetic pole of attraction for the oppressed.

Spitting boldly in the teeth of all Tory philosophy, the miners rallied round them all the movements, impulses and rebellions against that philosophy and against the system it defends. The miners inspired and gave focus to an across-the-board challenge to Toryism; and that challenge became an increasing part of their own awareness of the world.

Thatcher did have an "enemy within"! And hundreds of thousands, if not millions, of people rallied to it. Many of them were shocked by the Tories' remorseless drive to compel the miners and their families to let her offer them as human sacrifices to her savage god, Mammon, the god of profit and lucre; and shocked at the will of the police to use any means necessary to beat the pickets. They started to think about alternatives to Thatcherism.

Jenny Dennis, from Kiveton Park, Yorkshire, told *SO* in November:

"Mining communities are traditionally male-dominated. It's the men that work and the women that do: having babies, washing and making snap is our lot. Then it changed.

"It was as though we'd been sleeping for hundreds of years. We awoke, we realised a new political awareness:

"Organising food, raising money, speaking. Men have acknowledged that we, as women, are vital to that victory. We're an active part of that struggle, side by side with our men in the battle's frontline.

"We are witnessing something amongst the women which I can only compare with the suffragettes. We are living and making history. We won't

## "Outcasts of the state"

We, as lesbians and gay men, black people, the organised working class, are a threat to the power of the state — and their main weapon is the police and they use it.

We've got to fight together because there's no way we're going to be able to beat them if we're divided. The miners from Dulais Valley who've met us have said just that. They've said that they are now outcasts of the state — we've seen what the police and the media are like.

Mark Ashton and Mike Jackson of "Lesbians and Gays Support the Miners": *Socialist Organiser*, 4 October 1984 return to the status quo. We can't.

"Personally it has made me realise that not only must we fight our injustice but others too.

"Because we have lived through media lies we ask ourselves: 'What other lies have they made?'

"Look at the injustice in Ireland. What really happened in Toxteth? In Brixton? I realise the black community is struggling against injustice.

"After we win we must turn and right other injustices".

Lesbians and Gays Support the Miners set themselves up, and found miners coming to their meetings, saying things like: "Since the strike their ideas had really changed, and perhaps now the 'traditional' labour movement should go to black people and lesbians and gay men to relearn what socialism is all about" (*SO* 199). But the lesbians and gay men had things to learn from the miners too: the strike drew a class line among lesbians and gays.

Black groups organised to help the miners; and miners came to understand better what black communities feel about police harassment.

Frank Slater of Maltby NUM (Yorkshire) put it like this:

"What did we do when blacks were being harassed? We said — it's not us. But we're ethnic minorities now" (*SO* 200).

The local miners' support committees were never anywhere near having the weight, in official labour movement terms, to organise strikes in support of the miners.

Usually they were run by the Labour Left. The Communist Party organised its own activities, often trying to exclude or suppress more active people to its left. The Socialist Workers Party continued its "splendid isolation", pouring scorn on the "left-wing Oxfam" and "baked beans brigades" of the support committees, until October, when it readjusted and joined in. Militant [forerunner of the Socialist Party and Socialist Appeal] never joined in.

But, if the support movement was organisationally weak and ramshackle, it was the umbrella for a vast amount of individual activity. Workplace collections, door-to-door collections, street collections, pub collections, football ground collections; benefits, demonstrations, mass pickets; visits from miners, visits to pit villages...

The "Coal Not Dole" sticker, the bundle of *The Miner*, and the collecting bucket became the standard hardware of political life. Hundreds of thousands of people who did nothing more than give donations or wear a badge were stirred and inspired by the miners' fight. Labour activists miles from any coalfield found themselves talking, thinking, breathing, living the miners' strike week after week.

In Basingstoke, Hampshire, for example, the miners' support committee became the centre of political life. In May Carla Jamison reported on their links with the Notts strikers: "Long after the benefit night was over [one of the Notts women] was still sitting up talking over the issues with the *SO* supporters she was stopping the night with... It was a great and inspiring weekend for us [the visit of the first strikers' delegation], and hopefully for the delegation too...

"For us it hadn't just been a one-off visit, it has been very special and we will hopefully be seeing them again soon... they have probably done more for us than we did for them".

## Joe Green, Davy Jones: working-class martyrs

"There's blood on coal", people say, meaning that many miners die or suffer terrible injuries working to bring coal to the surface.

Now the saying takes on a different meaning, in the fourth month of the strike — the blood of miners killed and injured fighting to stop Thatcher and MacGregor wrecking the coal industry. The blood of working class martyrs in the fight against Toryism. The blood of militant prepared to stand up against the state.

Joe Green was the second miner to die in this strike. Joe was 55 and he died picketing Ferrybridge power station at Castleford, Yorkshire. He was pulled under the back wheels of a scab lorry and crushed to death.

Arthur Scargill, who was himself to be injured and hospitalised as a result of a police attack outside Orgreave, said this about the death of Joe Green:

"Joe Green gave his life for the right to work — every miner, every trade unionist in Britain must ensure that he did not die in vain."

On Thursday 15 March, Davy Jones, a 24 year old Yorkshire miner, was killed on the picket line outside Ollerton colliery Notts. Arthur Scargill wrote to Davy Jones' parents. "In a few years time, those who inflicted damage on our industry and were directly responsible for the tragedy that befell David will have been forgotten, while David will be remembered..."

*Socialist Organiser*, 21 June 1984

# May-July: the strike at its peak

Could the labour movement have been rallied to the miners in sufficient strength to tip the balance against the Tories? Yes they could — if our movement had been headed by leaders who wanted to fight. The response to the local and regional activities called (and inadequately campaigned for) by TUC bodies proves it.

Between 9 May and 13 July there were regional TUC days of action in every major region except the Midlands. Railworkers, hospital workers, council workers, dockers and shipyard workers struck; demonstrations in London and Manchester were up to 50,000 strong. But there was no centrally organised campaign to develop the potential shown by the days of action. Len Murray denounced the days of action in advance. The central TUC leaders stood on the sidelines, sharpening their talons, eyeing Scargill and Heathfield with hatred. But the miners, keeping their distance, had not yet approached the TUC.

## Arthur Scargill's demands

Last week, Arthur Scargill set out his demands for the pit strike:

- A complete withdrawal of the Coal Board's closure programme announced on 6 March aimed at reducing capacity by 4 million tonnes.
- A reaffirmation by the Board and the government of the Plan for Coal, the expansionist plan agreed between the government, Coal Board and unions in 1974.
- Development of 40 million tonnes new capacity.
- New investment to expand all existing pits.
- Rapid development on new coal burning technologies.
- The introduction of a four day week.
- A substantial increase in wages.
- Retirement age brought down to 55.
- A scheme to protect wage rates.
- Consolidation of the incentive bonus scheme

The demands for the four-day week and for scrapping the incentive scheme are particularly important as part of a working class programme to defend jobs and unite mineworkers.

*Socialist Organiser*, 21 June 1984

It was the miners' picketing that mainly drove the struggle forward. On 2 May the police (probably exaggerating) estimated 10,000 pickets at Harworth colliery, and on 3 May almost as many at Cotgrave (Notts). On 7 May 1,000 miners picketed Ravenscraig steelworks, near Glasgow. On 14 May, 40,000 marched in Mansfield. Between 29 May and 18 June thousands of pickets and police fought battles outside Orgreave coking plant, near Sheffield: coke runs from Orgreave were suspended on 18 June.

On 7 June the transport unions agreed not only to boycott coal and coke, but also to block substitute oil movements. On 9 June union leaders Jimmy Knapp and Ray Buckton persuaded railworkers at Shirebrook depot in Notts to follow this policy; by 13 July Knapp could announce that only 10 coal trains were running daily in Britain, out of a normal 356. On 25 June

## A Notts striker at Orgreave

There was plenty of blood. I went to the assistance of a young miner who was lying in the grass. He was bleeding profusely from the head. I knelt on one knee beside him. I could give no useful medical assistance other than trying to comfort him.

I called to the police for an ambulance. The police lines were no more than 15 yards from this injured man. An inspector shouted over, "We've got an ambulance coming, son". They made a gap in their ranks for an ambulance to come through.

I was still knelt there waiting for the ambulance when a black policeman ran through the gap and straight to me. As he reached me I looked up and he was above me and flashing through the air was his truncheon, which he brought down on the back of my neck. There was a sickening, deadening pain in my neck, and as I was trying to get to my feet I saw this black policeman run back through the gap in the police ranks. The police closed ranks and stood behind their riot shields.

As I was walking from the scene, a solitary policeman riding a grey horse rode his horse straight at me, swinging his baton freely. The horse knocked me down and the mounted policeman struck me across the right thigh and knee. He then rode off...

I got home at 8 pm. When I got sat down with a cup of tea I thought about my experiences since the strike began and determined that whilst I could stand, police violence would not keep me from the picket lines. I arose this morning, though on crutches and wearing a surgical collar and in severe pain, I made my way to Bevercotes Colliery to stand on the picket line. And when I can't walk, I'll crawl.

Notts striker Robert Cooper, writing
in *Socialist Organiser*, 28 June 1984

**Sit-in against job cuts at Cammell Lairds shipyard, Birkenhead. The occupation lasted from May to September 1984.**

railworkers stopped iron ore supplies to Llanwern steelworks (South Wales); on 28 June, to Ravenscraig.

From early June the Tories became visibly alarmed. They had schemed and prepared for years, waited patiently for the right moment to strike; they had split the miners; they had thrown many thousands of specially trained police at them; they had mobilised the entire press to engulf them in a barrage of lies, misrepresentation, libel and hate-filled propaganda — but still the miners remained in the fight and seemed to be advancing steadily, though slowly. They could fight epic battles like the one at Orgreave, near Sheffield, and hold the cops to a draw, forcing — temporarily — a halt to coke movements there.

Thatcher saw that, like some fabled "British square" of soldiers on the battlefields of the Napoleonic wars, the miners could take a tremendous pounding, stand in a swirl of smoke and shell, and then move forward on the offensive. The Tories had good reason to be worried. So they stepped up the counter-attack.

MacGregor sent a letter to every miner. The NCB talked about organising a ballot over the heads of the NUM.

There was a new and sinister development of police thuggery, directed not against miners on the picket line but against miners and their families in their home villages. Police began to act like a hostile army of occupation in some pit villages.

On the night of 16-17 May, 160 police in riot gear terrorised Thorney Abbey Road, Blidworth, Notts. Annette Holroyd and Pauline Radford told *Socialist Organiser* what happened:

"They managed to get Terry [Terry Dunn, a Yorkshire picket] over the driveway onto the road and about four or five got hold of his arms and got him into the van.

"Everyone asked why they were arresting him. They refused to give an answer and said, 'We don't have to tell you'.

"Then they chucked him in the van and all the men ran up to the van but they slammed the doors in their faces. One of the lads said, 'Come on, take me. If you're going to lift him you should lift the lot of us'. They just drove straight off.

"I went over to see my baby-sitter. She was terrified. It was my house just next door. I asked her what was the matter. She said, 'There's been five or six policemen knocking on the door, and asking questions: Where's my dad? Where's my husband? Where is everybody?'

"I calmed her down and by then there were thirteen or fourteen police vans out in the road. There were policemen lined up across the road. I've never seen so many policemen — hundreds of them.

"I was terrified, as was everyone else. I kept clinging hold of my husband so he wouldn't go through the gate. If they went through the gates they'd get lifted.

"All the men said, 'What are you doing here? We're not causing any trouble'. The police said they'd had a report about a disturbance — they need at least 13 police vans to check out a disturbance, 160 police in riot gear!

"The union official said he saw another 20 vans in the next street waiting to come round.

"I feel the police wanted all the Yorkshire lads to go over the gate into the road and get into a riot with the police, and then they'd do them all for rioting.

"It was definitely an act of deliberate provocation".

The tone of Tory denunciations got more and more shrill and hate-filled, until, on 19 July, Thatcher denounced the NUM as "the enemy within", a domestic equivalent of the Argentines she had fought in the Falklands war. Other Tory speakers followed up the attack, and the *Times* editorialised: "There is a war on".

On 13 June, with the battle of Orgreave still in full swing, Arthur Scargill had set out an expanded set of demands for the strike, including a four-day week. By 25 June, Tony Benn was calling over the heads of the union leaders for other workers to strike immediately alongside the miners, and the next day in Parliament Labour MP Martin Flannery spoke of an "inexorable march towards a general strike... now under way".

Tony Benn was right to appeal over the heads of the union leaders for workers to back the miners. But that it was Benn the MP who did it was also the measure of the weakness of the official trade union leadership.

The NUM special conference on 11-12 July was jubilant, endorsing Scargill's expanded demands and approving a rule change which could be used to discipline scabs.

Miners had a right to be proud of what they had so far achieved against great odds. They knew that if they could build on what they had done, and develop from where they were, then they could win. But the miners could not themselves do it — they could not at will generate the irreplaceable help of others in the labour movement. They didn't get the help. And the Tories counterattacked, putting the miners on the defensive.

## "It's woken the lads up"

The women's involvement in the strike... we couldn't have managed without it.

We've stirred a hornet's nest up. God knows how we're going to live with them when this dispute is over.

They're politically active and that's very important. If I'd gone down to our welfare a year ago and asked for women to go down to Greenham Common, I couldn't have got a car load.

Now if you go and ask, there's a bus load wants to go, because they have recognised what the women of Greenham Common are fighting for.

The tie up between what is happening in our dispute and what has been happening in Northern Ireland is becoming increasingly clear for us to see. People can also understand now the harassment that ethnic minorities have to put up with. And we can now see the reality of policing Northern Ireland for ourselves.

It's woken the lads up...

Paul Whetton, *Socialist Organiser*, 11 October 1984

# South Wales NUM funds seized

The forward-movement phase of the strike ended on 1 August, when the High Court ordered the seizure of the South Wales NUM's funds. The union had defied an injunction against picketing granted to two haulage firms.

The Tories were upping the stakes. The seizure of a trade union's funds was a matter for the whole labour movement, not for that trade union alone. It was an attack on the whole labour movement — and only the whole labour movement could hope to confront and beat the government that stood behind the courts.

Miners occupied the area NUM headquarters and demonstrators gathered outside to hear area president Emlyn Williams explain what the labour movement needed to do: "We hope trade unions will show solidarity with the miners, and as of today throughout the country there will be a general strike" (*SO* 190).

Arthur Scargill called on the TUC for "physical support". But nothing happened.

As *Socialist Organiser* commented: "The startling thing about the savage fine on the South Wales NUM is that the other unions haven't come to their defence. The cry for a general strike should have rung through the labour movement at every level. Instead we have a numb silence at the top" (*SO* 191).

After all the clamour and the uproar of the summer, suddenly there was numb silence. Some days later, Ron Todd of the TGWU did start talking about plans for a "big bang" of trade union solidarity, but nothing came of that. The same numb silence would happen again, and more damagingly,

## Uniting dockers and miners

We need to coordinate the action of striking port workers and striking miners. The best way to do this would be immediately to set up — in areas where that is practicable — action committees. We should also invite railworkers' and seafarers' representatives to join them.

United, dockers and miners can massively augment and increase each others' strength. We must unite. Unity will bring us victory.

Appeal from Paul Whetton to dockers' delegates, 24 August 1984 in November, after the central NUM funds were sequestrated, and in December after a Tory lawyer was declared "receiver" of the NUM's finances.

Why?

Just a week before the seizure of the South Wales funds, Notts striker Paul Whetton had observed this "numb silence" in microcosm. He told an *SO meeting* in Ollerton:

"I spoke with Dennis Skinner in Basingstoke, and of course everyone was clapping and cheering everything Dennis Skinner said.

"Dennis Skinner made the point that we were begging not only for money and for food, but for solidarity action. He said: there is nothing to stop you taking action now. And the applause stopped.

"People were taken right up to the edge of it, and when it was put point-blank to them, they hesitated and drew back. That's a natural reluctance. They fear the machinery of the state, they fear the machinery of the employers and all the rest of it" (*SO* 189).

So, by failing to respond to the seizure of funds, the movement went into retreat, and the miners began a new phase of their war of attrition with the government — the phase in which the balance, inch by painful inch, was turned against them.

The sceptics and defeatists will say: the NUM leadership should have known in advance that it would go like that; the labour movement was in no condition for an all-out fight. Some of them — like the Socialist Workers Party — will add that nothing better could have been expected from the TUC.

When something has already happened and is now history, then it naturally seems in retrospect to have happened inevitably — it seems that all the pieces fell into place as they had to in the circumstances. But that is to substitute hindsight for an examination of the actual course of events. There was nothing inevitable about the isolation of the miners.

At a number of points dotted across the middle of 1984, great possibilities for broadening the struggle came into existence, before vanishing unrealised. The most important of these were the two dock strikes, but there were others. The leaders of the NUM tried again and again to link up with other workers and broaden the struggle. Again and again they appealed for solidarity, to the broad labour movement or to particular groups of workers.

On 9 May Arthur Scargill appealed to railworkers, then due to start an overtime ban on 30 May: "If ever there was a time to join with this union, to come out on strike... now is the time".

In the event the NUR [forerunner of RMT] and ASLEF settled for a miserable 4.9% rise. Paul Foot later printed documents in the *Daily Mirror* showing that Thatcher had instructed the British Rail bosses to make whatever concessions were necessary to avoid a "second front" with the railworkers.

# Why wasn't there more action?

But the most dramatic point in the struggle to broaden the front came in July, when the dockers came out on strike on 9 July. Thatcher must have remembered the fate of Edward Heath.

Dockers struck against the use of non-dockers to unload iron ore for Scunthorpe steelworks at Immingham. The fire had jumped from the miners to the dockers.

Britain's dockers are in trouble. Shifts in trade patterns have redirected traffic away from the old ports and into new ones where dockers do not have the job security long ago established in the older ports and enshrined in the National Dock Labour Scheme. One Tory minister said openly in mid 1984 that the Dock Labour Scheme should be scrapped. The jobs of many dockers were — and are — under threat.

On the docks, as in the mines, the basic issue was jobs. Here were ready-made fellow-fighters for the miners. And dockers had the power to close down Britain very quickly. Within weeks of a solid docks strike the Tories would either have to surrender or use troops — and that would have escalated the conflict further.

Competent leadership could have welded the dockers to the miners in a common fight for jobs. The dockers' leaders, whatever good intentions they may have had, bungled it.

The TGWU did not even formulate clear demands for the strike. The basic demand should have been extension of the National Dock Labour Scheme to the new, unregistered ports.

When the strike was on, *Socialist Organiser* called for the creation of joint action committees of dockers and miners. But the NUM did not make much initiative to link up with the dockers. It was difficult for the NUM. The leaders of the TGWU were protesting that their dispute was quite separate from the miners', and would not have welcomed any such initiative.

On 19 July anti-strike lorry drivers threatened violence against dockers in Dover, where the strike was shaky anyway, and the dispute collapsed. The press that had been screaming against "violent" miners either gloried in the threats against the strikers or reported this in a matter-of-fact way: the police had no comment! Instead of organising flying pickets, the mighty TGWU crumbled.

As we have seen, solidarity also failed in the steel industry. The steel unions had been unresponsive from the start. When the NUM and the rail unions applied their blockade in June, Tommy Brennan, convenor at Ravenscraig, said he would work with scab deliveries of coal and iron ore. Peter McKim in Llanwern said the same. ISTC [steel union] general secretary Bill

Sirs, according to the *Financial Times* (2 July), "sounded almost like a British Steel spokesman".

From late June British Steel started running huge convoys of scab lorries into Ravenscraig and, especially, from Port Talbot to Llanwern. Miners' picketing in Port Talbot soon tailed off, and was token at Ravenscraig. The steelworks kept running at full, indeed increased, production.

Many miners were critical of the area NUM leaders on this. In South Wales, for example, where area president Emlyn Williams had publicly criticised Arthur Scargill's effort to mobilise for Orgreave, Mark Thomas of Penrhiwceiber NUM told *Socialist Organiser*:

"The leadership [of South Wales] — or the majority of them — are failing to give us a determined lead. This comes out most notably in the way they have handled the steelworks situation and the scab miners at the Point of Ayr colliery in North Wales. Increased picketing is not only essential to win the dispute but key to keeping the membership involved. Many people have drifted off, not because they have lost interest, but because of the token nature of the activity we are involved in.

"There are 4000 steelworkers at Llanwern. Not all of them can be Bill Sirs fans. [There should be] a regular bulletin attempting to speak inside the plant, leafleting of the pubs and clubs in the area..." (*SO* 187).

Stopping steel would have been difficult with the best tactics from the NUM, given the steel unions' attitude and the steel workers' recent experience. But some of the NUM leaders were so overwhelmed by the difficulties that they practically gave up.

In rail and docks, too, problems of leadership had combined with problems of confidence among the rank and file.

Having seen the miners on strike for four months, railworkers, dockers and steelworkers knew what was involved in a serious battle with the government — the risk of months of deprivation, legal threats, police violence. The prospect was especially daunting in the steelworks, where the workforce was a shattered remnant, reduced in numbers by a half since 1980.

Railworkers and dockers were still often willing to take a stand for principle: to show solidarity when they were asked to handle coal. But to link their fate more fully with the miners in an indefinite strike? There was, in Paul Whetton's words quoted above, "a natural reluctance". London dockers, for example, told *SO* that they just did not believe that the extension of the Dock Labour Scheme could be won under a Tory government.

In addition to all this there was the deadening effect of the Labour Party's role in the strike. The Party rank and file were with the miners. Labour Party activists, premises and equipment were involved in the miners' strike to a degree probably not seen in any dispute since the 1920s. The National Executive Committee backed the miners and called for a levy to support them. Conference condemned police violence and defied Kinnock's request to condemn pickets' violence.

But what most people saw, courtesy of TV, was the public weaseling of Kinnock, Hattersley and others. We should not underestimate the role played by this in dampening the spirits of the labour movement.

To rally around the miners and against Thatcher, the movement had to have the feeling of being a movement, the feeling that it could win, that its leaders wanted to win and would fight. It had to have its leaders saying,

## Why steel was crucial

British Steel chair Robert Haslam said after the end of the strike:

"I have the temerity to believe that if our employees and management had not responded so positively in the early days of the strike, our production would have been halted very quickly with immediate, serious ripple effects for the motor, food and many other key industries.

"Also, other unionised employees would undoubtedly have been encouraged to show much more solidarity with the National Union of Mineworkers. Thus the evolution of the strike would have been very different and the pressures on the National Coal Board and the Government would have been immeasurably greater."

Sir Robert said the corporation had to resort to extraordinary measures to keep going, including massive lorry convoys and the use of armadas of small ships delivering imported coal to small ports on the River Trent and the River Usk.

*Financial Times*, 13 March 1985

with political boldness to match the boldness of the NUM's industrial challenge to Thatcher: "there is an alternative to Thatcher". The leaders had to say it, mean it and fight for it, and in the first place back those already engaged in the fight against Thatcher.

A politically confident movement could have boosted the industrial solidarity by countering the fears, depression and hopelessness that held back many workers who sympathised with the miners from acting. Kinnock and his team played a fatal role here. Instead of creating a movement against the Tories around the miners, they made the emergence of such a movement impossible. They acted like acid corroding the links and sinews of the movement.

The leadership could have swayed it. A leadership which puts the issues squarely and is visibly prepared to fight to the end can rally the faint-hearted. In the charged atmosphere of summer 1984, there was a lot of potential militancy that could be rallied.

The union leaders were inadequate, too.

The ISTC leadership was positively opposed to a struggle. Having sabotaged the steelworkers' chance of saving jobs in their industry in 1980, Bill Sirs now preached no option except the strictest co-operation with management to preserve "viability".

The TGWU leadership had made some gestures towards supporting the miners. The ineffectiveness of its boycott on coal movements by road was partly due to the inherent difficulty in organising an industry like road haulage, with a multitude of small employers. But TGWU Scottish secretary Hugh Wyper is reported to have sent 52 union cards to scab drivers at Yuill and Dodds, the main firm involved in taking supplies into Ravenscraig. On payment of a £10 fine, the scab drivers have had full union membership restored.

And the way the TGWU leadership ran the docks strike was a disaster.

In July, and again in August-September, when there was a second docks strike, the TGWU did not even put forward any precise demands for the strike. It argued that the disputes had nothing at all to do with the miners. Nobody believed them, least of all the dockers whose solidarity with the miners had triggered the dispute. Many other dockers — men who could have been won to a fight which linked their own threatened jobs to the miners' fight for jobs — felt they were being manipulated.

In November, TGWU members struck again, at Austin Rover: the union leadership supported them, after a fashion, but did nothing at all as the AUEW and EETPU [forerunners of Amicus] pressurized the strikers back to work. When the High Court fined the TGWU for supporting that strike without a ballot as prescribed by Tory law, the union leadership again opted for masterly inaction. It didn't pay the fine, nor did it organise any action in defence of the union.

The TGWU leadership, in other words, did not fight to raise the confidence of their members. They reflected the lack of confidence, in the debased form of bureaucratic cowardice; and thus became a factor against action.

The rail union leaders likewise. They gave official support to a boycott of coal movements, although the militants in the front line of that boycott — as at Coalville — were highly critical of the lack of support from the leadership against British Rail harassment. But when they had a chance of going out in front themselves — over pay in May, and again over workshop closures in September — they shrank back.

If the NUM had had leaders like the rail unions or the TGWU, let alone the unspeakable Sirs, then the miners themselves would probably never have had a national strike.

As Dennis Skinner told *Socialist Organiser* in July: "I don't think the NUM would be on strike now if it hadn't had some very competent leadership" (*SO* 188).

The truth, as Dennis Skinner put it, is that only competent leadership got even 80% of the NUM out. The basic difficulty was not this or that tactical device, but that in the political and industrial situation of March 1984 the odds were extremely daunting.

At the start of the strike (editorial of 29 March) *Socialist Organiser* had said bluntly: "The strike cannot be won in the pits". Solidarity was irreplaceable. And on 4 April John McIlroy wrote: "It would be self-deluding to pretend that today's miners' strike is anything but an uphill struggle. The miners are divided. The price is now being paid for the weaknesses of the past period. Conditions are very different from those prevailing in the victorious struggles of the early 70s".

The editorial of 19 April added: "Only a general strike can stop the Tories. The alternative is to let the miners get mauled in a strike that could stretch into next winter".

Miners understood this too. No wonder sections with weak area leadership and more apparent security from closures — like Notts — were not keen to go on strike.

The wonder is not the weaknesses of the strike, but its strength — the stubborn courage with which the miners defied all the iron laws and the iron fists of this soulless government of exploitation and repression.

It is true that the NUM paper, *The Miner*, which had the job of rallying, encouraging and fortifying the striking miners, sometimes gave an impression of over-confidence, as if victory would be certain if only the miners stuck firm for a few weeks. But Arthur Scargill, in an interview on 15 June, made it clear that he had a lucid view of the odds.

"Faced with the Coal Board's closure plan, the progressive elements in the NUM discussed two options. One, you accept the plan and allow pits to close. Alternatively you fight it. If you fight and you have lost, at least you fought it..."

It is this combination of realism with willingness to stand on the line which raises Scargill — and the other NUM left-wingers — head and shoulders above the other leaders of the trade union movement. And Scargill consistently did what was necessary in the situation.

"If I am the last person left rejecting the closure plan, then that will be my position. If I am right, I'll stick there. I don't know how some people can fudge and compromise on... a principle" (*Financial Times*, 15 June).

And right from 14 April onwards Arthur Scargill appealed repeatedly and urgently for other workers to strike — both through their union leaders and over their heads.

He was not able to do more than make appeals. Scargill's great predecessor as NUM leader in the 1920s, A J Cook, was a leading figure in a cross-union rank and file movement, the so-called "Minority Movement", as well as being the miners' president. He thus had an organisation to campaign for solidarity in other unions. Scargill had no such organisation: one major lesson from the strike must be the need to build a new Minority Movement.

## Cooking Picket Pie

The Women's Action group has been working hard since the early weeks of the strike. We've been providing families with three food parcels a week, since we don't have cooking facilities in our club.

We started oil by raising voluntary funds ourselves — by going out in the street with the NUM banner and standing out all morning. We got some funny looks at first, but soon contributions started coming in.

We also go to Rotherham to collect, but the funds are drying up now. We've bled our own areas dry. If people are not unemployed, they're pensioners or strikers — mind you, some pensioners are our best supporters.

We also run a weekly coffee morning and jumble sale and run rallies all the time. Last month we had a good laugh holding a funny football match between the woman and the "flying pickets". We didn't raise much money but we got a lot out of our system.

We cook at home in my kitchen and so when pickets get back we have a home-baked meat pie and peas — it's called Picket Pie — and we can't cook anything else now, the men won't have it.

Some weeks we cook three or four times but because you don't always know when it's required, it's difficult to have a rota. Also you can't cope with more than two people cooking in my kitchen!

Ann Bowns interviewed in *Socialist Organiser*, 16 August 1984

# The balance begins to shift

The lack of such a rank and file movement was the basic reason for the failure to stop steel. By late June all the major steelworks were fully supplied, and set to stay that way.

The docks strike, the solidarity which stopped almost all coal trains, and the six well-supported regional days of action (well-supported considering the lack of official campaigning) offset the failure in steel.

On 16 July the well-informed *Financial Times* wrote: "There is now a substantial lobby in the Coal Board — though not in the government — for a settlement before the end of autumn, even if a settlement means conceding that pits cannot be closed on purely 'economic grounds'..." These tensions in the NCB would erupt later in sackings and resignations of top officials.

But, nevertheless, from early August, as we have seen, the balance began to shift. The government had used its legal bludgeon on a section of the labour movement, and discovered that it could get away with it without the TUC responding on behalf of the whole movement. Now it could confidently wait its time to use the bludgeon again.

The shift in the balance was, however, slow and unstable. The miners put up a fierce resistance. They were still solid, and would remain fundamentally solid until November.

No-one quite knew how near or remote power cuts were. The debacles at Llanwern and Ravenscraig had marked a reflux of solidarity, following its high point, but the rail action was still strong — and, indeed, additional solidarity action was still developing in late 1984 and early 1985, in the form of new mass pickets of power stations. In the huge furnace of the strike, new flames were constantly leaping up.

For example, at Florence colliery, North Staffs, the first women's picket in the Midlands took place as late as 11 October. "150 women descended on the picket line armed with song sheets, candles, streamers, and bags of enthusiasm. The all-male police presence were at first slightly bemused, but soon called in a couple of dozen women PCs.

"The non-stop singing and jeering turned three scabs back, but much more than that, the whole atmosphere generated vast quantities of energy, confidence and determination.

"As a grand finale, the 150 women joined together to form 'the Miners' Strike Conga', and danced and sang around the main road to the pit. The police found this 'intimidating'." (*SO* 201)

Meanwhile, the longer the miners stuck out, the more likely was a "second front" which would put the screws on the Tories. (The second docks strike, for example, ran from 24 August to 18 September).

From June, and more intensely from August, the Tories and the NCB mounted an offensive to break the strike. Backed by all the propaganda the tabloid press could put out — backed up none too subtly, though less crudely, by TV — they launched a back-to-work drive. Scargill-baiting and NUM-bashing became the obsession of the press, in a campaign of unbridled hatred against the miners' leader they could not cow.

To match and balance their demonology against the best leader any section of the labour movement has had in decades, the press in 1984 (in August, especially) discovered the representative working-class hero of Mrs Thatcher's new Britain — the scab.

An atmosphere of hysterical pressure was built up in the country, resembling almost the atmosphere in the big marquee during an evangelical revival meeting when the call goes out for sinners to get up and "testify for Jesus". Instant glorification, if not on-the-spot canonisation, awaited the man who would step forward to 'testify' for Thatcher and for strikebreaking. He would be dubbed with some would-be glamorising name like "Silver Birch", or the "Dockers' Silver Birch".

The back-to-work drive had little success in June. Then from July North Derbyshire NCB area director Ken Moses started a campaign of unprecedented ruthlessness. Miners living outside the main pit villages were singled out. They were written to, phoned, visited, systematically pressurised.

Moses' effort produced few results until November. But in late August a "National Working Miners' Committee" was set up, under the wing of Thatcherite whizz kid David Hart. A Notts "Working Miners' Committee" had existed since the end of May.

## The Scab as Hero

The typical hero of Mrs Thatcher's brave new Britain is the scab. No-one in Britain today is more honourable or respect-worthy, the mass-circulation newspapers tell us, than the "men who take their courage in their hands and, braving the violent savagery of crazy left-wing-led pickets"... crawl on their bellies to lick their bosses' boots and help them defeat and beat down their fellow workers.

No trade is more honoured than that of the scab-herder, no force more highly praised than the militarised ranks of police thugs who protect them.

No, the working class heroes are still the men and women who dare to take on this vicious government despite the pressures of slump and mass unemployment. They are the dockers who fight for their own concerns, but also want to help the miners. They are the millions of loyal trade unionists who resist the pressure and the hysteria with the grim determination of people who know what the capitalists and their government are trying to do in Britain right now.

Editorial, *Socialist Organiser*, 30 August 1984

Ominously, towards the end of August, a few scabs appeared in South Yorkshire. Huge numbers of police descended not only on the picket lines but also on the pit villages, which in the following months were transformed into mini police states.

Sue Carlyle penned this picture of life in Kiveton Park, where it sometimes seemed as if the entire might of the British state were being mobilised to ensure that seven scabs would get to work.

"To support and defend their right to scab, and help the Coal Board break the strike, the village has been turned into a mini police state.

"The scabs now have police guards back and front of their houses, or hiding in their garages and back gardens. After each shift the scabs are taken home in convoys consisting of from three to five transit vans loaded with police.

"As you look through the guarded windows at them speeding past, the scabs hold their heads down...

"Every morning, in the early hours, between 2,000 and 3,000 police drive in to barricade the pit from pickets. The picket line is physically pushed every morning from the pit entrance into a country road away from the village. The police make charges through the old people's estate and parade horses and riot gear through the main street, endangering local people, young and old."

From late August, a second wave of mass picketing was mounted by striking miners — not to spread the strike but to stop scabs at their own pits, where, as soon as one single scab could be found, the government would send hundreds of police to bully and intimidate the community.

**"The miners' strike is an extreme example of what we in the Socialist Workers Party have called the 'downturn' in the movement." — Tony Cliff, *Socialist Worker*, 14 April 1984**

# The TUC congress

This was the situation when, six months into the miners' strike, the TUC congress opened at Brighton on 3 September. By now even a David Basnett [leader of the GMB] was worried enough to make a seemingly sincere speech about the responsibility of the TUC to stop the government in its manifest desire to destroy the NUM.

The ball was at the feet of the TUC. There was still time to rally the working class to the miners. But, of course, the TUC leaders had made it clear months before that they would not support the miners. They wanted to get themselves in as mediators between the miners and the government, so that a deal could be fixed that would end the strike.

The congress, despite all its bureaucratic limitations, would want something better. The miners' strike had gripped the imagination of militants and activists throughout the movement. So the leaders trimmed and faked.

The NUM had put down an amendment calling for "industrial action involving all trade unions". The furniture union FTAT called for a 24 hour general strike. But, under pressure from the TUC leaders, these were withdrawn in favour of a near-unanimous resolution recommending — conditional on the agreement of each individual union concerned — a boycott of coal, coke or substitute oil moved across NUM picket lines.

The resolution was passed with great enthusiasm from the floor.

*SO* commented: "Either this TUC congress will mark the beginning of a new rallying of the working class around the miners. Or it will go down in history as one of the worst examples of vile left-talking fakery in the history of the labour movement.

"The reflex of every militant with an ounce of sense will be to regard the almost unanimous vote as mainly an exercise in left-fakery by the leaders of the TUC...

"[But] the TUC decision is a lever which miners can use to gain solidarity. For it to be effective rank and file militants should start organising to use it now" (*SO* 195).

Vile left-talking fakery it was. The railworkers and seafarers had already been giving such support for months. Some power-stations likewise. A few more power stations did start boycott action, but, as it turned out, not enough to be decisive. The EETPU and the power engineers' union voted against the TUC resolution and did nothing to implement it: the GMBU and the TGWU, who had the majority of coal-handling workers in power stations, did practically nothing.

Arthur Scargill complained in mid-January: "I did ask the leaders of the major power unions if they would arrange meetings of shop stewards in the major power stations. Although there was no rejection of this idea, it has not been put into operation" (*SO* 212).

The TUC resolution strengthened NUM appeals for solidarity, and was thus something to build on. But it wasn't much. The question arises: would it not have been better if the NUM leaders had pushed the call at congress for a general strike? It would have given a rallying point for the militants and the Left, at least. *Socialist Organiser* thought at the time that they should have pushed the general strike resolution, and in hindsight we think we were right.

But the lack of an organised rank and file movement was especially critical in the weeks after the TUC. This lack ensured that the solidarity produced was no more than the TUC leaders intended.

The first week after the TUC was occupied by talks between the NCB and the NUM — shifting to and fro between Edinburgh, Selby, Doncaster and London. Many rank and file strikers were bewildered and disturbed.

Stan Crawford of Bevercotes NUM, Notts, wrote in SO: "The main problem during the week of NUM-NCB talks was not knowing what was going

## The SWP's turn

The Socialist Workers' Party has made a "turn" from what they themselves now describe as splendid isolation — splendid, it wasn't! — to participation in miners' support committees and trade union Broad Lefts.

Yet for the first five or six months of the strike, the SWP played virtually no role in the Birmingham committee. A couple of individual SWP members turned up to the meetings, but the organisation itself took no part in the work. Leading SWP members privately dismissed its work as "left-wing Oxfam" (a reference to the food collections) and suggested that the leaders of the Trades Council were "minor bureaucrats" using the strike to further their careers.

Suddenly, all that has changed. SWP members now turn up in force at the Committee's meetings, and generally play a constructive role.

*SW* now carries frequent articles praising the work of the once-despised "baked beans brigade" (food collectors).

All this is to the good. But what about an explanation for this dramatic turn?

A cynic might point to the *Socialist Worker* sales report carried in the same issue as the article on Birmingham: "Birmingham SWP are actively involved in the miners' support group. When they first started they used to sell eight papers a week. Now that they have been working alongside other activists for a considerable time the sale has increased to 15".

However, we should welcome the comrades in.

Jim Denham, from *Socialist Organiser*, 1 November 1984

on... All we knew was what we saw on television or read in the papers. We were left to guess.

"I would like to see talks held in the open, as they were during Solidarnosc's negotiations with the Polish government four years ago. Then, the discussion was broadcast to the membership as and when it was happening" (*SO* 197).

Then, once more, the prospect opened up of other workers decisively tilting the balance in favour of the NUM. The pit deputies' (overseers') union NACODS decided on 12 September to ballot its members on strike action over the two issues of pit closures and pay being stopped for deputies who refused to cross picket lines. If NACODS struck, every pit in Britain would stop.

## Eric Heffer MP backs law-breaking miners

If you've got legislation of this kind, then it's quite clear that workers are bound to come up against those laws. They're bad laws, they're class laws.

Whether the Labour Party thinks they ought to come out against those laws or not, the workers are going to do so. And when workers are in struggle against bad laws, it is my feeling that the Labour Party has got to support those workers, while at the same time pressing for a change in those laws.

The Tolpuddle Martyrs — the people for whom we march around with banners saying how marvellous they were — they broke the law. We have a trade union movement in this country because people were prepared to stand up against bad laws and break them.

Eric Heffer speaking on TV-AM, 1 August 1984

# The Labour Party conference

The result of the ballot — 82.5% for a strike — was announced on 28 September. The same day the High Court declared whole NUM strike "unlawful" because there had not been a national ballot.

The Labour Party conference opened at Blackpool on 1 October. Labour Party conference is less tightly sewn up than the TUC, and it overturned and overruled the platform line on the miners' strike.

Arthur Scargill got a tremendous reception. Neil Kinnock had given the impression for six months of slinking around on the edge of the great working class battle, waiting for a good chance to savage Arthur Scargill; but now the Labour Party conference rejected his "statesmanlike" even-handed condemnation of violence, by which primarily he meant pickets' violence.

Conference condemned police violence, called for police to be removed from the coalfields, and thus implicitly sided with the pickets. (*SO* supporters originated the crucial clauses.)

Albert Bowns (Kiveton Park NUM commented: "We got the support we wanted from the rank and file, but we certainly didn't get the support we wanted from the leadership, particularly Kinnock.

"I thought he was very skilful, the way he skirted round the issue — it was a typical politician's answer.

"Kinnock is concerned only to put forward policies he thinks people will vote for and so, of course, he was worried about the violence. But the present situation is the perfect opportunity to put forward socialist policies. Instead the leadership... think that all working people are 'moderates'. But what is happening now is not moderation..."

Two scab miners had applied for a High Court declaration that it was unlawful for the NUM to run a national strike because its rulebook required a national ballot for a national strike. The legal action paralleled a new Tory anti-union law requiring ballots for all strikes. But that law was not actually used. The court took it upon itself to interpret the NUM's rulebook, and declared the strike unlawful.

On 1 October the NUM leaders were served with a court order, as they sat in the Labour Party conference, declaring that they were in "contempt of court" for continuing to call the strike official. They responded by insisting that the strike was official according to the rules of the NUM, and that they would not let the court dictate to the union. On 10 October the court fined the NUM £200,000. When the union would not pay, it ordered the seizure of the NUM's entire funds, on 25 October.

The day before, 24 October, NACODS had called off strike plans with a miserable compromise, slinking away while the miners fought for jobs. Now, for the NUM, blow followed blow.

Police violence in the Yorkshire pit villages was stepped up dramatically. The screaming, spitting gutter press was now witch-hunting and agitating about an NUM official's fund-raising visit to Libya (although many British firms, and even the NCB itself, have links with Libya). The TUC leaders did nothing to help the NUM. Congress was over for a year, so fake militancy and fake concern for the survival of the NUM was no longer at a premium.

TUC chair Jack Eccles said publicly that the TUC should pressurise the NUM into accepting the NACODS deal (for an "independent" non-binding element within the colliery review procedure). Several top trade union leaders agreed — off the record. TUC general secretary Norman Willis went through the motions of dissociating the TUC from Eccles' rambling. He did nothing to help the miners.

At the time union leaders who backed Eccles did not even dare go on the record about it. But now many people in the labour movement or on its journalistic fringes are trying to set up in business as wise men and sages with the thought that really the NUM would have been best advised to accept the NACODS deal in October. After all, the NUM did end up in February offering to accept that deal and being told by the Tories that now they had to have something worse.

Such a philosophy would rule out almost any serious struggle. In October the strike was still around 80% solid. The strikers were still confident and strong. The Coal Board was visibly in trouble: NCB official mouthpiece Michael Eaton was suspended on 29 October, and director of information Geoffrey Kirk was sacked on 31 October. A second front was about to be opened up by Austin Rover and Jaguar car workers striking over pay from 1 November. Only a faintheart could recommend settling for the miserable NACODS deal.

Even as it turned out — with the Austin Rover unions leaving their members in the lurch, and the TUC remaining inactive even when the High Court appointed a receiver over the NUM's finances — the miners did not end up worse than they would have done by settling in October.

If, by some quirk, the NUM leaders had gone for the NACODS formula and bulldozed the strikers into accepting it, then many miners — certainly, the militants who were the heart and soul of the strike — would have gone back feeling let down and shamed, if not betrayed. They would feel that they had accepted defeat in mid-battle. Such an outcome would have been worse for the miners, and for the labour movement as a whole, than the defeat which actually happened. In any case, there was not a single voice within the NUM for accepting Eccles' fine. Right-winger Trevor Bell talked about a ballot on the NCB's proposals in mid-November, but that was all.

## Scab-herding in North Derbyshire

From the start of the strike, the management armed itself with names, addresses and telephone numbers of workers and plotted their residence and likely attitudes on large maps. The plan was to concentrate on workers living outside the immediate area of the pit villages. The management also drew up lists of men believed to be strongly hostile to the strike, or even those who had worked a lot of overtime and might therefore be finding things particularly difficult financially. The management began telephoning and visiting those likely to return. After organising the men into groups, buses were arranged to pick them up at central points.

"Putting transport on was a key", said Mr Moses. So was the growing role of the working miners themselves in breaking the strike. Mr Roland Taylor, from Shirebrook and a member of the national working miners' committee, was responsible for court actions preventing disciplinary action by the union. He said: "Everything that is happening now has been tried in Derbyshire. I've thought things through with management at my own pit. They suggested we use phones to call people up, they gave us lists and lent us vans. Shirebrook has been a well-oiled team."

NUM activists complain that the area has three working miners on full pay doing nothing but knock on people's doors. "We try to go round and counter it, but we cannot provide them with the instant gratification of over £600", said Mr David Crowther, an NUM delegate from Warsop.

The scab-herding operation in North Derbyshire, as described in the *Financial Times*, 14 November 1984

# November: on the defensive

With the start of November, the strike went decidedly onto the defensive. After months of chipping away, the Coal Board finally claimed a break-through with scabbing in North Derbyshire. The NCB offered a massive Christmas bribe to miners — who had not had a wage packet for eight months, and were now suffering serious hardship — if they returned to work. By 19 November the NCB was claiming a record 2282 miners returning to work on a Monday. Two pits which come under the Yorkshire NUM but are geographically in Notts — Manton and Shireoaks — suffered major back-to-work moves.

The NUM was organising a series of regional strikers' rallies. These showed the tremendous continuing determination of the hard core of the strike, but also their bitterness about the official leaders of labour. At Aberafan on 13 November a symbolic noose was dangled in front of TUC general secretary Norman Willis; "Ramsey MacKinnock" was pilloried for refusing to speak at the rallies.

Now there was a growing note of anguish in Arthur Scargill's appeals: "We have to translate resolution into action. I am not going to appeal to the barons of the TUC — I want to ask the ordinary men and women of this country to give industrial action support to this union.

"How much longer can you stand to one side and see this union battered? We are asking you to come out now and stop scab coal being delivered into power stations" (Birmingham, 14 November: *SO* 206).

At police-battered Kiveton Park, there were still only 26 scabs in mid-November. But branch delegate Albert Bowns, a leading militant, told *SO* how things now looked to him:

"I think a general strike is less likely at the moment than it has been in the past... I just can't see anything happening through the TUC.

"I was hoping for something more from the national delegate meeting [of the NUM on 5 November] than these rallies. I was hoping for, perhaps, a national mass picket on particular collieries or particular areas. Now, we're just sticking to our own collieries and it's making us weaker... " (*SO* 206).

The labour movement was shamelessly leaving the NUM to its fate in the struggle against the government. So the Tories pressed relentlessly on.

On 30 November the Tories delivered what they hoped was a knock-out punch. Tory lawyer Herbert Brewer was appointed by the High Court as receiver of the NUM's finances. Brewer declared, "I am the NUM".

Legally, he was the NUM. But there was another NUM, not the notional legal entity now embodied by the High Court in the unlikely figure of the former Tory councillor, but the 140,000 striking miners and their families.

And that NUM refused to go down under the new blow. They refused to surrender the union's money, which they had moved overseas.

Four days previously, on 26 November, the High Court had fined the TGWU £200,000 (to be paid by 10 December) for supporting the Austin Rover strike without a ballot in Tory-prescribed form. All the other car unions wriggled out (including the Communist-Party-led TASS, whose general secretary, Moscow-liner Ken Gill, told the court that he had wished to obey the injunction to withdraw support from the strike — but since he had not been supporting it anyway, he had not known what to do). But the TGWU would not pay the fine.

Unfortunately, it would not do anything positive either. The meeting of its executive in early December decided to take no action against the threat to the union. If passive endurance could beat the Tories, then the TGWU would have done the workers of Britain a great service in 1984. But passivity — even defiant passivity — is not enough.

Now Arthur Scargill's efforts to rouse the labour movement and to make it aware of what was happening reached a new peak of desperate urgency. Again and again he appealed for industrial action to back the miners. "There must be the most massive mobilisation of industrial action our movement has ever known, and we must have it now.

"There is no other way to stop the court's attempt to destroy the NUM" (*SO* 209).

Other voices on the left augmented and supplemented Scargill's. Tony Benn (reportedly on the private urging of Scargill and Heathfield) called for a general strike; so did Dennis Skinner.

But the TUC leaders did nothing. Neil Kinnock had earlier refused a request by the Labour Party NEC to speak at the November series of NUM rallies. Now he condescended to speak at a miners' rally in Stoke on 30 November, to put "the case for coal" (as distinct from the case for the miners!) and — faced with jeering, baiting demands from Thatcher and her press that he do so — to denounce pickets' "violence".

Things were going badly for the miners, but, despite all the miners' difficulties, the Tories were still scared of a second front. That was shown very clearly by the careful way the courts handled the TGWU, using an official called the "Queen's Remembrancer" to take £200,000 rather than seizing the union's whole funds. Despite everything, even a limited initiative from other unions could have swung the balance against the government.

*Socialist Organiser* proposed a campaign for a recall TUC, which might call the leaders to account for their failure to implement the decisions of September. A campaign for a recall TUC could be used to focus discussion of the miners' strike in the trade union branches. We argued that, if a full general strike were not possible immediately, then as a first step a 24 hour general strike should be called by the pro-NUM unions or even by the NUM itself.

"I'm not sure", objected Paul Whetton. "It's a hell of a gamble. A call for a strike could rebound on the NUM if the NUM itself called it... For the NUM to call a one-day general strike would be the last card. It always is the last card in a shop steward's or a branch secretary's hand — if you call a strike and nobody answers, then you have played your last card" (*SO* 210).

That "last card" could have rallied and helped to organise the hundreds of thousands of active supporters that the NUM had won in the labour movement. But scepticism was understandable. Albert Bowns, for example, disputed the demand for a recall TUC. "We all hoped that we would get a good reaction from the TUC when its congress met. We hoped that they would get everyone out alongside us. Since that hasn't happened, I just can't see anything happening through the TUC" (*SO* 206).

"I think we've got to call for a recall TUC conference", said Paul Whetton, but without any illusions — "put the arguments again and give them one last chance to come in with us".

The NUM leaders followed up their November rallies with a speaking tour in the pit villages during December. The back-to-work drive tapered off, collections increased as Christmas came nearer, and at Christmas itself the pit communities celebrated with defiant solidarity. Despite all the hardships, many strikers and many strikers' wives insisted that it was their best Christmas ever, because of the warmth and comradeship. Instead of isolated families, each slumped in front of their television, whole communities came together to support each other and celebrate.

But the turn of the year brought back the grimness. Energy minister Peter Walker confidently claimed (29 December) that there would be "no power cuts in 1985". Although the City and East London were blacked out for some hours on 7 January, the policy of oil-burning and maximum use of nuclear power did in fact see the Central Electricity Generating Board through to the end of the strike without any crippling cuts.

As if to rub brine in the miners' wounds, the Tories marked New Year's Day by giving peerages to Len Murray and former electricians' leader Frank Chapple — the symbols and representatives of everything in the labour movement that had combined with the slump and effects of mass unemployment to allow the Tories to impose the sufferings of a ten month strike on the miners and their families, and would ultimately allow them to win the strike.

The steady dribble back to work was now usually to be measured in hundreds per day. Neil Kinnock decided that the strike had gone near enough to defeat for him to visit a picket line (by chauffeur-driven car) in the same way that he might attend commemorations for the Tolpuddle Martyrs.

But the miners were very much alive. The indomitable spirit of defiance of capitalist "normality" was still strong.

At Kiveton Park the strike started to break up seriously from 21 January, after 10 months out and five months of heavy police occupation of the village.

When people set out together on a difficult, testing struggle, and some of them break and give up or change sides, those who continue to fight are forced to think hard and define for themselves and others just what they think they are doing. Albert Bowns did that when Reg Moss, a branch official at Kiveton Park, started scabbing in late January and allowed the *Daily Express* to proclaim the fact and use him against the strikers. Albert Bowns published an open letter to Moss — and to others who had given up the strike — in *Socialist Organiser*:

Reg Moss had said he wanted to return to "normal life". But: "What is normal about having to accept mass redundancies? What is normal about having to accept pit closures on economic grounds (possibly Kiveton Park)?

"What is normal about craftsmen being de-skilled ... ? In effect, what is normal about running to accept every crumb which the management might, and I say might, condescend to offer us?

"That is the 'normality' which you will have to return to if the rest of us follow your example.

"The Kiveton Park NUM was directed to fight against this kind of 'normality' and will continue to do so until the final outcome" (*SO* 214).

*Socialist Organiser* tried to present an accurate picture of the stages the strike went through as it unfolded. We refused to voice any of the pessimism or defeatism rampant in sections of the Left (in *Socialist Worker*, for example). Even so, by 6 February we had to admit: "Whatever the exact number of new scabs, it is true that a steady stream of strikers seem to be giving up and letting themselves be driven back to work. Inevitably this drift back puts pressure on the strikers and encourages Thatcher's belief that her lust for the NUM's blood can be satisfied" (*SO* 215).

In this adverse situation, South Wales NUM official Kim Howells floated the idea of a return to work without an agreement (6 February). Whatever the possible merits of this as a tactic once the union was collectively convinced that a further attempt to maintain the strike would only tear shreds off the NUM, to raise it there and then through the hostile media was highly counter-productive.

Paul Whetton commented: "To make that statement on the eve of a crucial meeting of the executive showed exceedingly bad judgement, at best, and at worst an attempt to scupper any cohesive policy... When it came over on the news, the reaction amongst the Notts striking miners was one of horror. Absolute horror... In fact the Notts striking miners lobbied the executive meeting... to oppose the suggestion coming out of South Wales" (*SO* 216).

The executive did not even discuss the idea, and Kim Howells was removed from his job as an area NUM spokesperson. But damage had been done. And then the TUC stepped in with its final blow.

# Tories out to shred the NUM

On 19 February seven TUC leaders scurried to Downing Street, not even bothering to conceal their glee that they were back in contact with the people who had just sent Len and Frank to the House of Lords. They eagerly took on the job of acting as messenger boys to the NUM. The message from Thatcher said, in essence: "surrender, or else. No negotiations, no concessions: surrender!"

When the NUM rejected this document, the TUC let it be known that they were washing their hands of the miners, and retired to let Thatcher urge her surrender terms under the title of "the TUC document".

Few things in the strike were more sickening than the cat and mouse games played by the government from November to the end. First, they offered the Christmas bribe to needy miners, and howled with indecent glee when some miners deserted the strike. They were showing their displeasure with Scargill's undemocratic methods, said the press, as the broken men slunk back to work.

Then the Tories played the game of the on-off negotiations, raising the hopes of the miners and then, having softened up a few, slamming the door and waiting for more miners to give in. Having said for months that the NACODS deal was on offer to the NUM, they withdrew it at the point, at the end of the strike, when Arthur Scargill said he would accept it.

The Tories now did not want a settlement. They wanted to shred the NUM.

Commenting on the great Dublin lockout of 1913, the employers' leader in that struggle, William Martin Murphy, cynically identified the fundamental disadvantage for labour in any long industrial war of attrition. The workers, he pointed out, soon have difficulties getting enough to eat; the employers rarely have that problem. By March 1985 Britain's glorious miners had that problem.

The Tories had all the resources of the ruling class at their disposal. The miners, some two per cent of the labour movement, had to fight 100% of that centralised ruling-class power with insufficient support and sometimes downright sabotage from the leaders of the other 98%. That was the cause of the defeat.

On 3 March the eighth NUM conference since the strike began met to decide what to do. South Wales proposed a return to work without an agreement. Arthur Scargill opposed the return to work, and so did the executive. They argued instead that, with over 50 per cent of miners still out, the strike should continue until 700 sacked strikers got their jobs back.

The majority of delegates felt that there was a danger that a big acceleration of scabbing would further erode the union's bargaining power on the 700 (and everything else), and result, ultimately, in a return to work with the union in tatters. They decided to stop that happening.

Starved, battered, but still defiant, they voted by 98 to 91 to return to work without a settlement, but as a still-intact union.

To go back without the 700, and fight for their reinstatement in local negotiations, was a bitter and agonising decision to have to take. In the circumstances the conference had little viable alternative. This was confirmed a few days later when the first wave of Labour councils failed to deliver on their promises of opening up a second front, instead collapsing ignominiously.

Once the decision was taken, Scargill and the left-wingers on the executive urged a united return to work, and most areas went back on Tuesday 5 March.

Kent, and a few pits elsewhere, stayed out for a week after the national return to work. Polmaise, in Scotland, the first pit out in 1984, did not go back until Tuesday 12 March, after one year and four weeks on strike.

The greatest strike in British history was over. But the miners' strike was one battle in a war, and the war is far from over. "The fight goes on", said Arthur Scargill after the decision to return had been taken. The NUM has been forced to retreat to "guerrilla" struggle — "like the Resistance in World War Two", as Scargill put it.

# The fight goes on

It was a defeat; and what we said during the dispute about the heavy implications of a defeat for the whole labour movement was true. But it was not just a defeat; nor was the struggle in vain. And it is not the end of the fight.

Despite all the horrors and hardships suffered by the pit communities during the strike, and the further horrors and hardships that will be imposed on them and on the whole working class in the immediate period ahead as the Tories improve on their victory, many good things have already come or can yet come out of this struggle.

In the first place, the Tories were shaken. We still do not know how close they were to crippling power cuts at the end of the strike. They certainly had to sacrifice over £5 billion for the dispute, and they have built up a vast fund of working-class resentment against themselves.

Thatcher's success so far will reconcile the ruling class to the huge costs of this strike as a "worthwhile investment" in crushing class struggle once and for all. But class struggle never can be crushed once and for all. And the ruling class will not lightly agree to Thatcher taking them into further ventures if they look like rousing resistance similar to the miners'.

History shows a standard pattern after serious working-class defeats in struggle: first, a period, often not very long, when matters go from worse to worse and reaction reigns; then a revival during which it sometimes becomes clear that the defeated struggle chastened the ruling class more than at first seemed.

Studying the very terrible defeat of the Paris workers' uprising in 1871 (30,000 supporters of the Commune were massacred, and many others deported), Marxists later argued that despite defeat the uprising actually did achieve limited gains, in that it tipped the scales towards a republic in the long debate during the 1870s on whether France should be a republic or a monarchy, and helped thereafter to safeguard France's republican constitution.

They also hailed the uprising as a great political inspiration for future generations.

The 1984-5 miners' strike will inspire not only future generations but this one. The miners have shaken Britain and remodelled the political landscape. Class conflict, class bitterness, and class hatred on a level not seen here for a very long time have been brought into the centre of British politics. The ruling class starved men, women and children for a year, and now Mrs Thatcher gloats in public over her triumph. But the miners' strike has stored up memories and hatreds — not only among miners and their families — that the ruling class and the Tories will live to regret.

Tens of thousands have learned that capitalism is a soulless system that sacrifices people for profit; tens of thousands of new militants have learned to hate capitalism and those who run it.

Coming out of jail after a week of being locked up simply because she insisted on picketing, despite police "cautions" and despite bail conditions, Nottinghamshire striking miner's wife Brenda Greenwood spoke the language and expressed the feelings that live in thousands who have gone through the miners' strike.

This is not, as the editorial writers fondly believe, the language of the past, or of a stage in the history of the labour movement which the miners' strike has brought to an end. It is the language of the future.

"The shattering experience of being sent to prison will be etched on my memory for as long as I live. But I am in no way deterred, nor has my spirit been broken.

"The time has come for the working class of the 1980s to stand up and be counted. We must not be afraid to face the machinery of the state head-on in defence of our rights.

"We must fight on every front in defence of all the rights and standards that have been won for us in blood, sweat and tears by the working class of the past.

"It is our duty to defend, protect and uphold all these rights and standards, and it is our proud heritage to hold them in trust for future generations of our class".

# The strike, week by week

**Socialist ORGANISER**

Paper of the Socialist Organiser Alliance No.169 March 8 1984 25p Claimants and strikers 10p

**Inside**

Centre pages: The Iran/Iraq war
Page 4: International Women's Day 1917 – and 1984
Page 3: Benn wins in Chesterfield
Page 4: Youth fighting back
Plus more reports, reviews, letters, controversy.

## SUPPORT THE MINERS

By Martin Thomas

THE miners and Tory hatchetman Ian MacGregor are squaring up for a full-scale fight. South Yorkshire miners are already on strike against the closure of Corton Wood and Bulcliffe collieries.

The National Union of Mineworkers executive meets on Thursday 8th to discuss action against 21,000 job cuts planned for the next year.

Coal Board boss Ian MacGregor has said bluntly that he may go for sackings. Until now, however fast the run-down of the industry, in theory at least every miner at a closed pit has had the option of transferring to another pit.

The area executive in Scotland, where Polmaise miners are already on strike over the planned closure of their pit, is calling for an area strike from Friday.

Mick McGahey, national vice-president and Scottish area president of the union, has predicted a 'domino effect' with strikes spreading from area to area, creating a national strike faster than the formal procedure of a pithead ballot could.

If miners, on this issue, can match the tremendous response of other groups of workers on the GCHQ issue on February 28 – and there is little doubt that they can – then we will have a major national battle against the Tories.

And the miners can win.

There are big coal stocks. Just like there were when the miners' strike began in 1972. But flying pickets and solidarity action by other trade unionists can tie them up.

That solidarity, and those pickets, will be unlawful. But only one group of employers, out of hundreds affected, has dared to go to law over the equally unlawful February 28 strike. If trade union solidarity action is strong enough and determined enough, then no words the Tories write in the statute book can stop it.

MacGregor is determined and hard-faced. But the miners made the Tories back down before, in February 1981, by brushfire spreading strike action.

And now the Tories, beset by scandals and internal divisions, look far less strong than they did a few months ago.

But there are problems.

The NUM leadership has failed to get action on many test-case pit closures since 1981, like Kinneil and Lewis Merthyr. Those failures have left it unsure and unconfident.

In Scotland the area leadership has let Bogside close and delayed the call for solidarity for Polmaise again and again. Nationally, Arthur Scargill has made no definite call for action.

In 1983-4 already 22 pits have closed or been merged, as compared to 11 in 1981-2 and seven in 1982-3.

It is going to need a bold turnabout and a determined leadership to defeat MacGregor and the Tories. There is still time to turn the tide. But that time must be seized, now.

*Pickets in South Yorkshire*

## BREAK LINKS WITH TORIES!

**8 March 1984. South Yorkshire miners strike against closure of Corton Wood and Bulcliffe collieries. Miners at Polmaise colliery in Scotland are already on strike over planned closure of their pit and are calling for an area strike. As the Coal Board gears up for many more pit closures miners spread the strike from area to area into a national strike.**

# Socialist ORGANISER

Paper of the Socialist Organiser Alliance No 170 March 15 1984 25p Claimants and strikers 10p

## Support the pickets who DEFY THE TORY LAWS!

### By Eric Heffer MP

**THE miners should be given every possible support. They are defending not only their jobs and their industry, but in a sense they are defending the entire working class trade union movement, because they have the power and the strength to do it.**

By their efforts they are also helping to combat the government's policies against trade unions and their industrial relations legislation. The entire movement has to give them every possible backing.

It is very interesting how much the press recognises this and have for example, encouraged miners' wives to come out against them going on strike and so on.

I think this is a crunch situation as far as the miners are concerned. If the miners don't come out of this successfully it could be disastrous not only for their future but for the entire trade union movement.

The miners have been very generous to the Labour Party over the years. Their union has been one of the staunchest supporters of the Labour Party.

How practically can we help the miners? Well we shouldn't do anything without the miners themselves wanting us to do it.

But if the miners want us to give them facilities in areas, whether it is the use of our rooms, helping in the propaganda, whatever it is we ought to be prepared to give it.

**If the miners come up against the anti-union legislation, although the government may not be too happy to push their legislation against the miners, I would hope that the miners would respond in a totally positive way.**

I was only sorry to see the divisions in the movement in the past. The movement has learnt something. There were some who took the view that we ought not to break Tory legislation, or at the very least were half-hearted about it.

I think that has to some extent changed because of government policy over GCHQ.

So I hope not only the miners will respond positively but the whole movement have got to do everything possible. That means if the miners call upon other unions to come up with positive action, then they should be prepared to do it.

Eric Heffer was talking to John Bloxam

JOHN HARRIS

*Pickets in Yorkshire*

## TUC: break links with the government! Fight the Tories now!

THE TUC General Council meets on Monday 19th to decide on its attitude to 'tri-partite bodies' — joint committees with the bosses and the Tories.

It looks as if their angry words after the GCHQ affair will end in a wimper rather than a bang.

The TUC has decided to boycott the National Economic Development Council but the TUC employment committee on March 12 recommended staying in the conciliation service ACAS and the Manpower Services Commission.

Several unions are still attending the industry sub-groups of the NEDC, though the GMBU and others, are boycotting them.

And the TUC is not even discussing withdrawal from its talks with the government over new anti-union laws.

Plenty of union leaders have all sorts of other links with the capitalist class — lucrative jobs on the side.

For example, according to the latest reference books, Geoffrey Drain (ex-NALGO) is a director of the Bank of England. Clive Jenkins of ASTMS is a member of the National Research Development Corporation and the British Overseas Trade Board. Gavin Laird of the AUEW is on the BNOC Board, as well as the Industrial Development Advisory Board.

Roy Grantham of APEX is a director of Henley Management College.

The trade unions need to fight the Tories, not plead with them. And you can't fight the fundamentals of Tory policy seriously if you're chatting with them about the details the next day.

## Solidarity can beat MacGregor

AS WE go to press, Coal Board boss Ian MacGregor has obtained a High Court injunction against the National Union of Mineworkers to stop flying pickets.

But flying pickets are moving across the country with great success. Some three-quarters of the country's miners are estimated to be out — called out on strike, or picketed out.

The miners are clearly moving towards a national strike against the threat of pit closures and 21,000 job cuts over the next year.

The National Union of Railwaymen executive has said that railworkers should refuse to cross miners' picket lines, and the TGWU has also called on members not to allow movement of coal.

This puts some of the most powerful sections of the trade union movement directly on collision course with the Tory anti-union laws which ban solidarity action.

The right wing Nottinghamshire area executive of the NUM has called its members away from the picket lines, but NUM national president Arthur Scargill has said he will never submit to the laws.

This could be a crucial battle. If the whole labour movement rallies round the miners, ready to take solidarity action, then it could be as important a defeat for Thatcher's Tories as the miners' and dockers' struggles were in 1972.

The TUC and the Labour Party, at every level, must give full support to the miners and to defiance of the Tory laws.

## ORGANISE FOR A GENERAL STRIKE!

**15 March 1984. Flying pickets are moving across the country, three-quarters of the pits are now out. The Coal Board has obtained a High Court injunction to stop the NUM organising flying pickets. The bosses' use of the law raises the stakes. Getting solidarity action from other workers and other unions is critical.**

# Socialist ORGANISER

Paper of the Socialist Organiser Alliance No. 171 Miners' strike special. March 22 1984 20p

NUM president Arthur Scargill denounced the police moves as "almost tantamount to a para-military state".

# POLICE STATE TORIES

"THERE IS no longer a soft option. We will use aggressive action against intimidation to enable miners to go to work" – Peter Joslin, Chief Constable of Warwickshire.

The Government and the police, in their determination to break the miners' strike, have turned whole areas of Britain into virtual police states.

In a massive centrally-coordinated operation, thousands of police (over 8000 according to New Scotland Yard's own figures) have been mobilised to prevent flying pickets reaching strike-breaking coalfields.

Roadblocks have been set up, and Kent miners were stopped at the Dartford tunnel and warned that they would be arrested if they crossed the county border.

Chief Constable David Hall, head of the New Scotland Yard strike-breaking 'nerve centre', told the press on Monday that his 'clearing house' was handling 400 calls per hour from Chief Constables throughout the country, outlining requirements for officers.

### Enforce

"We arrange their movement from one area to another. We are determined to enforce that mass picketing is not permitted".

In addition, phone calls coming into the Yorkshire NUM headquarters have been interrupted by the police, and call boxes in Nottingham being used by pickets have been cut off.

So much for the image of the good old British bobby, non-political, impartial, and never taking sides in an industrial dispute.

The police know who their paymasters are. As the NGA pickets found out at Warrington, the cops are ruthless, well-organised and determined upholders of the 'rights' of scabs, the property of employers, and the whole anti-working-class offensive of the Tory government.

**By Jim Denham**

The Tories like to present themselves as upholders of democracy. But to defeat the miners they have been prepared to tear up the elementary rights of a citizen to travel freely round the country (of course British governments, Labour and Tory, long ago ended the equally elementary right to travel between countries) and of trade unionists to picket strike-breakers.

### Contempt

It is the same contempt for democracy that the Tories have demonstrated in their proposals to abolish the Greater London Council and the metropolitan county councils. For this government all the cant about 'democracy' goes out of the window when it comes to dealing with their political opponents.

Despite the police, the flying pickets still managed to bring the majority of pits to a halt. And the Coal Board's decision not to proceed with its High Court injunction against the NUM was almost certainly due to the militancy of the pickets.

But there is no room for complacency. As Yorkshire area president Jack Taylor says: "On the surface this appears to be a victory for the Yorkshire miners and those who have been supporting them. But we are under no illusions.

"The main struggle – against pit closures and for jobs – will have to be continued with renewed determination"

For the striking miners, the immediate tasks are clear: to picket out every pit, and to stop the movement of coal to the power stations, docks, and depots.

The rest of the movement must give the miners every possible support. Trade union branches and Labour Parties should be raising money for the strikers, providing accommodation for pickets, and organising trade union boycotts of coal.

Trades councils should be forming support committees in the areas.

Most importantly of all, we must be urging defiance of the anti-union laws at every level – from solidarity action at rank and file level to the demand for the TUC to break collaboration with the Tories and organise for a general strike.

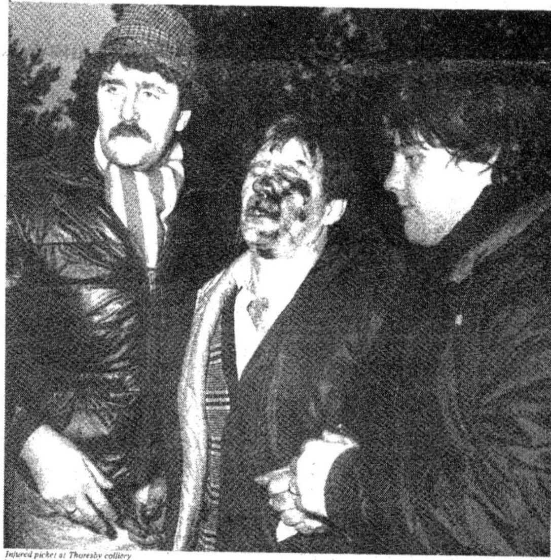
*Injured picket at Thoresby colliery*

# ORGANISE FOR A GENERAL STRIKE!

**22 March 1984. The government is operating with a centrally co-ordinated police force. Thousands of police have been mobilised to prevent flying pickets reaching strike-breaking coalfields. The police set up roadblocks, (illegally) preventing miners from travelling between counties. But the majority of pits remain closed.**

# Socialist ORGANISER

Paper of the Socialist Organiser Alliance No.172 March 28 1984 25p Claimants and strikers 10p

## Liverpool

## BENN SAYS: DEFY THE LAW!

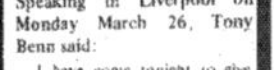

Speaking in Liverpool on Monday March 26, Tony Benn said:

I have come tonight to give 100% support to the decisions of the Liverpool Labour group. I have done that because I believe you are right, and I would like to say very simply why, as somebody who does not live or work in Liverpool, I believe that to be the case.

First, Liverpool has suffered enough already. The Tory government say they have no money, but they have enough money to spend £12 billion on the Trident.

They export £12 billion a year of capital, profits made by the workers of this country, including the workers in Liverpool. They are ready to spend £17 billion a year on dole money to pay people to do nothing, £3 billion to be spent on the Falklands. And the oil revenue of £20 billion or more – every penny of it has been spent on paying for the cost of unemployment.

That is the first reason.

And I think that Liverpool has suffered more than most areas of the country from the deceit of the Liberals, who have gone round on the doorstep promising that every problem that is raised will be dealt with, and then going to the council chamber or the House of Commons and voting to see that the money to meet those needs is stopped.

Liverpool, which is a very creative and a very imaginative city, and a very famous city, has created a lot of wealth for other people – and that money has left that city and gone abroad and to people who do not live in the place. Liverpool is the graveyard of capitalism and, I believe, the birthplace of socialism in Britain.

Comrades, the second point is very simple and very important too. It is that Labour was elected in Liverpool to protect jobs and services, and it must keep faith with the people who put their confidence in the Labour council. That is absolutely essential.

In 1981 the people of Toxteth took to the streets. In 1984 the Labour council must stick to their guns. And that is the way in which it will be seen by people up and down the country.

I believe what you are doing is morally right. It cannot be right for anybody – for any councillor

Continued on page 3

## SUPPORT THE MINERS!

# STOP ALL COAL

THE PIT strike is biting deep. The Coal Board says it isn't, but British Steel at Scunthorpe has had to cut production by half because coal isn't getting through.

The coal-fired Aberthaw power station in Wales is also short of coal because of effective picketing.

The rail unions NUR and ASLEF, members of the coal-rail-steel Triple Alliance, have asked their members not to cross miners' picket lines. NUR general secretary Jimmy Knapp has pledged that the railworkers' support for the miners must be "totally effective".

In South Yorkshire, representatives from the NUR District Council have met with the rest of the Triple Alliance, and have since stopped coal getting into British Steel's Orgrave Coking Plant.

The plant has been picketed by miners from Treeton Bridge.

Coming into London a train driver stopped when he saw a miners' banner draped over a bridge. The train went on only after coal wagons were unhooked and left.

British Rail have so far not dared to send home union members who refuse to cross picket lines, despite earlier threats that they would.

The TGWU has promised to support members who won't deliver coal to stockpiles. Scottish NUM leader Mick McGahey has called for workers to "stop the importation and transportation of coal'", and for the TUC to organise support.

Ravenscraig steel workers have given £1000 to the Scottish miners, and the Clyde area of the steel union ISTC has called on general secretary Bill Sirs to come out in public support of the miners.

The executive of the Society of Civil and Public servants has promised to give organisational and financial support to the miners, remembering the "magnificent support received from NUM members in the day of protest for the staff of GCHQ".

The miners can win – if this solidarity is spread at rank and file level, and at the same time we demand that the leaders of the TUC and the Labour Party come out in active support and stand on the line with the miners.

Stop all coal!

Picketing Lea Hall power station in Staffordshire

## Free Sarah Tisdall!

WIDESPREAD anger has greeted the six months' sentence imposed on Sarah Tisdall for leaking government documents to the Guardian.

Neil Kinnock called it malevolent. "a mixture of malice and weakness that is characteristic of all bullies"

It is clear that Sarah Tisdall's case was chosen to be a show trial by the government.

The labour movement must protest against Sarah Tisdall's imprisonment. We must oppose the Official Secrets Act which is there to be used in cases like this. We must fight for a Freedom of Information Act, which is Labour Party policy.

Sarah Tisdall

**29 March 1984. The strike is beginning to bite. Power stations are running short of coal because of effective picketing. Railworkers bringing in coal refuse to cross picket lines.**

Socialist ORGANISER

Paper of the Socialist Organiser Alliance No.173 April 5 1984 25p Claimants and strikers 10p

## Enforce unions' decisions

# DON'T MOVE COAL!

### Police out of the coalfields!

A demonstration has been called in Nottingham on Saturday April 14, 11am from the Forest, on the slogans 'Police out of the coalfields' and 'Support the miners'. An ad hoc 'Nottingham coordinating committee against the police presence' called the march, but support is expected from the NUM in Yorkshire and maybe wider. Contact: Ivan Wels, 11 Osborne Ave, Sherwood, Nottingham (0602 624827).

By Rob Dawber (Sheffield City NUR)

THE miners are fighting for the life of their industry. They fight for their jobs and for their future. Indirectly they are fighting for all of us.

For the first time since the steel strike of 1980, a section of workers with the weight, the muscle, the experience and the will to humble the Tory vandals has gone into a stand-up fight.

They have laid it on the line for Bloody Margaret and for Ian MacGregor, her trained pit-butcher.

MacGregor, the sinister professional industrial thug who rampaged through the steel industry for Thatcher, throwing tens of thousands of workers and their families onto the dole. MacGregor, the fifth horseman of the Apocalypse, who ruthlessly fought Mrs Thatcher's class war against the steelworkers and without shame, conscience or humanity brought ruin to the steel communities of South Wales, South Yorkshire, and elsewhere.

Now the militant majority of the miners are saying to Thatcher and MacGregor. No you don't. We've had enough. You are not going to bring destruction, unemployment, poverty and hopelessness to Britain's mining communities.

We can stop you. And if we can't, we'll go down fighting rather than go peacefully and quietly to join the dole queue.

The miners' fight is every worker's fight. For five years we have suffered defeat after defeat. The slump, and rotten leadership, led to setbacks and retreats, which brought depression and even some demoralisation to the movement.

Now the miners have given the signal for an attempt to turn the tide. Listen to the Sunday Times on what's at stake for them.

"If Mrs Thatcher loses, she will be left presiding over a country which is not worth governing".

They know that despite the police they can be beaten.

The Times wrote: "If, for example, the Yorkshire miners, assisted by large numbers of sympathetic trade unionists, decided to besiege the big coal burning powers stations in the Trent Valley and Doncaster area, the backbone of the national

Continued back page

*Lea Hall, Staffordshire*

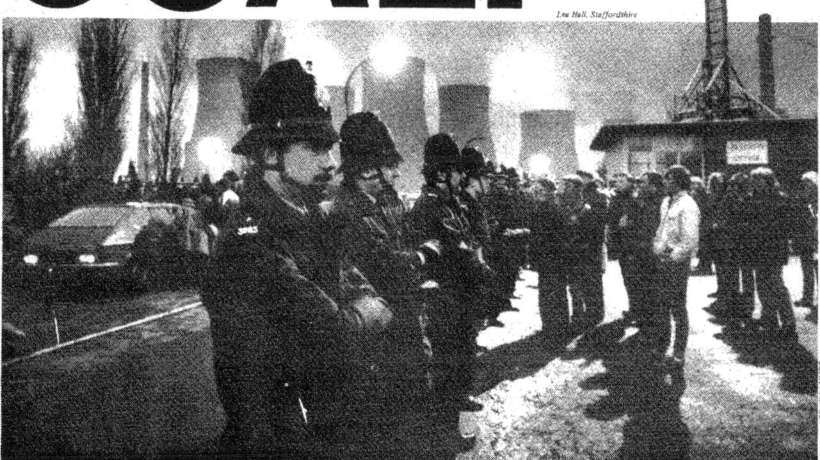

**5 April 1984. Transport unions — NUR (rail), ASLEF (train drivers), NUS (shipping), TGWU (lorry drivers) — decide to defy the law and refuse to move coal, to stop supplies to the power stations. Workers in those unions had been and would in the future be affected by the Tories' job-cutting economic programme.**

Socialist ORGANISER

Paper of the Socialist Organiser Alliance No 174 April 12 1984 25p

Demonstrate this Saturday

# POLICE OUT OF THE COALFIELDS!

## SUPPORT THE MINERS!

**12 April 1984. North Nottinghamshire now looks like a police state. Police transit vans and coaches full of police drive around the countryside, stopping vehicles and ordering people to return home. Lines of police surround the pits that are still working. Many miners are arrested for offences such as shouting "scab". A demonstration has been called in Nottingham. 4,000 miners from Yorkshire join 3,000 striking Notts miners and their supporters, demanding "Police out of the coalfield".**

Socialist ORGANISER

INSIDE: Pages 3, 6 and 7: miners' strike. Page 2: international — Nicaragua, US, India. Page 4: Blacks organise in the Labour Party. Page 5: Labour students. Page 8: Is Thatcher a Bonaparte? Page 9: 'Silkwood' reviewed. Page 11: Industrial reports.

Paper of the Socialist Organiser Alliance No.175 April 19 1984 25p
Claimants and strikers 10p

# STOP THE PITS!

"Stop merely saying you support us. Come out and join us. We are facing a fundamental challenge to the whole working class, not merely miners. We are facing the organised might of the state machine. There is a police state in Nottinghamshire".

Arthur Scargill,
speaking in Nottingham last Saturday, 14th.

The Scottish TUC is calling on all its members to act in support of the miners. The date has not yet been set but it looks like the day of action will be May Day (May 1).

That's the way to help the miners and beat the Tories!

Now we must fight to make it a Day of Action throughout the whole of Britain.

Demand that the TUC comes off the fence and organises a national strike on May 1.

Demand that individual unions support the Scottish TUC.

Convince your mates to come out with the miners on May 1.

# STOP THE TORIES!



**19 April 1984. Arthur Scargill poses issues for a special NUM delegate conference. Conference is lobbied by tens of thousands of miners. It votes to ignore the bosses' propaganda about "democracy" and the lack of a national strike ballot. The conference calls on every area to join the strike.**

# Socialist ORGANISER

**Stop all coal!**

**Industrial Special**

# VICTORY TO THE MINERS!

BY ROAD, rail or sea — all movement of coal must be halted.

The decision of the TGWU, the National Union of Seamen and the rail unions to instruct their members not to touch coal provides a vital means of pushing the miners' strike forward.

In particular it can provide the means for a breakthrough in Nottinghamshire by closing the 'merry-go-round' system which links the pits to the power stations.

But despite setbacks this requires an intensification not a relaxation of flying pickets. Head Office instructions are in themselves insufficient. They must be policed and deepened by miners on the ground.

Our job is not only to halt all movement of coal but to use this to take the argument into the power stations and explain to the workers there that the miners' struggle is their struggle and the struggle of every worker in Britain.

There is tremendous latent support in the wider movement. It must be mobilised.

The lies of the media must be answered. Even the yellow press, Mail on Sunday, publishes a poll which shows that when 'don't knows' and 'won't says' are excluded 60% of miners want a national strike.

Every local Labour Party, every union branch, every stewards' committee must in the next few days put the miners' strike at the centre of all their activities.

*Victory to the miners!
*Intensify the picketing!
*Boycott all coal movement!
*Bring out the power stations!
*TUC: call a 24 hour general strike!
Organise for an all-out general strike.

Dews Hill, Warwickshire: miners arriving for work by coach meet police and pickets

**26 April 1984. Campaigning to persuade the labour movement to actively back the miners.**

Socialist ORGANISER

Inside

[illegible]

Labour Party Young Socialists conference [illegible]

Eric Hobsbawm and the new [illegible]

[illegible]

Paper of the Socialist Organiser Alliance No.176 April 26 1984 25p Claimants and strikers 10p

SOLIDARITY!

ORGANISE FOR A GENERAL STRIKE!

**26 April 1984. Miners rally outside Sheffield NUM headquarters. The picture suggests miners storming the capitalist citadel — exactly what they were doing nationally!**

# Socialist ORGANISER

Paper of the Socialist Organiser Alliance No.177 May 3 1984 25p Claimants and strikers 10p

**Inside**

Pages 2 to 7: Miners' strike. Page 2: Swing Labour behind the miners. Build support committees. Page 3: May 9 day of action. Pages 4 and 5: Front line Nottingham. Pages 6 and 7: Women and the strike.
Page 8: International – Libya, Hong Kong, Ireland.
Page 9: Reviews – the true history of Africa; does nature move in leaps?; behind the IMF.
Page 10: Liverpool vs. the Tories. EEC elections.

## Swing Labour behind miners' strike

# MOBILISE!

"The time has come to say to other unions: Yes, we want your support, but not only financial contributions. When we're faced with Thatcher, MacGregor, the CBI, the Institute of Directors, we're entitled to say to colleagues in other unions join us, come out with us in dispute".

Arthur Scargill



## Strike with the miners on May 9!

**3 May 1984. On the 25 April the Labour Party National Executive votes to support the strike; Party members are asked to donate 50p a week. Individual Party members are joining, and in many areas are the backbone of the local support groups.**

# Socialist ORGANISER

Paper of the Socialist Organiser Alliance No. 178. May 10 1984. 25p Claimants and strikers 10p

**Inside**



# ORGANISE FOR A GENERAL STRIKE!

## Scargill says: bring rail out!

Miners President, Arthur Scargill, said [illegible] demonstration in Mansfield, Notts, on May 7 said:

MAKE NO mistake, we're winning this battle. The fact that there is feeling inside the steel industry means that it is effective.

But the other sections of the trade union movement have got to become more involved in this dispute. There is no doubt that the support given by ASLEF and NUR has been magnificent.

But I know that the NUR and ASLEF are not only pressing for a wage increase. They are also fighting against the threat of redundancy.

And I would appeal to both the NUR and ASLEF. If ever there was a time to join with this join, not merely in an expression of solidarity, but to come out on strike in support of your own claim and join it with other, now is the time – and I call on you to do so.

On the 14th of this month – next Monday – I want to see in this town the greatest demonstration of trade union solidarity, both from miners and the wider trade union movement, that we have ever seen.

And I also want to see every single striking miner not merely on strike but actively engaged in picketing ports and wharfs and power stations to bring this dispute to a swift and successful conclusion.

I wish to say, from all the miners, to the wives and to the families, and to the wider trade union movement, that the solidarity that has been displayed in this dispute has been an inspiration to our movement. It's the first fight back that Thatcher has ever seen. Make no mistake, we are going to win this dispute. Comrades, it's a privilege to lead you!

JOHN HARRIS

*Marchers in Mansfield on May 7. Even if the comparison of the Tories with the Nazis is not scientifically precise, it expresses what people feel about the "Notts police state".*

## AUEW calls for TUC day of action

THE AUEW National Committee last Tuesday, 1st, called for a national TUC day of action in support of the miners.

Scotland has a day of action on the 9th. The Wales TUC on Friday 4th decided to organise a day of action in Wales. The Yorkshire and Humberside regional TUC has called for a 24-hour strike in support of the miners on Monday May 21, and the Sheffield AUEW district committee has already supported this call.

Arthur Scargill has called for all workers to rally for the greatest trade union demonstration in years at Mansfield, Notts, on Monday 14th.

The TUC's duty now is to pull these initiatives together with a call for a full 24 hour general strike in support of the miners.

Such a call could rally the labour movement and help prepare for an all-out general strike capable of stopping cuts and closures and getting rid of the anti-union laws.

In the meantime we need to organise at rank and file level for maximum support on May 14 and May 21.

**10 May 1984. The strike is reaching its peak. There are regional TUC days of action, one-off strikes by other groups of workers and many demonstrations. But there is no organised labour movement campaign to develop the potential of this action into a generalised fightback against Thatcher.**

# Socialist ORGANISER

Paper of the Socialist Organiser Alliance No 179 May 17 1984 25p Claimants and strikers 10p

**50 face 'riot' charge**

**Miners Special p. 5-8**

# SOLIDARITY WILL WIN!

RAILWORKERS will begin limited industrial action over pay from May 30. The teachers' unions already have selective strikes underway.

The Yorkshire and Humberside regional TUC has called a 24 hour strike in support of the miners for Monday May 21. The Wales TUC has scheduled a 'day of action' for June 12. These regional actions would be better for being coordinated into one national event, but they can still be used to increase the pressure on the Tories.

Printworkers have struck a blow for solidarity by forcing the Daily Express to give Arthur Scargill the right of reply, and blocking a witchhunting anti-Scargill picture and headline in the Sun.

And the miners' union leaders themselves, after consultation with the transport unions are stepping up their struggle by turning the pickets towards the power stations.

It is still a long hard fight ahead, and there are still problems. Jimmy Knapp of the rail union NUR told the press that his union's action was not a response to Arthur Scargill's call for railworkers to strike alongside the miners.

**TUC action**

But don't believe the media stories about the pit strike weakening. The bosses' paper the Financial Times last Thursday, 10th, quoted the Coal Board's Midlands marketing director as saying: "The rail action is biting harder than has been generally acknowledged."

The TUC general council meeting next Wednesday, 23rd, should decide on solidarity action starting with a 24 hour general strike. But if the leaders won't lead, then the rank and file must

**ORGANISE FOR A GENERAL STRIKE!**

**17 May 1984. Strikes by workers fighting on their own demands continue. In May and June some regional TUCs call 24-hour general strikes in support of the miners. Printworkers force the *Daily Express* to give Scargill a right of reply and block a witchhunting anti-Scargill picture and headline in the Sun. The picture appears to show Scargill giving a Nazi salute.**

# Socialist ORGANISER

London Health Emergency
NHS: DAY OF ACTION AGAINST CUTS AND CLOSURES
Saturday May 26
Morning: local campaigns in most of London's 31 Health Districts will be out on the streets with leaflets and exhibitions.
Afternoon: Demonstration at St. George's, Hyde Park Corner, 3pm.

Paper of the Socialist Organiser Alliance No. 180 May 24 1984 25p Claimants and strikers 10p

# TUC: OFF YOUR KNEES!

THE MINERS' strike is biting.

Top Tories are pressing the Coal Board to shift its ground — or at least to give the appearance of shifting its ground. Cabinet ministers, reports the Guardian, "are privately advocating a slowing of the colliery closure programme".

And media-boosted 'back to work' movements have flopped.

Arthur Scargill has made it plain that the miners are interested, not in slowing down job cuts, but in stopping them.

TUC and Labour leaders, however, have shown that they are interested only in finding a formula — any formula — to end the struggle.

Len Murray demonstrated the style in which he intends to conduct his last few months as a lame-duck TUC general secretary by denouncing the Yorkshire/Humberside strike for the miners on May 21, and the Welsh day of action on June 12. The TUC finance and general purposes committee, and the Labour Party/TUC liaison committee, endorsed Murray by their silence.

Neil Kinnock and his energy front-bencher, one-time leftist Stan Orme, have been busy playing compromise-brokers. While local Labour Parties across the country are collecting funds and organising support activities for the miners, Kinnock and Orme are trying to engineer what the dissident Tories want — a deal in which the Coal Board appears to give some ground but actually concedes nothing.

The TUC has been angling to get itself in as a mediator between the miners and the Tories.

That's what the 'new realism' means — the labour movement's leaders not mobilising the movement against the Tories, but trying to negotiate away any struggle.

Now that we are beginning to get the Tories rattled for the first time in a long while, the last thing we want is to give them escape clauses. What's needed is to develop the struggle towards a general strike. And if the TUC and Labour leaders won't do that, then the rank and file must.

## Rail should unite with miners to beat Tories

THE rail unions NUR and ASLEF are due to start an overtime ban in pursuit of their pay claim on May 30. The action is long overdue (the settlement date was April 16) and it does not include Sunday working or workshops staff — who, with guards, are the section most under threat of closure or privatisation.

16,000 workshops staff are due to go by 1986 — and at the workshops grades conference they voted unanimously to be in the action due to start on May 30.

The overtime ban could still have a substantial impact. But what is the point of dribs and drabs? All out strike action now, alongside the miners, is the way to save both rail workshop and pit jobs, and win the pay claim.



**24 May 1984. The tide seems to be turning in favour of the miners. Instead of fully backing the miners so they can finish the job, the Labour Party and the TUC urge that the strike be brought to the swiftest posssible conclusion.**

# Socialist ORGANISER

Paper of the Socialist Organiser Alliance No. 181 May 31 1984 25p Claimants and strikers 10p

## Vote Labour on June 14

Centre pages: Against the bosses' Market, against bosse Britain, for a socialist united Europe!

# Police and courts help the Tories

*Police at Orgreave*

# JOIN THE PICKETS

## Help the miners win

By John Bloxam and Dan Duncan

Orgreave coking plant on Tuesday, 29th, from 4 am, was the scene of the fiercest confrontation between police and pickets yet seen in the dispute.

The police were determined to protect the scab lorries taking coke to the BSC plant in Scunthorpe. They sealed off the exits from a nearby motorway, and they swamped the entrance to Orgreave with up to 2,000 police.

Clements, the South Yorkshire Assistant Chief Constable said: "If it takes every man in the South Yorkshire police force and the surrounding police forces, that's what we shall do."

When the first convoy of scab lorries appeared at 9 am, sandwiched between ranks of police vans, the police by the gates reinforced the weight of their numbers by what Arthur Scargill later described as "almost unbelievable" scenes of police brutality.

Dogs, truncheons and horses were used against the two main groups of pickets, herded into two separat areas opposite the main gat of the plant and up the hill Riot shields were also pro duced for the first time, a the police waded in. Th performance was repeate when the second convoy turned up in the afternoon.

The 83 reported arrest and 41 injured pickets only give a hint of the damage th police tried to inflict. T cheers in the crowd, number of police wer injured as pickets defende themselves.

Other miners wer attacked before they even go to the picket line. We saw on miner going back down th approach road to the plant holding his bleeding head. H had never got to the picke line. The police had seen h was on his own and clubbe him from behind.

Thousands of pickets – mainly miners and wome from the mining communitie – had responded to the week end call to turn the picket a

Continued page 4.

**31 May 1984. On 29 May miners mount their first mass picket outside the coking plant at Orgreave near Sheffield. The coke is used at a major steel works in Scunthorpe. Orgreave is the scene of many battles by miners against the mass ranks of the police. At this first picket over 80 are arrested and 40 injured. There will be many more until on 18 June coke runs are suspended.**

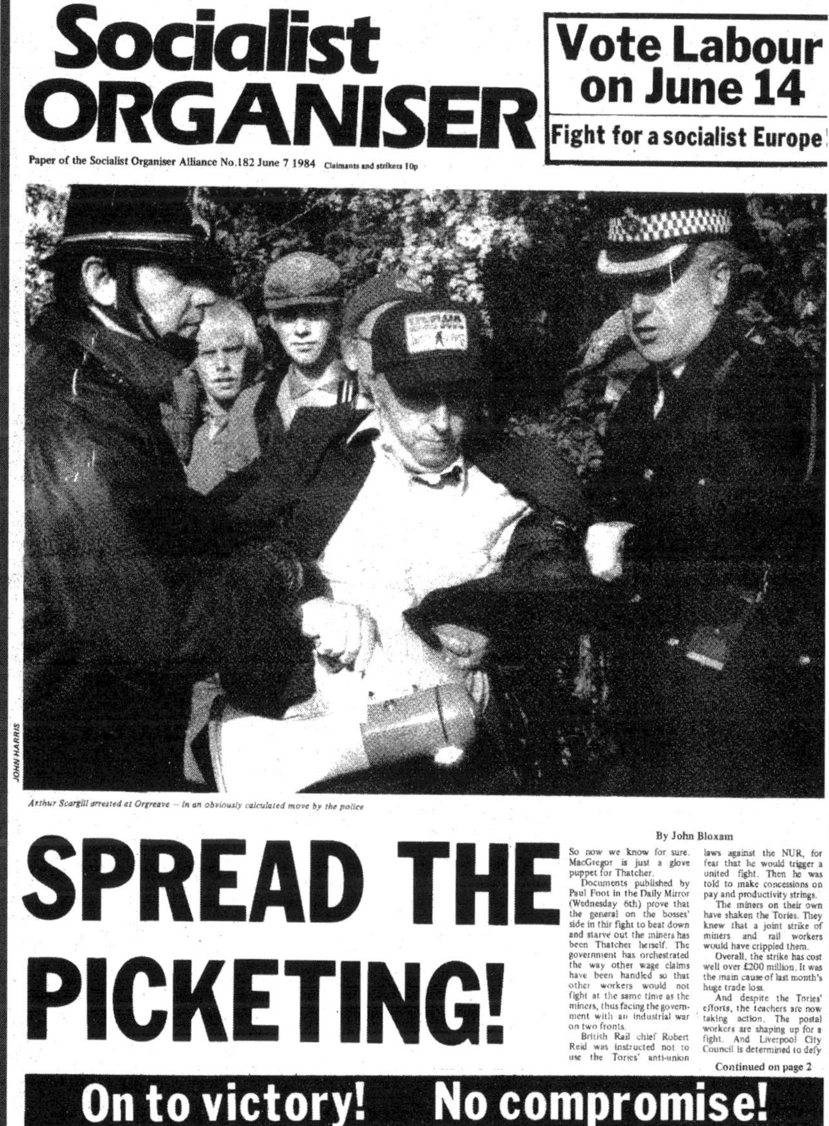

Socialist ORGANISER

Vote Labour on June 14

Fight for a socialist Europe!

Paper of the Socialist Organiser Alliance No.182 June 7 1984 Claimants and strikers 10p

JOHN HARRIS

*Arthur Scargill arrested at Orgreave – in an obviously calculated move by the police*

SPREAD THE PICKETING!

By John Bloxam

So now we know for sure. MacGregor is just a glove puppet for Thatcher.

Documents published by Paul Foot in the Daily Mirror (Wednesday 6th) prove that the general on the bosses' side in thir fight to beat down and starve out the miners has been Thatcher herself. The government has orchestrated the way other wage claims have been handled so that other workers would not fight at the same time as the miners, thus facing the government with an industrial war on two fronts.

British Rail chief Robert Reid was instructed not to use the Tories' anti-union laws against the NUR, for fear that he would trigger a united fight. Then he was told to make concessions on pay and productivity strings.

The miners on their own have shaken the Tories. They knew that a joint strike of miners and rail workers would have crippled them.

Overall, the strike has cost well over £200 million. It was the main cause of last month's huge trade loss.

And despite the Tories' efforts, the teachers are now taking action. The postal workers are shaping up for a fight. And Liverpool City Council is determined to defy

Continued on page 2

On to victory! No compromise!

**7 June 1984. On 30 May Scargill is arrested at Orgreave. The Tories now step up their attack: the Coal Board talks about organising a ballot over the heads of the NUM, the government works to hold off the pay disputes of other groups of workers.**

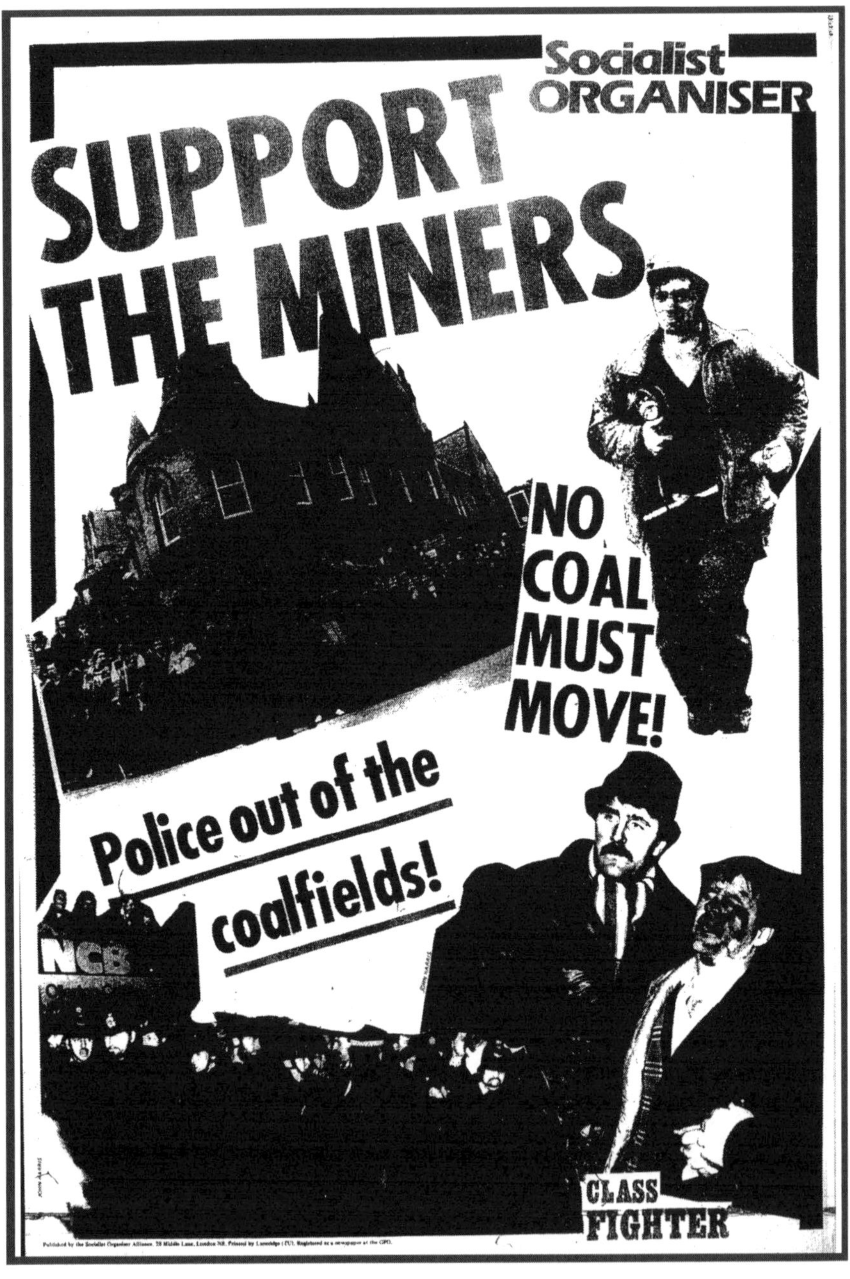


**Poster, June 1984**

Socialist ORGANISER

Paper of the Socialist Organiser Alliance No.183 June 14 1983 25p Claimants and strikers 10p

**On to victory! No compromise!**

# Troops against the miners?

By Tony Benn

There has been a great deal of hypocrisy about the government not intervening. They are deeply involved. The police are preventing peaceful picketing. They have set up road blocks, introduced curfews in the villages and provoked on the picket lines. There have been cavalry charges against unarmed pickets. That is a disgrace to the British police for the which the government are responsible.

This afternoon I asked in the House about the use of troops, and the Leader of the House was very evasive. At the beginning of the dispute, I asked the Leader of the House whether the armed forces had been alerted, and he gave a categorical assurance that they had not.

Now the Prime Minister has written to me. I had asked her whether the troops were involved. She used a very skillful phrase. She said that there has been no authorisation. She did not say that the troops were not being used, and she admitted that the army and the armed forces are supplying facilities and transport as part of a joint police and military operation. Either the Leader of the House or the Prime Minister was misleading the House.

The magistrates have come in and introduced bail conditions that amount to a sentence – a sort of exclusion zone – for those who have been convicted of nothing. Much has been made of the crudity of the way in which the government have turned off every source of funds, including social security, to starve the miners back to work. They have "deemed" that the miners have been getting strike pay when in fact they have not. They have cut maternity grants and excluded from strike pay workers who have been only indirectly involved and were never employees of the NCB. One case that came to my attention was of the government stopping a retired miner benefiting from the redundancy payment scheme because, for a short while, he was on the NCB's books before the strike began. The government think that by starving the miners, or bribing them with thousands of pounds, the miners will respond.

*The arrest of this miner outside St Stephen's entrance to Parliament sparked off an hour's fighting between miners and police last Thursday*

The miners know that the large sums of money that are given to them is not real money. It is a lump sum payment for future social security benefits as they will not get those benefits until the redundancy pay has been spent. Neither the tightening of the screw through the Department of Health and Social Security nor the attempted bribery through redundancy pay will affect the miners.

The most remarkable thing that has occurred in the coalfields is that the miners are fighting the present policy and will go on doing so and the government can do nothing whatever to stop them.

Young miners know full well that if, at 29 or 30, they take the money that is offered, there will be no work for them, their children or their grandchildren in the areas in which they live.

Continued on p.2

**14 June 1984. The police are now acting like an army of occupation in many pit villages. Striking miners believe soldiers in police uniform are being used on picket lines. Cabinet papers released in January 2014 will show that Thatcher had made contingency plans to use troops to move coal stocks.**

# Socialist ORGANISER

**If they use anti union laws – general strike!**

Paper of the Socialist Organiser Alliance No. 184 June 21 1984 25p claimants and strikers 10p

# STOP STEEL!

*Orgreave: A woman from the Sheffield support group shouts for an ambulance for an injured miner. A mounted policeman in riot gear swears at her and hits out with his truncheon*

*Orgreave: The policeman continues hitting out and she backs away...*

## Orgreave pickets beat police violence

By John Bloxam

**THE miners' strike has suddenly escalated.**

**The Government has given signals to employers to go ahead and use the anti-union laws to sue the NUM. Such moves will make it starkly clear that the Tories' aim is not just to shut pits but to beat down the whole trade union movement. They should be answered by a renewed and more urgent campaign for a general strike!**

For 100 days, the Tories have been persuading bosses not to use the courts because they fear the effect — both on those miners still scabbing and on other trade unionists. Now, as the NUM moves to take serious action to stop steel production, they have decided to play this card.

On Monday 18th a nationally coordinated effort was mounted to shut off Orgreave coking plant. The Notts area sent pickets for the first time. Despite the police brutality, the size of the picket and improved organisation resulted in a decision to suspend coke runs from the plant. The NUM won the first 'battle of Orgreave'.

This followed directly from the breakdown of talks last Wednesday 13th.

Government pressure must have been behind MacGregor's hardline and provocative approach. According to Arthur Scargill, "we gained the impression" from the first two sets of talks, "that the plan to close the pits announced on March 6 was no longer applicable — they wanted to see the thing negotiated and a settlement achieved". Using the losses because of the strike, and a wide definition of closure due to 'exhaustion' and 'geological difficulties', the Coal Board negotiators were looking for a tactical retreat.

But the government could not accept the implications of even an *apparent* miners' victory.

The break-up of the talks meant that Thursday's NUM executive meeting, and other regional and national meetings on the same day and Friday, were about stepping up the dispute. They produced immediate results.

A rule change at the forthcoming Special Delegate Conference was discussed to put clearly in the hands of the national union the power to discipline officials who scab. Steel dispensations were put firmly in the hands of the national coordinating committee.

Those area leaderships who had gone along with local agreements to permit large-scale steel production were firmed up. On Tuesday South Wales president Emlyn Williams was publicly disagreeing with Scargill on the issue. By Friday he was calling for a tighter blockade on Llanwern steelworks.

The leadership of the steel union ISTC was given until today (Wednesday 20th) to agree an effective deal for 'care and maintenance' only in the steel plants – the level that existed during the steel strike. If they rejected this, a

Continued on page 2

## POLICE OUT OF THE COALFIELDS!

**21 June 1984. The Tory counter-attack continues. On 18 June in the "Battle for Orgreave" police run amok. The government pushes the Coal Board to threaten to expand the use of the anti-union laws. They have so far held back from this tactic for fear it will lead to an eruption of solidarity action in support of the miners.**

Paper of the Socialist Organiser Alliance No.185 June 28 1984 25p Claimants and strikers 10p

**Ian MacGregor**

He has a deceptively simple view of the future of the NCB. He takes the example of the US Mid West coalfields which used British-developed longwall mining techniques to get ten times the UK's productivity by carefully selecting only thick rich seams, working them out, and leaving the rest, while all the time introducing computerised mining equipment underground.

"That kind of future does not offer Scargill's members much security as miners. The kind of industry he (MacGregor) is striving for should... go the way of steel, motor manufacture and other capital-intensive, labour-shedding sectors".

*From the bosses' paper, the Financial Times, June 22*

# SOLIDARITY!

# GENERAL STRIKE!

*Pickets at Ravenscraig steelworks in Scotland. (Photo: Rick Matthews, IFL)*

## SUPPORT THE MINERS!

**28 June 1984. Railworkers' action grows. On 7 June the transport unions agree to block rail and road movements of oil (the substitute for coal).**

Socialist ORGANISER

**Stop the coal trucks**

Paper of the Socialist Organiser Alliance No.186 July 5 1984 25p Claimants and strikers 10p

# BLOCKADE!

"To those unions with members in the power stations I say — tell them not to handle coal.

Demonstrations are important, but there is one thing that is more important, and that is participation on the picket lines. Irrespective of legislation, I want to see all workers joining our picket lines.

We're on the way to victory. But do not underestimate the forces of the state.

I want to see in every town and village in Britain miners' support committees set up — to support the miners in their fight for jobs".

Arthur Scargill

"If we say that the miners are fighting for all of us, then it is up to all of us to give support in our own way to the NUM. I've personally paid tribute to the transport workers... but politically the most important action has been and is when workers in Fleet Street say that they are no longer prepared to print lies about miners.

We're going to win a great victory. But don't think the battle ends when Cortonwood opens again. The battle is a real battle to change our society.

It is a battle to get work for everybody. It is a battle to see our children get education... for a good health service... to give dignity to retired people... for the democratic control of our society — of local government, of our industries, of the police, of the mass media. We want a country controlled by the people who produce the wealth."

Tony Benn

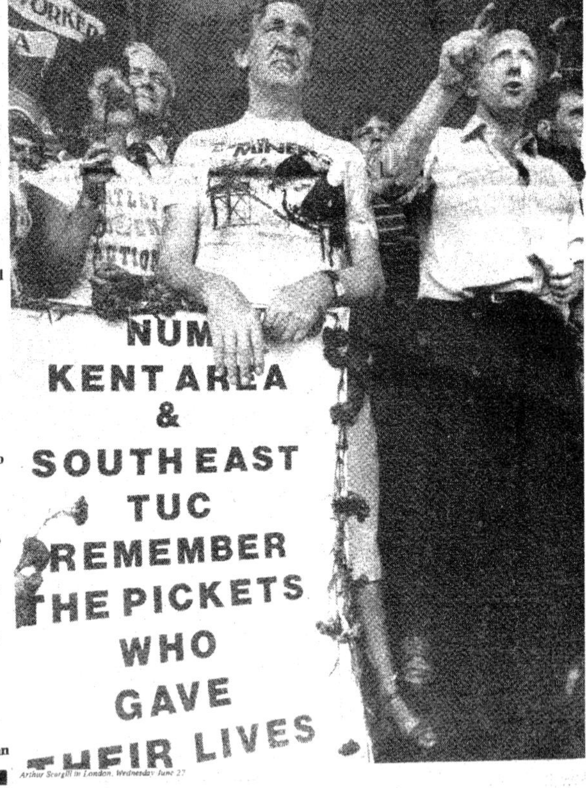

NUM
KENT AREA
&
SOUTH EAST
TUC
REMEMBER
THE PICKETS
WHO
GAVE
LIVES


Arthur Scargill in London, Wednesday June 27

**5 July 1984. Arthur Scargill makes a direct appeal to non-miner workers to join the strike; he calls for a four day week and ask workers in the rail, steel and power stations to refuse to handle coal.**

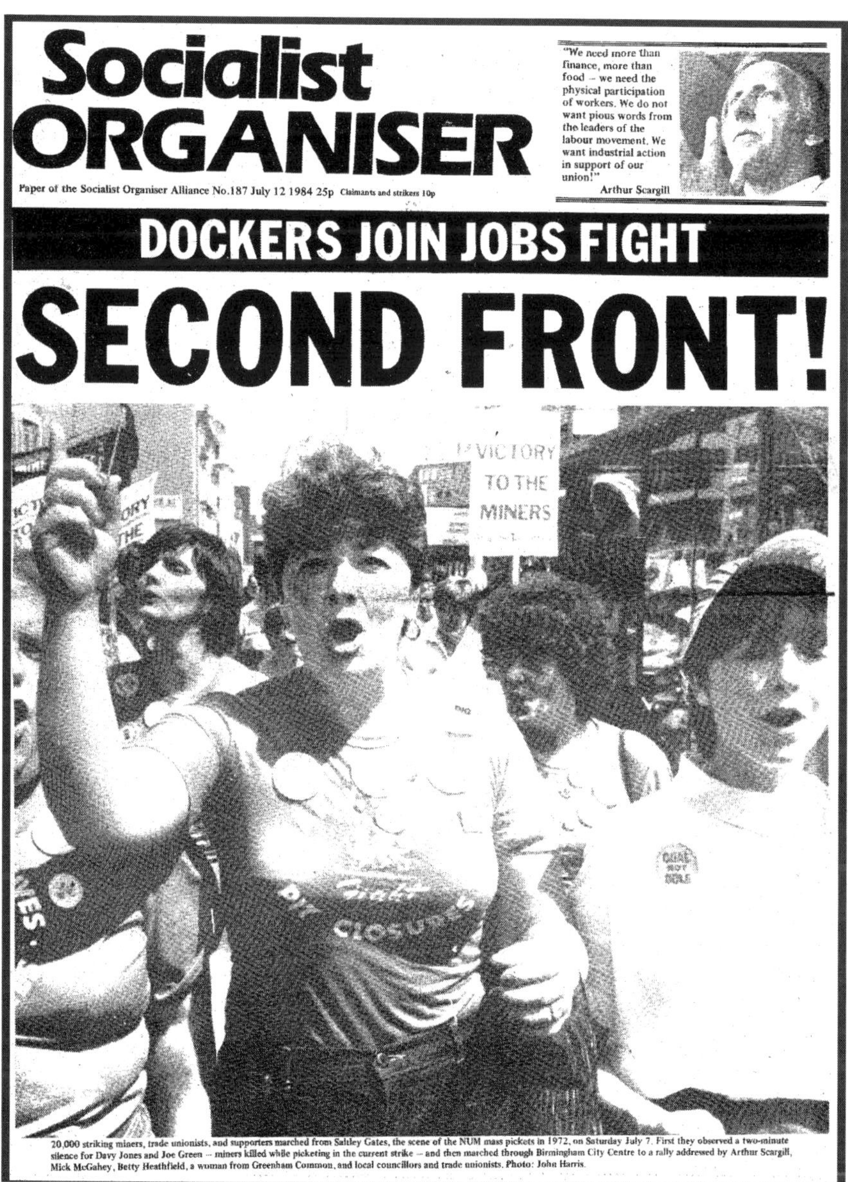

Socialist ORGANISER

Paper of the Socialist Organiser Alliance No.187 July 12 1984 25p Claimants and strikers 10p

"We need more than finance, more than food – we need the physical participation of workers. We do not want pious words from the leaders of the labour movement. We want industrial action in support of our union!"
Arthur Scargill

DOCKERS JOIN JOBS FIGHT

SECOND FRONT!



20,000 striking miners, trade unionists, and supporters marched from Saltley Gates, the scene of the NUM mass pickets in 1972, on Saturday July 7. First they observed a two-minute silence for Davy Jones and Joe Green – miners killed while picketing in the current strike – and then marched through Birmingham City Centre to a rally addressed by Arthur Scargill, Mick McGahey, Betty Heathfield, a woman from Greenham Common, and local councillors and trade unionists. Photo: John Harris.

**12 July 1984. When dockers at Immingham refuse to unload iron ore in solidarity with the miners, British Steel tries to unload it using non-dockers. This prompts a national strike of 35,000 dockers.**

# Socialist ORGANISER

Paper of the Socialist Organiser Alliance. No. 188. Thursday July 19, 1984. 25p (Claimants and strikers 10p)

# Tories talk of using troops



RICK MATTHEWS (IFL)

Dock strike picket at Glasgow's King George V docks – 12 July

# Time for a general strike!

STEFANO CAGNONI (IFL)

Durham Miners' Gala – 14 July

**19 July 1984. On 15 July Tory Transport Minister Nicholas Ridley threatens to use troops against striking dockers. The dockers' strike collapses.**

Socialist ORGANISER

**Lobby the TUC**

LOBBY THE TUC
Monday September 3 1984
8.30 onwards at Conference Centre, Brighton
Called by Broad Left

Organising Committee
Join the Socialist Organiser contingent
*Full support for the miners!
*For a general strike!

Paper of the Socialist Organiser Alliance. No. 189 July 26 1984 25p Claimants and strikers 10p

# OUR ENEMY WITHIN

By Gerry Bates

THE Tories know the facts of the class struggle. However much they use phrases about 'national interest' for public consumption, they are not fooled themselves.

They know that there is no common national interest between workers and bosses. Workers have a common class interest with workers of other nations, bosses have a common class interest internationally and indeed organise through bodies like the EEC and NATO to enforce it.

Last weekend the Tories denounced Arthur Scargill and the miners as 'the enemy within', and compared the coal dispute with the Falklands war.

From their point of view they are quite right: the miners are a much deadlier enemy to the interests, power and privilege of the British ruling class than the Argentine government could ever be.

What we need is for the leaders of the labour movement to see the class war in equally clear terms, and to advance the interests of our class as vigorously as the Tories advance the interests of theirs.

The Tories' fury reflects increasing anxiety on their part about the effects of the strike and the failure of their attempts to sponsor a drift back to work.

An important sign of the mood of the capitalist class was the Times editorial of July 20 – "There is a war on" – and, even more so, on Monday 23rd by Samuel Brittan – brother of Tory minister Leon Brittan, and one of the most serious and influential economic journalists of the ruling class.

Brittan considers himself an enlightened liberal. But his article is undiluted class fury.

Conciliators in the Coal Board management should be cleared out, he says. "There can be no excuse for tolerating . . . 'sources within the board' who brief the media towards appeasement".

The government "should permit the free import of coal, now and for ever". It should start closing "uneconomic" pits immediately. And "the green light needs to be given to any concern, nationalised or other, which wants to take any union to court for secondary picketing".

"Nor should legal action be confined to the civil side". If the law does not permit jailing Arthur Scargill for 'violent picketing', then too bad for the law. "If there is no way of bringing to trial the instigators of violence at the highest level there is something wrong either with the criminal code, or more probably with those who advise on its enforcement".

The other plank of Brittan's programme is: "not to 'cease from mental strife' to ensure that Labour as now constituted, should never again form the government of Britain".

So the capitalist class is clearing the decks and rallying its ranks for battle. It's about time the labour movement did the same, instead of having our Labour and TUC leaders dithering in the middle and posing as compromise brokers.

Victory to the miners! Organise for a general strike!

## HELP MINERS FIGHT TORIES

## Councils face the crunch

STRUGGLE or surrender: mobilise direct action against the Tory government or become executors for Tory cuts.

That alternative is now facing Labour councils very starkly and immediately.

Three authorities – the Greater London Council, the Inner London Education Authority, and Greenwich – have been told to cut their budgets by 6% in real terms. 15 others have been told to cut by 4½%.

Those 18 have no choice within Tory law: bigger rate rises are banned. Other councils would need huge rate rises.

Several Labour councils have already said that they will set a budget according to what is needed in their areas, and refuse to set a rate.

This is a step towards a struggle. But the council leaders seem to see their tactic in terms of brinkmanship with the government – a gambit to strengthen their hand at the negotiating table.

More will be needed than tough negotiating. The Tories will be defeated only by direct action from council workers, other workers and tenants.

Labour councils can play a big role in leading that action – but only if they take a clear stand now, supporting the council workers' unions rather than confronting them as so many left councils have done, and pledging that they will not impose rate rises above the rate of inflation.

**26 July 1984. Comparing the Falklands conflict to the miners' strike, Thatcher declares the miners are "the enemy within".**

# Socialist ORGANISER

Paper of the Socialist Organiser Alliance No.190 August 2 1984 25p Claimants and strikers 10p

# GENERAL STRIKE!

# HIGH COURT SEIZES MINERS' FUNDS

AS WE go to press, court officials are due to seize the assets of the South Wales area of the miners' union.

The High Court issued the order to seize the assets because the South Wales NUM refused to pay a fine imposed on it as a result of a case brought under the Tory anti-union laws by two haulage firms.

The labour movement should answer the seizure of the miners' assets with a general strike.

The full force of the law is now poised to come down heavily on the miners if they continue to use the methods of struggle which they need for victory — flying pickets, trade union boycotts, solidarity action, all of them unlawful under the Tory anti-union laws.

The heroic miners say that they will continue to use those methods.

So now either the laws will strike down working class solidarity — or solidarity will strike down the laws. Either the NUM will be defeated by crippling blows from the bosses' courts, to bankrupt the union — or the labour movement will rally round the miners and escalate the struggle against the Tory government.

When the courts jailed five dockers under a previous Tory anti-union law in 1972, 250,000 workers struck immediately without waiting for the union leaders. This spreading strike movement pushed the TUC into calling a one-day general strike.

The Tories caved in and freed the dockers, and the Tory law was in tatters. The Labour government scrapped it in 1974.

Mass strike action now to back the miners can do the same to the anti-union laws and to the government as we did in 1972.

Already railworkers and some other transport workers have boycotted coal and iron ore movements, and faced up to reprisals from their employers, in solidarity with the miners.

The dockers struck last month in a dispute closely connected to and parallel with the miners' strike. Hundreds of thousands of other trade unionists have joined one-day strikes to back the miners or have given food and money to help them.

Workers in many smaller disputes have been boosted and encouraged by the miners' stand.

21 weeks of the miners' strike have stirred up the labour movement, and roused it to the point where a general strike is possible.

Immediate rank and file action, spreading across the country, can do now what it did in 1972. But we must also demand that the official leadership acts.

Two TUC leaders appeared on TV on Monday 30th. Alan Sapper of ACTT called for 'a generality of strikes' in support of the miners. Alan Tuffin of the UCW said that the situation was heading towards a general strike, and a special conference of the TUC should be called to avoid it.

The TUC should be calling a general strike in support of the miners and to smash the anti-union laws — pledging itself to continue the action until *the miners* are satisfied. The NUM has already put down a resolution for the September TUC congress calling on all trade unionists not to cross NUM picket lines.

Now is the time for every trade unionist with an outstanding claim, demand or grievance to act to help themselves, the miners, and the whole working class.

Merseyside County Council workers are striking on August 7 in protest against the Tories' attacks on local government, and Greater Manchester NALGO members on August 9. These action should be tied in with the test of strength between the miners and the State.

A general strike could not only force the courts to back off the miners, but also wipe the anti-union laws off the statute book.

Indeed it could go much further. It could make the country ungovernable for the Tories, and even for the whole capitalist state machine.

Such a prospect frightens the TUC leaders, and if a general strike gets underway

continued on back page

# SMASH ANTI-UNION LAWS!

**2 August 1984. On 31 July the High Court fines South Wales NUM £50,000 for defying an injunction granted to two haulage firms against picketing. The courts then seize the area's assets. Class law backed by state violence is the Coal Board's response to the workers' methods of pickets, boycott, solidarity action. General strike is possible but it is a dangerous moment in the strike.**

Socialist ORGANISER

No. 191. August 9 1984 25p Claimants and strikers 10p

DEFEND THE NUM!

SMASH ANTI-UNION LAWS!

**9 August 1984. The broad labour movement does not respond to the seizure of the South Wales NUM funds. The Tories feel able use the courts more freely. Two scab miners bring a writ against the NUM to force them to call a national ballot and outlaw picketing.**

Socialist ORGANISER

No. 192. August 16 1984. 25p Claimants and strikers 10p

"In view of what happened in Northern Ireland at the weekend, I want to warn the mining community here that the police tactics that are being developed and used in Northern Ireland would represent the next stage in Britain."

*Northern Ireland:*

**TORY POLICE STATE!**

JOHN HARRIS (IFL)

Orgreave, June 18

Belfast, August 12

**Belfast today-Britain tomorrow**

**16 August 1984. A man is killed with a plastic bullet, fired by police on demonstrators in Belfast. This front page draws a parallel with increasing recklessness of police violence in Britain. In Nottinghamshire the coalfield resembles a police state.**

# Socialist Organiser

**STOP PRESS: NATIONAL DOCK STRIKE LOOMS**

BSC has announced that it intends to provoke a national dock strike over the dispute at Hunterston. It will begin on Thursday morning (August 23) to use unregistered labour to unload coal from the Ostia for Ravenscraig steelworks. There will be a national dock workers' delegate meeting on Friday to decide a response.

Paper of the Socialist Organiser Alliance No. 193. August 23, 1984. 25p Claimants and strikers 10p

## TUC: don't rat on the miners

# SUPPORT THE NUM PICKETS

By John Bloxam

THE hollowness of the NCB's massively publicised strike-breaking attempts is underlined by events in the coalfields and by MacGregor's own latest outburst.

Ten days ago MacGregor was boasting that the wind was now at his back and the strike was beginning to crumble. On Tuesday his desperate 'lock Scargill up' speech was a tacit admission of failure. It was a compliment to the effectiveness of the picketing.

Outside the main scabbing areas, the numbers returning to work over the past week have been tiny. Only hardened, isolated, unrepresentative right wingers have returned.

They have used everything except helicopters to get them to the pit top. Even then, some have been turned back. The solitary scabs in Kent and South Wales gave up after one day, and the one at Easington (Durham) was turned back by pickets on Tuesday.

The NCB have to lie even to get their figure of 0.15% working in the 'solid strike' areas. Most of the numbers given by the NCB come from Bilston Glen, and they are claiming more than three times the figure given by the local NUM. And at Castlehill (Fife), the local strike committee said the two scabs claimed by the NCB were in fact nurses the union had told to return.

A further indication of the strength of the strike came after a special lodge meeting at the South Celynen pit (South Wales) on Tuesday. Threats to close the pit within a year and leave a nearby pit working the same seam open had led to reports of a possible revolt in the branch. But of the 200 at the meeting, only eight insisted on a ballot and a return to work.

Continued on page 3

## Lobby TUC Sept. 3rd

John Harris (IFL)

John Harris (IFL)

**23 August 1984. Winter is approaching and the National Coal Board steps up its propaganda, claiming (untruthfully) that there is a big drift back to work. The TUC annual congress is also approaching and the miners are looking for help; but the TUC leaders want to wind up the dispute.**

**LOBBY THE TUC!**
**September 3**
**Assemble 8 a.m. Brighton Conference Centre**

Paper of the Socialist Organiser Alliance No.194 August 30 1984 25p Claimants and strikers 10p

# TUC: support miners and dockers

(Photo: Martin Shakeshaft, IFL)

*Miners' wives and children march in Maerdy, in the Rhondda. Monday August 27.*

# DON'T RAT, FIGHT!

**NEXT week Brighton could look like the pit villages of Nottinghamshire.**

**Police talk of sealing the town off, mounting road blocks, and flooding the area with their men.**

In short, Frank Chapple and his like will get the same sort of protection from pickets and militants as the 'Silver Birch' brigade in Notts.

Very appropriate, too. Many top trade union leaders have been stabbing the NUM in the back just as viciously as the scabs in the coalfields – only more subtly and suavely.

Trade unionists will be going to Brighton to demand that their union leaders give real support to the miners. The current ballyhoo in the Fleet Street press about "the scab as hero" makes it clear that the battle between the Tory government and the miners is not about the details of conditions in the pits. It is a battle for the life or death of effective trade unionism. The Tories are out to break the NUM – and if they succeed, no other union will be spared.

There can be no better time than *now* for other trade unionists to enter battle for their own demands and for the common cause. And if we do not fight with our full strength now, we will be seriously weakened in every future struggle.

Proposals before the TUC include an appeal to respect the NUM picket lines and a call for a one-day general strike. Both should be supported: indeed, what we should be working towards is a full-scale indefinite general strike.

But the trimmers and class-collaborators of the TUC leadership must not be allowed to use the call for solidarity as a lever to get control. For months they have wanted to end the dispute at all costs. AUEW general secretary Gavin Laird said on Monday 27th: "If an affiliate, be it the NGA, the NUM, or any other union, wishes to involve the movement and receive total support, then there must be the total involvement of the General Council. No union has the right unilaterally to adopt a course of action, pursue its own strategy, circumvent the leadership of the movement, and expect the same leadership to give unconditional support on demand".

It's the same argument as the working miners in Notts used against the appeal for solidarity from Yorkshire and other areas hit by closures: except that now the people who demand to vote on miners' jobs are not even miners from other areas, but top officials of other unions, themselves safe in a job for life! All support from the TUC must be with the clear understanding that *only miners* can agree a settlement to their dispute.

The striking dockers also need full TUC support. The main weakness of the dock strike so far is the weakness of its leadership. At the press conference after the TGWU docks delegate

continued on page 3

**30 August 1984. With the press behind the government, praising scabs and demonising strikers, the political stakes in the strike have become very high. Will delegates to the TUC congress vote for solidarity action to help the miners?**

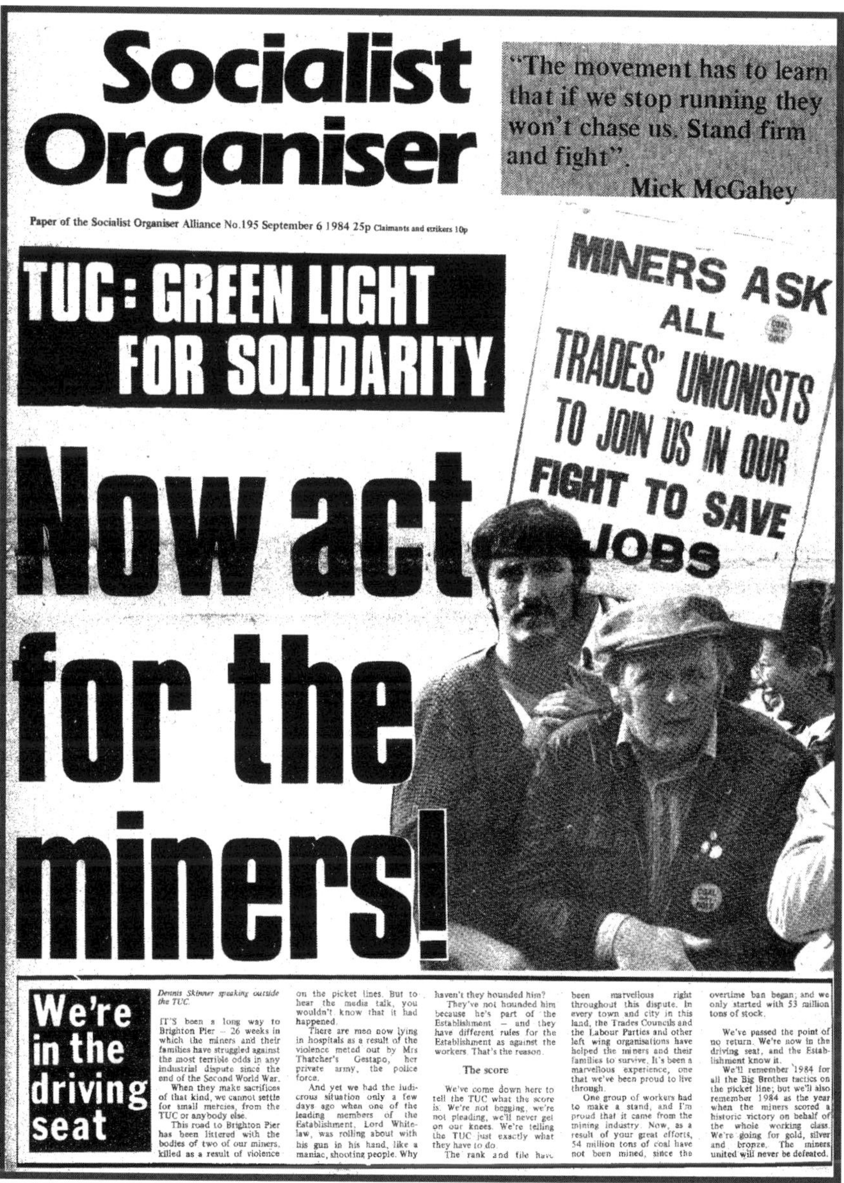

# Socialist Organiser

"The movement has to learn that if we stop running they won't chase us. Stand firm and fight".
Mick McGahey

Paper of the Socialist Organiser Alliance No.195 September 6 1984 25p Claimants and strikers 10p

## TUC: GREEN LIGHT FOR SOLIDARITY

# Now act for the miners!

MINERS ASK
ALL
TRADES' UNIONISTS
TO JOIN US IN OUR
FIGHT TO SAVE
JOBS

## We're in the driving seat

*Dennis Skinner speaking outside the TUC.*

IT'S been a long way to Brighton Pier — 26 weeks in which the miners and their families have struggled against the most terrible odds in any industrial dispute since the end of the Second World War.

When they make sacrifices of that kind, we cannot settle for small mercies, from the TUC or anybody else.

This road to Brighton Pier has been littered with the bodies of two of our miners, killed as a result of violence on the picket lines. But to hear the media talk, you wouldn't know that it had happened.

There are men now lying in hospitals as a result of the violence meted out by Mrs Thatcher's Gestapo, her private army, the police force.

And yet we had the ludicrous situation only a few days ago when one of the leading members of the Establishment, Lord Whitelaw, was rolling about with his gun in his hand, like a maniac, shooting people. Why haven't they hounded him?

They've not hounded him because he's part of the Establishment — and they have different rules for the Establishment as against the workers. That's the reason.

### The score

We've come down here to tell the TUC what the score is. We're not begging, we're not pleading, we'll never get on our knees. We're telling the TUC just exactly what they have to do.

The rank and file have been marvellous right throughout this dispute. In every town and city in this land, the Trades Councils and the Labour Parties and other left wing organisations have helped the miners and their families to survive. It's been a marvellous experience, one that we've been proud to live through.

One group of workers had to make a stand, and I'm proud that it came from the mining industry. Now, as a result of your great efforts, 54 million tons of coal have not been mined, since the overtime ban began; and we only started with 53 million tons of stock.

We've passed the point of no return. We're now in the driving seat, and the Establishment know it.

We'll remember 1984 for all the Big Brother tactics on the picket line; but we'll also remember 1984 as the year when the miners scored a historic victory on behalf of the whole working class. We're going for gold, silver and bronze. The miners united will never be defeated.

**6 September 1984. Unions at the TUC pledge to give financial support to the miners and to refuse to handle coal, coke or oil. The key battle front is to stop all work at power stations and steelworks. But that requires the union leaders to do more than pass a TUC resolution. They give no practical support and betray the miners.**

# Socialist Organiser

Paper of the Socialist Organiser Alliance No. 196 September 13 1984 25p Claimants and strikers 10p

## Build joint action committees

Dockers, miners and all workers supporting them – seafarers, railworkers, drivers – face a common Tory enemy, determined to hammer them into the ground. Dockers, miners, railworkers and drivers should therefore link arms firmly by organising joint action committees.

## Dockers and miners can



# GET THE TORIES ON THE RUN!

This open letter wa written by Paul Whetto on behalf of the Nott Rank and File Strik Committee.

After six months on strike the Notts. strikers wish to make it clear that we are not prepared to accept any compromise, or face-saving settlement or anything less than 100% total victory. We have come too far, and suffered too much, to contemplate anything else.

We realise this will entail further hardship and suffering, but if we are to achieve a worthwhile victory, this is something we are readily prepared to accept.

We therefore strongly urge the National Executive to accept no compromise on the question of pit closures and further, to insist on full implementation of the package as presented to the NCB prior to the present industrial action being undertaken by our members.

By that we mean:

*Full rate protection scheme.

*Early retirement.

*Shorter working shift.

*A four day week.

*Extra holidays, extra rest days.

*The implementation of a technology agreement for the benefit of all workers.

There is however an exception, and that is in regard to the pay rise. We would respectfully suggest that the question of a pay rise for the year November 1, 1983 to November 1984 be abandoned. A pay rise for that period would be of benefit to those who have worked in defiance of the National Executive's call for a united front against the NCB.

We urge that a pay rise be negotiated that takes cognisance of the financial loss of wages of our members, due to the intransigence of the Board, to be implemented on a full return to work and not before.

The pledge that all members dismissed during the course of the dispute will be reinstated, must be honoured.

We further urge, that as a sign of good faith by the government, the Chairman of the Coal Board, Mr. I. MacGregor be dismissed, and that a new plan for coal be negotiated that will give cast iron guarantees by this or any future government, of an expanding and prosperous coal industry.

We urge these things in the full knowledge that the miners are on the road to victory. That victory will be the most momentous ever achieved by the working class of this country, and the terms of the settlement must be seen by all to underline this.

The National Executive must recognise the depth and strength of feeling in the rank and file of our union and deliver a just and honourable settlement that reflects this feeling.

We address this appeal to the National Executive in the full confidence and knowledge that you will not fail us.

**13 September 1984. Dockers are once again on strike. Solidarity action is being organised by railworkers and seafarers. Paul Whetton, chair of the Notts Rank and File Strike Committee, writes this open letter to the National Executive of the NUM. Paul testifies that, despite the hardships, miners are still prepared to fight and want no compromise on pit closures.**

# Socialist Organiser

Paper of the Socialist Organiser Alliance No. 197 September 20 1984 25p Claimants and strikers 10p

## Tories call TUC's bluff

# STOP ALL COAL!



*Left: Notts striking miners at a demonstration by the print unions in Nottingham against union-busters David Dimbleby (on poster) and Christopher Pole-Carew. (Photo: John Smith, IFL).*

## 'It's them and us'

**Tony Benn speaking at Barnsley on Saturday**

A week before the Americans withdrew from Vietnam, they launched the biggest attack on the Vietnamese people that had been seen in the whole war. I believe that this is what is happening today in the miners' dispute in Britain.

When the Home Secretary said recently that miners convicted of picketing offences might well serve life sentences, that was an indication of the desperation that the government felt and they knew when they said that, that they could never, never, never beat the National Union of Mineworkers.

We know that they planned this strike. Nigel Lawson said in the Commons that he could have had a strike in 1981 when he was energy secretary. Why didn't they have a strike in 1981? Because they were not ready. They had other things they wanted to do first.

They had to get the law changed so they could starve the miners when their strike came. They had to recruit more police. They had to pay the police more for the work they knew the police would have to do.

They had to make an allowance in their public expenditure for the cost of the strike. And Lawson, who is now Chancellor of the Exchequer, said in the Commons two months ago, that the investment in this strike has been well worthwhile.

This is a struggle between them and us. Nobody can separate themselves out from this struggle – it is one big struggle with the miners in the forefront.

Everything hinges on the support that the labour movement, every trade unionist, every single member of the Labour Party, and millions of others, give to the miners now.

We have three sources of strength. One is solidarity – do not cross a picket line. Another is struggle – because all the gains that have ever been made by working people have been made by struggle. Thirdly the power to understand what is happening.

**20 September 1984. The leadership of the dockers' union sues for peace and bring their strike to an end on 18 September. The Tories are strengthened. Now they refuse to enter into talks with the NUM.**

# Socialist Organiser

Paper of the Socialist Organiser Alliance no.198 September 27 1984 25p (*Claimants and strikers 10p*)

## Defend Lairds!

By Lol Duffy, secretary, Lairds Occupation Committee

THE High Court in Manchester ruled today, Wednesday, 26th, that the 43 workers occupying Cammell Lairds shipyard on Merseyside must leave the vessels in the yard by midnight. Sunday 30th, or face arrest.

The response of the workers has been firm. We will not leave the vessels or the yard.

We are calling a mass picket for 7 a.m. on Monday morning, October 1. And we are calling for a national shop stewards' conference of shipbuilding unions.

In the event of any of the 43 workers occupying the yard being arrested, we call on the Merseyside trade union and Labour movement to take industrial action to defend trades unionism and defeat the law.

## This is class war, Kinnock:

*Police at Maltby, 22 September. Photo: John Harris, IFL*

## OFF THE FENCE!

**Paul Whetton is secretary of the Notts rank and file miners' strike committee and a delegate to the Labour Party conference in Blackpool. Here he writes — in a personal capacity — an open letter to Neil Kinnock.**

Dear Neil Kinnock,

Did you hear Margaret Thatcher on Radio last week laying it on the line against the miners? Did you see the headlines in her lap dog press next day? "I will never give in" and "No surrender" were two of them.

Mrs Thatcher is tough, nasty, brutal, spiteful, single-minded and very hostile to the labour movement — but a good, tough, committed fighter for her own cause and capable of being an inspiring leader for her own side. Mrs Thatcher knows how to lead.

There is no double-talk from Thatcher about the miners' strike. She is out to beat us down and crush the NUM. She leaves her supporters in no doubt about it.

When Thatcher denounces "violence" she doesn't feel obliged to be "impartial" and denounce the police as well as the pickets who stand up to them. She denounces us — she praises, lauds and defends the army of police thugs she sends to beat us down. She knows a bitter class war is being fought — and she knows which side she is on.

The contrast between Thatcher's conduct during the miners' strike and yours, Neil Kinnock, is a devastating one.

You have rightly blamed the Tories for the strike. But your backing for the NUM has been vague and equivocal at best. You have added your voice to the vile chorus of Tory orchestrated propaganda against picketing miners who are, in fact, victims of police thuggery. You denounce us for defending ourselves against the police and for trying to stop the police herding scabs to break our strike.

Whatever your intentions you thereby help Thatcher and MacGregor in their war to beat us down. You boost the Tory propaganda campaign which is designed to stop other workers giving miners the solidarity action that would make such a difference to our strike.

Thatcher is a Tory pig, but I find it impossible to compare Thatcher's performance on her side with yours on ours without a feeling of deep disappointment in you.

One reason why Thatcher knows how to lead is that she does know which side she is on. No messing, no weasling, no equivocation. For her there is no hint of doubt in her own side of this class war. She is determined to do everything she can to make sure her side wins. She will do nothing that gives aid and comfort to the miners.

Mrs Thatcher faces the just charges we hurl at her with a hard face, impregnable self-confidence and skin as thick as a rhinoceros. No doubt you have seen it close up.

When Mrs Thatcher talks of 'Britain', she means her part of it, her class, the Tory party.

We accuse her of starving miners' families to break the NUM, but does she care?

**Continued on back page.**

## Labour must back the miners

**27 September 1984. On the eve of Labour Party conference Paul Whetton urges Labour leader Neil Kinnock to get off the fence and back the miners. Against the leadership, the conference votes to condemn police violence and calls for police to be removed from the coalfields.**

# Socialist Organiser

Paper of the Socialist Organiser Alliance no. 199. October 3 1984 25p Claimants and strikers 10p

# TO HELL WITH THE COURTS!

## Strike to defend our unions

TWELVE trade unionists from Cammell Lairds are in Walton Jail. The leaders of the NUM – Scargill, Heathfield, McGahey – are threatened with heavy fines or jail for contempt of court because they insist that no court will tell their union how to run its affairs.

Lol Duffy

> "The Tories' class law does not frighten us. The occupation will continue. We will not be browbeaten with threats of prison or with courts." Lol Duffy
>
> Jailed secretary of the Cammell Lairds shipyard occupation committee

By John O'Mahony

They agree with what Lairds occupation committee secretary (and Socialist Organiser supporter) Lol Duffy said in the message he sent from Walton Jail to the Labour Party conference:

"The Tories' class law does not frighten us. The occupation will continue. We will not be browbeaten with threats of prison or with courts".

This is the spirit that will beat the Tories.

Right now contempt – open, avowed, belligerent, unpurgeable contempt – for the courts is the beginning of wisdom for the labour movement.

Neil Kinnock can go on as he did last Tuesday about sticking within the strict limits of legality and ballot-box politics. He doesn't want to fight the class struggle as it has to be fought. He wants to play parliamentary games and to waffle.

He should listen to the representatives of the ruling class. They know what's what and some of them even say it out loud.

Listen to the Master of the Rolls – and former chairman of the anti-union Industrial Relations Court, set up by the Tory government in 1972 – Sir John Donaldson, speaking last November:

"The legal system (is) not in practice even-handed as between employers and unions; current functions put the courts almost entirely in the business of restricting and penalising the latter, and not of remedying their grievances."

### Class war

Exactly! The law and the courts are – like the armies of lawless, scab-herding policemen in the coalfields – now being used in industry as a naked weapon on the bosses' side in a class war that becomes more open, more embittered, and more uncompromising – on both sides – with every day the miners' strike continues.

We owe naked class law no deference.

We owe the courts neither respect nor obedience when they are playing this blatantly partisan role in industrial affairs.

But, cautious people will say, we should beware of the damage the courts can inflict on the labour movement. Yes, we should. But the worst damage the courts can do to the labour movement is to break our spirit and make us docile and pliable towards an outrageous, vicious, and anti-working class government. That is what they are trying to do.

To be cowed by the fear – or the certainty – of fines or imprisonment is to let the courts peacefully do what they have been brought into industrial relations to do – neuter and house-train the labour movement.

Nothing the courts can do to us would be worse than that. The movement will survive fines and jailings. We can even survive a serious defeat. But the labour movement we have now will not survive if it surrenders peacefully to the rule of blatant class law in the court rooms and of a licensed bully-boy police force in industrial disputes.

### Fight back

The labour movement has no responsible alternative but to resist and fight back, defying the Tory government and the law courts.

Not to fight back is to open the way for a full spate of Tory attacks on every section of the working class – on wages and conditions, on the welfare state, on democratic rights.

If the labour movement rouses itself and mobilises we can defy their law and break its back like we did in 1972.

The movement is in worse shape now because of mass unem-

Continued on page 3

**3 October 1984. On 28 September the High Court declares the NUM strike "unlawful" because there has been no national ballot. Meanwhile 12 trade unionists from Cammell Lairds shipyard are in jail for organising an occupation against job cuts. Socialist Organiser supporter Lol Duffy translates what the paper is saying into appropriate words of defiance.**

Socialist Organiser

DECEMBER 1

Day conference called by Socialist Organiser on:
'FIGHTING THE TORIES: SOCIALIST ANSWERS'
In London. Sessions include: How to fight for jobs; the Alternative Economic Strategy; winning the Labour Party to socialist policies; police accountability; alternatives to the police; debate on Defence.
Details from. SO, 214 Sickert Court, London N1 2SY

Paper of the Socialist Organiser Alliance No. 200 October 11 1984 25p Claimants and strikers 10p

SCARGILL IS RIGHT

ON Wednesday October 10 the High Court fined the National Union of Mineworkers £200,000, and Arthur Scargill £1,000, for "contempt of court" in defying an earlier court ruling that the miners' strike is official.

The miners' leaders have refused to bow down to the court's class law – and the Judge said that if the fines were not paid within two weeks he would impose further penalties, maybe seizure of the union's funds.

As at Cammell Lairds shipyard in Birkenhead, the courts are trying to say that fighting for jobs is a crime.

The labour movement's answer must be to prepare for general strike action if the courts seize the NUM funds or jail the miners' leaders.

Trade unionists should demand that the TUC calls a general strike. At the same time, the rank and file cannot wait for the TUC: organise now for strikes if the courts do not back down.

ARTHUR SCARGILL SAYS:

"We've got unelected judges dispensing not justice, but class justice, against our people who are involved in a struggle to maintain jobs and maintain the communities in which they live.

There's been a gauntlet thrown down. That gauntlet has been picked up.

The miners' union has been told after seven months of official strike action that the strike is no longer legal or official.

If there is any ambiguity, or any doubt, let me now dispel it. The National Executive Committee of the NUM, meeting on Monday October 1, 1984, were told that there were writs issued against the NUM seeking sequestration of the funds of the union, and also against the National President seeking to commit him to Pentonville prison.

Following a full discussion, the NEC unanimously agreed the following steps:

1. To fully endorse and support the views and comments expressed by the National President during the interview on Channel Four News on Friday September 28, 1984:

2. Irrespective of the High Court decision the Executive unanimously reaffirms its determination to continue to deal with

Continued on page 4

It's class law
Defend the NUM

ORGANISE FOR A GENERAL STRIKE

**11 October 1984. The High Court fines the NUM £200,000 and Scargill £1,000 for "contempt of court". Scargill calls these moves "class justice", against people attempting to fight for their jobs and communities.**

# Socialist Organiser

**Miners appeal to deputies**

Paper of the Socialist Organiser Alliance No.201 October 18 1984 25p *Claimants and strikers 10p*

## Threat to seize miners' funds

# CLASS LAW CLASS WAR

**By Paul Whetton, for and on behalf of the Notts Miners' Rank and File Strike Committee.**

**With the breakdown of the talks between the mining unions and the NCB, the Notts Miners' Rank and File Strike Committee calls upon our comrades in NACODS to turn their ballot result into action and join us on the picket line.**

**It is quite obvious that the chairman and the rest of the Coal Board have no intention of taking any notice of the workers within the industry and by their intransigence have clearly stated that they are merely puppets of the Tory government.**

**This blatant attack upon the mining industry must be answered in the only language that the Tories understand – total solidarity of all workers in withdrawing their labour.**

**Only by standing together can all the workers bring this dispute to a speedy and successful conclusion. Join us now and together we can save our jobs, our industry and our communities.**

**NOW is the time for the TUC to deliver the solidarity it has promised to the miners.**

Next Thursday the funds of the miners' union could be seized, because they have refused to pay a fine for "contempt of court".

Talks at the government arbitration service ACAS broke down on Monday 15th, and compromise is off the agenda for a while at least.

The Coal Board was not even willing to concede enough to satisfy the very moderate pit deputies' union NACODS. NACODS has now decided to activate their 82% ballot vote for strike action as from next week.

The conservative leaders of NACODS are still looking for a deal to avoid action, but at present Ian MacGregor is not even giving them that.

If the deputies strike, they will shut every pit in the country, and bring much closer the day when the Coal Board has to try to move stocks from the strike-bound pits, maybe using troops.

Stockbrokers Simon and Coates reckon there could be power cuts before the end of November.

All the biather about ballots has been exposed. The same newspapers that say it is wrong for the NUM to strike without a ballot are urging NACODS to stay at work despite a ballot vote to strike. 'The deputies didn't really mean to vote to strike', says Fleet Street.

The press is also encouraging individual pit deputies, in Nottinghamshire especially, to defy the NACODS strike if it goes ahead. And the scab miners in Notts, after all their cries that 'we want a ballot', talk about doing the deputies' work if they do abide by the ballot decision!

All's fair in class war, they clearly believe.

The issue is no longer just pit closures, but one of the development or crippling of effective trade unionism. The High Court is claiming the right to overrule the NUM conference on whether or not the miners' strike is official. The unelected, Tory-minded judges are threatening to seize all the NUM's funds and maybe jail its leaders unless they call the strike off.

Unions at the TUC pledged to stop all movement and boycott all new supplies of coal, coke or substitute oil. Contacts must be made at rank and file level to implement these decisions, at the same time as we press the official leaderships to put their full weight and authority behind the action.

Railworkers are stopping almost all coal movements by rail in Notts. A visit to Notts by rail union leaders Jimmy Knapp and Ray Buckton — later than it should have been, but effective nonetheless — was crucial in getting that action.

David Basnett, Moss Evans and Ron Todd, leaders of the GMBU and TGWU, should be visiting the power stations.

And if the High Court does seize the NUM's funds, the answer should be a general strike — to force the courts to back down, to gain victory fo the miners, and to smash th anti-union laws.

The TUC should be pre paring for action. But if the TU will not lead, then the rank an file must.

Spontaneous spreading strik action in July 1972 forced th Tories to back down on their us of the law against picketin dockers. Similar action no could bring quick victory for th miners.

## ORGANISE FOR A GENERAL STRIKE

**As deputies decide to strike, the truth on coal stocks - p.3**

**18 October 1984. The NUM now face having their funds seized for refusing to pay the fine. Meanwhile talks between the NUM and the Coal Board have been on-and-off for a while; they falter again and the pit deputies union NACODS looks set to strike.**

Paper of the Socialist Organiser Alliance. No. 202. October 25 1984 25p (Claimants & strikers 10p)

# Socialist Organiser

## Class law on the picket line

## Tory court set to seize miners' funds

# STRIKE BACK!

## JUDAS!

NACODS secretary Peter McNestry:

AS we go to press the courts seem set to grab the assets of the miners' union, because the NUM has refused to pay a £200,000 fine.

And the strike by the pit deputies' union NACODS, set for 6 am on Thursday, 25th, has been called off. Had the supervisors come out, they would have closed all the coalfields, shortened the miners' strike and brought victory over the Tories much closer.

The details of the settlement are still secret but it is unlikely that NACODS have got any reliable guarantees against pit closures.

For the leaders of NACODS to settle on their own like this, after 80% of supervisors voted for strike action, is the dirtiest piece of shameless treachery seen in the British labour movement for a very long time.

McNestry is nothing but a working class Judas!

Striking miners will be bitterly disappointed and very angry.

But many of them expected a stab in the back. Notts rank and file leader Paul Wherton explains the spirit in which militant miners watched the manoeuvres between NACODS leaders and the Coal Board:

"We've told as many of our lads as possible not to build their hopes on a NACODS strike, to believe it when they see it. The man who expects nothing is never disappointed." (See page 2).

Hardened by eight months on strike, miners and their families are unlikely to let disappointment lead to despair. The strike will go on. Over 140,000 miners and their families will continue the fight because they know they have no alternative except surrender.

Arthur Scargill says that the only deal the NUM will accept is one in which the Coal Board withdraws its closure plans, agrees to keep open pits marked for closure and produces "a definition of pit exhaustion that does not contain the economic connotation that the Coal Board has been seeking to include since the beginning of March this year."

That principle – that people come before economics – makes the miners' strike a fight on behalf of the whole working

Continued on back page

Rossington, Yorkshire: This picket was knocked over by a police horsebox and then run over by a police transit van. Photo: John Harris

## ORGANISE FOR A GENERAL STRIKE

**25 October 1984. NACODS call off their strike, just at the moment when the union of their fellow coal workers has its funds seized by the courts. 24 members of the NUM Executive are made liable to pay the £200,000 fine.**

No. 203.
November 1 1984
25p. Claimants and strikers 10p.

# Socialist Organiser

**Inside**

**Stop the millions starving p6&7**

**Fighting racist attacks p8**

**Yorkshire miner's wife: 'determined to win'**

# Stand by the miners!

## Unions must deliver on TUC promises

TUC chair Jack Eccles has blurted it out. The TUC leaders are not committed to a miners' victory. They just want to end the strike.

They want a settlement — any settlement, just so long as it ends the risks and agitation of the dispute.

In a radio interview on Tuesday 30th, Eccles said that the TUC should pressurise the miners to settle on terms similar to the pit deputies' deal.

That deal committed the Coal Board to nothing but "considering" concessions. But BBC Newsnight on Tuesday revealed that seven top union leaders had said they agreed with Eccles.

Because of rank and file support for the miners, six of those seven spoke only "off the record". And TUC general secretary Norman Willis said Eccles was "not speaking for the TUC. I do not share his views".

But Eccles' statement showed clearly enough why the TUC promises of support for the miners have remained largely a dead letter. At the TUC Congress in September union leaders promised to stop movement and handling of coal and of substitute oil. They have done almost nothing to keep that promise.

Eccles is an official of the GMBU, one of the crucial unions in the power stations.

Rank and file trade unions have to call our leaders to order, and demand that they deliver on their promises.

Militants must organise in every workplace and every trade union branch to make sure that the TUC decisions are actually implemented. No coal or coal substitutes must be allowed to move; picketing must be spread, especially at power stations, and the rule of not crossing them must be enforced. Trade unionists have to be convinced of the urgency of the tasks before us now to win support and victory for the miners.

The Tories are not just trying to close pits. They are out to break the back of effective trade unionism. Every union should back the miners.

*Miners on picket of Didcot power station* *Photo: John Harris (IFL)*

**BACK THE PICKETS STOP ALL COAL AND OI**

**1 November 1984. The miners are now on the defensive. A small trickle of miners go back to work. The TUC leaders want an immediate end to the strike.**

No.204. November 8 1984. 25p. Claimants and strikers 10p.

# Socialist Organiser

**Inside**

Centre pages: world poverty and a socialist energy policy.
Pages 4-5: report from a Yorkshire pit village.
Page 10: US threats against Nicaragua; the reasons for the slaughter in India.

## After NGA, GCHQ, Lairds, courts move against NUM and carworkers

Mass picket at Warrington

Scargill being arrested at Orgreave

Picket at BL Longbridge

# STOP THE TORY UNION-BUSTERS!

NO trade union is safe. The Tories are out to break the back of effective trade unionism.

The TUC's failure to deliver on its promises of support for the miners has given them the go-ahead. Now six unions in the car industry have had writs telling them that their strike at Austin Rover is against the law because the strike vote was not in Tory-approved form.

If they refuse to return to work and accept that workers can strike only by permission of the Tory-dominated courts, then these unions could have their funds seized.

The NUM's national funds are already being seized. Court cases are now underway which could lead to NUM area funds being seized, too, and individual NUM executive members being fined.

It is the latest stage in a developing offensive from the Tories, encouraged at each stage by the weakness of the official leaders of the labour movement.

Last December it was the print union NGA, beaten down by the courts after it tried to stop Eddie Shah's scab print-works in Warrington.

In March it was civil servants at GCHQ, told that they could no longer be union members.

In August the South Wales miners' area funds were seized. In October 37 shipyard workers from Cammell Lairds, Birkenhead, were jailed for occupying to defend their jobs.

Dockers in Cardiff now face legal action because they are boycotting the haulage firms that took the South Wales NUM to court.

Neil Kinnock has chosen this moment to distance himself from the miners, saying that he "hasn't got time" to attend support rallies. He is only giving a further boost to the Tories.

Despite Kinnock or against Kinnock, the labour movement must defend its rights. Start organising now for solidarity action with the car workers and the miners!

**8 November. Arrested miners now begin to appear in court. NUM area funds may be seized. Many other groups of workers are being hit by Tory anti-union laws and the courts.**

No. 205 November 15 1984. 25p. Claimants and strikers 10p.

# Socialist Organiser

## Miners' solidarity – conference Dec 2

Called by the Mineworkers' Defence Committee. Speakers include Arthur Scargill and Tony Benn. At Camden Town Hall, London NW1 [opposite St. Pancras Station] from 11.30 to 4.30. Delegates and observers invited from all labour movement organisations. Fee: £2 for first delegate, £1 for each additional delegate and for observers. Write to Jane Stockton, 31 Cranwich Road, London N16 or phone 01-981 3289.

## TUC must back miners and carworkers

# UNIONS ON TRIAL

**By John Bloxam**

SPEAKING at a miners' rally in Shirebrook, North Derbyshire, last Friday, 9th, NUM vice-president Mick McGahey appealed for support "over the heads of the trade union leaders."

"The NUM will win this strike", he said, "but we will win it quickly if the movement responds to our demands".

This week Austin Rover are having the TGWU and five other unions hauled up for contempt of court, because they called a carworkers' strike on the authority of mass meeting votes rather than the Tory-prescribed secret ballot. It's clear that the Tories are out to break effective trade unionism across the board.

But the TUC leaders are doing nothing. After two meetings last week with the NUM, they did no more than plan a trip to Holland to try to halt coal imports.

The defence of trade unionism rests in the hands of the rank and file.

At power stations in the south-east — West Thurrock, Tilbury, and Kings North — workers are refusing to accept coal or substitute oil. Seafarers are also refusing to deliver. West Thurrock has been switched out of the national grid.

It was reported at the NUM delegate conference that power shop stewards in Scotland have agreed to implement the TUC guidelines. And there is solid support in the big coal-fired Yorkshire stations, which are still being picketed by the Yorkshire area NUM.

In the Trent Valley power stations there has been a poor response so far, but the Notts miners' rank and file strike committee has decided to mount 16-hour, 7-day pickets on all of them. Up to now there have been pickets on some of them irregularly.

This is a difficult period for the miners' strike — and the TUC and Labour leaders are helping to make it difficult. But a tremendous potential for victory is still there.

The great turn-out by London council workers last Wednesday for a strike to defend jobs and services, for example, shows that under the surface there is a fund of militancy, built up by the inspiration given to other workers by the miners' heroism over eight months.

At the NUM rally in Sheffield on Thursday 8th, angry miners shouted tauntingly, "Where's Kinnock?" Neil Kinnock — and most other TUC and Labour leaders — clearly agree with the Tories that the miners are losing, and they want to distance themselves as much as they can.

Even the TGWU — left-wing in TUC terms — has just sat quiet and said nothing while Austin Rover moves towards getting its union funds seized.

Continued on page 3

Mass picket at Cortonwood — JOHN HARRIS (IFL)

## Thatcher threatens new police powers

SPEAKING at the Lord Mayor's banquet on Monday, 12th, Margaret Thatcher threatened new powers for the police.

In her own language she made it plain that justice had nothing to do with it. The police will be given *any powers necessary* to defeat the working class.

"If the police and courts are lacking the powers necessary to keep order in a free society, and necessary to protect the weak against the strong, then we shall introduce measures which give them what they need."

While declaring themselves that they will use "any measures necessary", the Tories make an outcry about the violence of miners trying to defend their picket lines against masses of police.

In this doublespeak 'the weak' are Ian MacGregor, the Coal Board, the Tories, and the whole ruling class: 'the strong' are the miners, equipped with nothing but their own courage and determination and the solidarity of other workers.

But the warning is unmistakeable: let the miners lose, and the whole working class will face a fierce new array of police measures.

**INSIDE**



**15 November 1984. Attack after attack, yet still the TUC leaders do nothing. The NUM organises a series of local rallies and the trickle of miners going back to work tapers off. Militants start to campaign for a recall TUC to call them to account for failing to implement the September decision.**

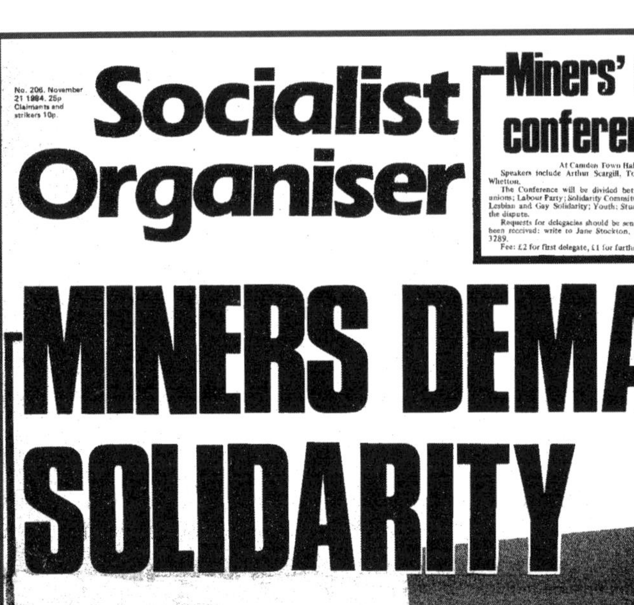

No. 206. November 21 1984. 25p Claimants and strikers 10p.

# Socialist Organiser

## Miners' solidarity conference Dec 2

At Camden Town Hall, London NW1, 11.30 – 4.30.

Speakers include Arthur Scargill, Tony Benn, Betty Heathfield, Kay Sutcliffe, Paul Whetton.

The Conference will be divided between plenary sessions and workshops on: trade unions; Labour Party; Solidarity Committees; Women Against Pit Closures; Black Solidarity; Lesbian and Gay Solidarity; Youth; Students. There is also a workshop on the police and the dispute.

Requests for delegacies should be sent off as soon as possible. Almost 400 have already been received: write to Jane Stockton, 31 Cranwich Rd., London N16, or phone 01-981 3289.

Fee: £2 for first delegate, £1 for further delegates and for observers.

# MINERS DEMAND SOLIDARITY

**"We have to translate resolution into action. I am not going to appeal to the barons of the TUC — I want to ask the ordinary men and women of this country to give industrial action support to this union.**

**"How much longer can you stand to one side and see this union battered? We are asking you to come out now and stop scab coal being delivered into power stations."**

That was Arthur Scargill's message to the rally in Birmingham (November 14). The same week, in Aberafan a symbolic noose was lowered in front of TUC general secretary Norman Willis.

He – and the rest of the 'TUC barons' – deserve it. After Willis' Kinnock-type speech, putting an equals sign over police thuggery and picket line self-defence, trade union leaders started to crawl out of the woodwork to tell the press how much they agree with him.

Now, as before, they want control of the strike. Without that, they will do next to nothing to make sure the decisions of TUC Congress are implemented.

Power workers in Yorkshire and the London area have agreed not to accept new supplies of coal – making power cuts likely by January.

A meeting of transport and power unions at the TUC has taken place. They have reaffirmed the decisions of TUC Congress.

But Arthur Scargill is right. The power to implement these decisions lies with the rank and file.

MARK SALMON

**INSIDE**

Miners' strike — Standing Firm Pages 4-5

Labour Party workplace branches Page 2

South African workers fight apartheid Page 10

Poverty and exploitation in the Third World Centre pages

**22 November 1984. Arthur Scargill demands solidarity from the TUC. TUC general secretary Norman Willis delivers a speech equating police thuggery with picket line self-defence. Other trade union leaders back him up.**

No. 207. November 28 1984. 25p. Claimants and strikers 10p.

# Socialist Organiser

## Miners' solidarity conference Dec 2

**From 11.30am at Camden Town Hall, Euston Rd, London NW1.**
**Inside: special four-page broadsheet**

## T&G FINED; TORY ASSAULTS ESCALATE

*Askern Colliery, Doncaster: police stand by while picket hut burns in the colliery yard. They deny setting fire to it, but as the police were in occupation it seems that no-one else could have done it. The hut was used during nine months of peaceful picketing. Photo: John Harris, IFL.*

# Every union is at risk

THE Transport and General Workers' Union's General Executive Committee – a broadly-based committee of working members – meets next Monday, December 3.

It will discuss the union's response to the £200,000 fine imposed by the High Court on Monday 26th, with two weeks to pay.

It has a heavy responsibility.

Made bolder by the TUC's weakness, the government is out to get a spectacular show of obedience from the TGWU.

Other unions involved in the Austin Rover strike have convinced the company that they 'disavowed' the strike. TASS is trying to persuade the court that it did not 'encourage' or 'promote' the strike.

The TGWU has been fined for contempt of court because it defied an injunction to call off the strike, which had been called without the ballot required by Tory law.

If the TGWU doesn't pay – and it is bound by union conference policy not to pay the fine – then its funds could be seized.

Behind this case stands not only the threat of Tory-enforced ballots for every future strike, but a whole string of court actions against the NUM.

Scabs are trying to get control of NUM area funds in North Derbyshire and Yorkshire passed to receivers. And they are trying to get the national executive members made personally responsible for the £200,000 fine against the union.

The TGWU's actions so far have encouraged the Tories. Although the TGWU did not disavow the Austin Rover strike, it certainly did nothing to encourage it. Clearly top TGWU officials hoped that the strike would die and that having beaten the strike Austin Rover would call off their court case.

Austin Rover – and behind them the government – are not interested in that sort of gentlemanly play-acting. They want the TGWU on its knees.

If the TGWU submits, it will be stacking the odds against every future strike in Britain, and betraying the NUM.

The TGWU should start off by calling a 24 hour strike, which it should appeal to other unions to make a general strike. It should explain to its members, and all other trade unionists, that the attack on the TGWU is inseparable from the Tories' assault on the miners, and that every union is at risk.



**29 November 1984. The TGWU is fined £200,000 for supporting a strike at Austin Rover. The TGWU does not fight back.**

No. 208. December 5 1984. 25p Claimants and strikers 10p.

# Socialist Organiser

## INSIDE

Pages 4-7: report from the 2000-strong Miners' Defence Committee conference last Sunday. Speeches by Tony Benn, Paul Whetton, etc.
Pages 3-4: More on the miners' strike
Page 2: National Union of Students conference
Page 11: CPSA conference, and other trade union reports
Page 10: International — Grenada, Uruguay, famine in Africa

# TUC: back the miners!

**"I am not asking for moral support, or resolutions, but a campaign of industrial action. The trade union movement only emerged because people fought unjust laws".**
**Arthur Scargill**

*Scargill at the first of the delegate conferences during the strike. Photo: John Harris*

"I have a right to the money. I am the NUM".

Despite those words, lawyer and Tory party official Herbert Brewer has so far failed to get hold of the miners' funds deposited in Luxemburg. His credentials as receiver in charge of the NUM funds, appointed by the High Court because the NUM has refused to obey court rulings and call off its strike, did not convince the bankers.

The NUM will continue to wage the strike without funds if it has to — in Arthur Scargill's words, "like the Tolpuddle Martyrs, with difficulty but with success".

### Tory lawyer

But as Arthur Scargill has also said, the appointment of a Tory lawyer to say "I am the NUM" is an attack on trade union rights unprecedented in Britain.

A series of further legal threats is following fast behind it. Scabs in South Wales have started moves to get the strike declared unofficial in that area. North Derbyshire and Yorkshire areas could have receivers put in to control their funds.

Another court case seeks to make the national executive members personally responsible for the fines on the NUM, and thus to open the way for jailing them if they refuse to pay.

Now that the back-to work movement has petered out — with very little increase in scab production — the focus of the Tory offensive has switched to court actions.

### Offensive

It is an offensive not only against the miners but against the whole working class. The TGWU is next in line behind the NUM.

It has been fined £200,000 because it didn't call off the Austin Rover strike when the High Court told it to. The TGWU executive is deciding its response this week. The union faces the prospect of having its funds seized like the NUM's — unless it betrays the miners and the whole working class by toeing the Tory line.

Bill Whatley the right-wing leader of USDAW, said that Monday's NUM conference decision to stand firm was "most unfortunate". Unless the NUM backs down and makes a "reasonable compromise", said the wretched Whatley "they are going to see many more in the trade union movement moving away from them".

Such attitudes will sabotage not only the NUM but also the whole trade union movement. The TUC must fight back now, or have its sinews cut by Tory law.

### Record

So miserable has been the TUC's record since the resounding declarations of support for the miners at its September congress, that talk of a general strike now seems far-fetched to many activists.

But if the TUC leadership — and especially the TGWU — turn round and start fighting, then they can quickly change the mood of defeatism.

### The time

The rank and file cannot afford to wait for the TUC, and the miners have made it plain that they will appeal over the heads of the top officials if necessary. If this is not the time for solidarity action, there never will be one! Pressure on the official leadership should go hand in hand with rank and file initiative.

*Call industrial action now, organise for a general strike to support the miners and to smash the anti-union laws.

*Recall the TUC congress. Rally the movement; call the leaders to account. End collaboration with the Tory government!

*Victory to the miners! Victory to the working class!

# Strike to defend our unions

**5 December 1984. The NUM moves its funds to an account in Luxembourg, frustrating the court-appointed receiver now in charge of NUM funds. An NUM conference votes to stand firm. Some union leaders are now actively trying to sabotage the strike.**

No.209 December 12 1984 25p (Claimants and strikers 10p)

"There must be the most massive mobilisation of industrial action our movement has ever known, and we must have it now.

"There is no other way to stop the court's attempt to destroy the NUM."

Arthur Scargill

*The miners will fight on: the whole movement should join them. Photo: John Harris, IFL.*

# Demand a general strike!

ACTIVISTS from the Mineworkers Defence Committee will be lobbying the TUC General Council meeting next Wednesday, 19th, to demand industrial action in support of the miners.

The courts have put a reciever in charge of every item of spending by the miners' union. A series of other legal actions coming up soon could put receivers in charge of the funds of NUM areas, and make NUM national executive members personally responsible for the £200,000 fine imposed on the union.

The TGWU could have its funds seized within the next weeks for not having paid a £200,000 fine imposed on it because it did not tell the Austin Rover strikers to go back to work.

The Tories are out for a showdown. Price Waterhouse, the firm appointed by the courts to seize the NUM's funds, could quite well lay their hands on £200,000 of NUM money if they wanted to. But they're out to get the lot, and the government has made it plain that it will finance the operation as far as is needed.

## Lightly

Nobody is going to be let off lightly. The Tories want a public, unequivocal act of submission by the unions to their laws restricting strikes and banning solidarity.

They won't get it from the miners, and they won't break the strike. But plenty of TUC leaders are r[illegible] to submit.

They [illegible] stopped supplying [illegible] to the NUM. A warning l[illegible]ter about illegality was enough to frighten them off.

They have increased their pressure on the NUM to back down.

According to the Tory laws all solidarity strikes are unlawful. All picketing except at your place of work puts you on the wrong side of the law. No strike is legal unless there has been an individual ballot in the form prescribed by the Tories. If we allow them to enforce these laws all the most effective methods of trade union struggle as it exists today will be outlawed.

Now is the time for all trade unionists to rally in self-defence and in defence of the miners.

The Mineworkers' Defence Committee will demand the TUC does an about-turn and starts organising for industrial action. The TUC should cam-

Continued on p.3



**12 December 1984. At the beginning of the month Ian MacGregor announces plans to privatise the pits that remain under the NCB after he has pushed through closures. The aims of the government could not be any clearer yet the unions stay passive. Activists from the Mineworkers' Defence Committee lobby the TUC General Council to demand industrial action.**

# Socialist Organiser

# Murray gets his reward...

Paper of the Socialist Organiser Alliance No. 210. January 2 1985 25p. Claimants and strikers 10p

# LORD SCAB

Len Murray is going to the House of Lords. Harold Jones is in Armley prison.

Harold Jones is one of 9,000 miners arrested during the strike, and hundreds in prison. Len Murray . . . well, let him speak for himself.

"I was not looking for this or hoping for this – but I wasn't surprised when it came. It's just one of these things that happen".

Len Murray has been made a Lord, alongside Frank Chapple, for services to the Tory government – for his blatant betrayal of ASLEF and the NGA, and his more subtle treachery to the health workers, the GCHQ workers and the miners.

Harold Jones has been jailed for being a loyal trade unionist and getting in the way of the police.

Lions led by donkeys? At least the First World War generals who got called 'donkeys' did not accept decorations from the other side in the midst of the battle!

Now Len Murray's successor, Norman Willis, is well on course for the House of Lords himself – mouthing words of sympathy for miners like Harold Jones while doing nothing to deliver the solidarity promised by TUC congress decisions.

On Wednesday December 19 the TUC General Council met to consider its response to the legal offensive against the miners' union, and in particular the appointment of a receiver to take control of the NUM's finances.

Arthur Scargill had called for "the most massive mobilisation of industrial action our movement has ever known". The TUC leaders called no action at all.

The only action was when the police cleared a lobby from the Mineworkers Defence Committee off the steps of Congress House.

Is it worth bothering with such cowards and traitors? The answer is yes – because they still have authority with many workers.

It is often difficult to remember that these same cowards and traitors called a General Strike 12½ years ago. Of course, that only happened after 300,000 workers had come out because five dockers were put in jail – but it happened and it was enough to get the Tories to surrender.

The TUC leaders did it because they were pushed, and because they were frightened of losing control. They can be pushed again.

Continued back page.



## And will Norman Willis make it as Baron Traitor of Cortonwood?

STEFANO CAGNONI (IFL)

# ...miners get jail!

Sheila Jones

Sheila Jones's husband Harold was arrested after police invaded their village – Frickley, Yorkshire – to get scabs into the pit on November 3.

Once the clashes between police and pickets had died down, the police started arrests, apparently picking up anyone in sight.

Harold, with two others, was taken to the pit office. They were laid face down and beaten with truncheons – one of the miners being knocked unconscious as the pit manager watched laughing.

Harold was beaten until he 'confessed' to possessing a petrol bomb – even though no such bombs had been seen in the village.

Later, at Pontefract Hospital, he had to have stitches in wounds on his head. He also had black eyes and heavy bruising.

Harold had been a regular picket for over nine mouths. He has never been in trouble with the law before, and says that he is completely innocent.

Send messages of support to Harold Jones, 677335 A2-14, HM Prison, Armley, Leeds.

Photo and story by John Harris (IFL).

**2 January 1985. Christmas is celebrated with defiant solidarity but the turn of the year does not bring cheering news. A life peerage is given to Len Murray, former leader of the TUC. Meanwhile many strikers are being arrested. Harold Jones from Frickley was beaten up by police until he "confessed" to possessing a petrol bomb.**

# Socialist Organiser

No.211 January 9 1985 25p Claimants and strikers 10p

MINEWORKERS DEFENCE COMMITTEE
NATIONAL CONFERENCE

Octagon Centre, Sheffield
Saturday February 9, 11.00 a.m. – 5.30 p.m.
Delegates: Two per trade union organisation
One per other organisation
Confirmed speakers include:
Peter Heathfield, Betty Heathfield, Tony Benn
John Tocher, Phil Holt
Accomodation, credentials and creche:
Mineworkers Defence Committee, c/o 31 Cranwich Road, London N16. Or phone 01-981 3289

## Yorkshire names the day

YORKSHIRE and Humberside regional TUC has called a 24 hour general strike in its area on February 11, and is appealing to other regions to join in.

Several Regional TUCs called days of action for the miners last summer, despite Lord Scab Murray denouncing them. Unfortunately they were on different days.

Now Yorkshire and Humberside is calling for united action. It is asking workplaces for all-out strikes if possible, or if not, then the donation of a day or half a day's pay.

### Pickets

Trades Councils are being asked to coordinate demonstrations on the 11th — but instead of rallies in town centres, the regional TUC wants pit picket lines to be the rallying point.

Socialists must work hard to build for February 11 and spread it from there.

MINERS ASK
ALL
TRADES' UNIONISTS
TO JOIN US IN OUR
FIGHT TO SAVE
JOBS

Andrew Wiard (Report)

INSIDE

Mineworkers Defence Committee page 3.

Which side are you on? Ken Loach's latest. page 9

Where is Tribune going? page 10

The Belfast engineers' strike 1919 Centre pages

**9 January 1985. Yorkshire and Humberside regional TUC calls a 24 hour general strike for 11 February. It is too little and very late.**

# Socialist Organiser

No. 212. January 16 1985. 25p. Claimants and strikers 10p.

## Support the miners

# Answer Scargill's call!

**By Tony Benn**

THE TIME has now come for a major political campaign in support of the miners.

The solidarity shown, and the financial support given, have been much appreciated, but it is not enough. The movement must do more, and do it urgently, if we are to sustain the miners and their families.

We need to win acceptance of the principle that you do not cross a picket line and to extend industrial action into related activities — especially power stations and road transport of coal and oil.

We need to step up the financial support and make it systematic, perhaps by regular levies, or the contribution of a day's pay, by those at work, on a regular basis.

We must also provide an effective political campaign to get the miners' case across to the general public, and link it with other attacks on working people including unemployment, health and education cuts, privatisation, reductions in the living standards of the old and the young, threats to women's interests, to civil liberties and to the democratic role of local authorities.

What are needed are political campaigns with public meetings, rallies, canvassing, collections and street-corner gatherings exactly as is regularly done in general election or by-

Continued on page 2

"We are not getting the support we want..."

"How much longer are you going to stand at one side and see us continually battered?"

Arthur Scargill

**INSIDE**



**16 January 1985. There is a steady flow of miners going back to work but two-thirds are still on strike. The miners are still hitting the government where it hurts. There are coal shortages at power plants.**

Socialist Organiser

No. 213. January 23, 1985. 25p (Claimants and strikers 10p).

Tories target rail unions

NUR/ASLEF picket at Coalville. Photo: John Harris, IFL.

WHO'S NEXT?

IN REVENGE for last week's one-day strike on the railways, British Rail will sue the NUR for half a million pounds, using the anti-union laws. Austin Rover is suing 12 unions for damages from the strike last year.

In last Sunday's 'Telegraph' (January 20), Ian Waller gave an insider's account of the thinking behind the British Rail decision and the tactics of the Tory government which pulls strings in the background.

"Since the start of the miners' strike (British Rail) has handled the rail unions gently, turning a blind eye to illegal blacking, shelving controversial productivity talks and even giving a better than expected pay increase last year. It suited Mrs Thatcher, who desperately wanted to avoid a battle on two fronts. It kept 95% of the trains running".

Now, however, British Rail has decided "to face up to the unions with a blunt warning of large-scale job losses over the whole freight business and no money for this spring's pay claim.

**The railway and car unions are being sued for damages under the Tory anti-union laws. Sheffield railworker Rob Dawber appeals to carworkers and railworkers to combine with the miners for a common response to the Tory attack on the working class.**

"The flashpoint that could precipitate a national strike (which the government would feel more sanguine about as the coal strike crumbles) would be when British Rail sues the unions for the losses caused by (last week's) stoppage".

Their attitude has change now because they think the miners' strike is crumbling.

If the miners are smashed, it will be the railworkers' turn. Then the car unions. And then...? 'One at a time', says Mrs Thatcher to the union leaders. 'Don't crowd me. I've got rope enough for every union in Britain'.

But the Tories and British Rail may have miscalculated. The miners are not beaten.

It is still not too late for railworkers and others to link up with the miners and turn the tide against the Tories. If the rail unions do not respond *now* to the threat from the courts, then the courts will grind them down. If they join the miners, then together they could bring the government to its knees and smash the anti-union laws, as well as defeating the Tory drive to break the NUM.

"THESE are hard times for our people", as Tony Benn said last week. It is easy for militants to get discouraged.

But last week's one-day rail strike showed that there is stomach for a fight in the rail unions. British Rail's attack through the courts leaves us no alternative but to fight — or surrender and bow down before the Tory drive to shackle the labour movement and destroy

Continued on page 2

All out for the miners Feb 11

INSIDE

Is a general strike possible? Debate: centre pages

The breakaway union in Notts, and other miners' reports: pages 3-5.

Our history: the Glasgow general strike, 1919. Page 10.

A workers' plan for jobs: how it could be done. Page 4.

**23 January 1985. British Rail are suing the railworkers' union for £500,000 in revenge for a one-day strike action. This is a shift in tactics from BR who had last year turned a blind eye to railworkers stopping fuel movements.**

# Socialist Organiser

No.214 January 30 1985 25p (Claimants and strikers 10p)

## All out Feb 11

By Stan Crawford
(Bevercotes NUM, Notts

WHAT is an "honourable settlement"? After all this time, it is the winning of the demands we came out on strike for last March. And we should not return to work without all the men being reinstated, without break in

their service. Arthur Scarg has said that there won't a sell-out. Mick McGahey h said the same. They've l magnificently so far, so don't think there's reason doubt what they're sayi now.

The strike is still soli although of course there h been fraying at the edge We'll still end up with majority out on strike.

We can still win by getti more support, some form second front – by oth workers going out on stri for their own grievances, b linking the action to the fa that the miners are still strike.

February 11 has got to worked for – hard. A lot people will put money in buckets, but what we need physical support. We need get round to trade unionis everywhere. We can get the out.

Then we need to find wa to give the best publ demonstration of suppo One idea is to have a rally the beginning – all rank ar file speakers, from differe workplaces on strike. Then to the nearest power static to picket.

The Notts scabs are st very much an issue. Exp sion is still on the car They have still got to expelled because, on Dece ber 20, the Notts Ar decided to delete Rule 3 and therefore refused abide by the national rule Whether we are still on stri or back at work it will ma no difference – because t Notts Area is trying to bre away.

## STAND FIRM!

DAILY EXPRESS THE VOICE OF BRITAIN

"I went to jail for Scargill, but now enough is enough"

A striking miner's reply to Reg Moss, the Kiveton Park miner who broke the strike and gave his story to the Daily Express.

THE miners' strike is in its 11th month.

Eleven months of great hardship for striking miners and their families. Eleven months during which striking miners have stood up to everything Thatcher and MacGregor have thrown at us. Eleven months of police violence, press lies organised scab-herding.

Eleven months during which the striking miners and their families have shown what they are made of and refused to let the Tories and their imported pit butcher MacGregor ride rough shod over us.

### By Albert Bowns
### Branch delegate Kiveton Park NUM

It's been a hard fight and it is harder now than ever. But the only alternative is surrender so we were right to fight and right to continue to fight.

I believe, Reg, that striking miners and our families have a right to be proud of what we have done over the eleven long and bitter months we have been fighting for our jobs, for our children and for our communities.

That fight is not over yet. We are still fighting to win. But you have changed sides.

This letter would not have been necessary if you had just deserted the strike, for whatever reason, but you have used a newspaper, whose vitriolic attacks on the striking miners and the working class movement is well known.

When I first read this article I wondered if you had realised the consequences. Did you think of your colleagues on strike? Did you think of your friends in London, especially in Stepney and Tower Hamlets? Friends who fed you and sheltered you on your four visits there.

I find it hard to believe that you didn't realise how it would hurt all these people.

#### Community

The article implies that you went on strike just for your union. I thought that you went on strike, as we all did, for your job, your pit and your community.

It is possible that this is what you also really believe but the Express puts its own distorted opinions first

I find it incredible that you should choose to air your views on this turnaround of principles in a Tory government mouthpiece. You are not ignorant of the support given by the Express to the Tory government and MacGregor's plan to decimate the coal industry.

The article itself, and the context in which it is written, is probably not the way in which you wanted your opinions put across. Even now, you might be saying that it is not what you really wanted to say.

Unfortunately, that is the price you pay for thinking that the national press and the Express in particular, will give a former union supporter an unbiased review.

The leading headline in the article justifies me in my opinion that you apparently don't know what you've been on strike for in the first place.

"I went to jail for Scargill but enough is enough". Having been arrested with you on the three occasions you speak about, and having spent two weeks in Lincoln Prison with you, and having been to London on fund-raising missions, speaking to various support groups with you, I have lost count of the number of times I have heard you state that our fight is for pits and communities and jobs.

If you did believe this at the time, although this article implies otherwise, then that is the reason you went to jail, not for Scargill!

#### Political strike

You say, maybe it is a political strike. Of course it

Continued on back page

## INSIDE



**30 January 1985. Eleven months of hardship are taking their toll and the Tory press, keen to exploit every division, publishes a story by a striker who has gone back to work after serving time in jail for his picket-line activities. Hundreds of miners have also been jailed and many will remain locked up long after the strike is over.**

Socialist Organiser

No. 215. February 6 1985 25p (Claimants and strikers 10p)

# STOP THIS LYNCH MOB!

"I call on our members to intensify picketing and on the wider movement to give greater industrial support of all kinds in the face of the government's blatant determination to destroy not only workers' jobs but trade unionism itself."

Arthur Scargill

OVER 100,000 miners and their families are still defiantly telling the government that they aren't beaten yet.

But the Tories have the scent of blood in their nostrils. NUM blood. Labour movement blood. Working class blood.

The Tories are going for the kill. They think it is only a matter of time before the miners are crushed and beaten back to work. They are confident that the official labour movement will not lift a finger to help the miners.

The Tory press is already setting up a howl of indecent triumph.

Mrs Thatcher publicly purrs with malicious joy such as she hasn't felt since she sent the Belgrano and 350 of its crew to the bottom of the South Atlantic.

The pin-striped Tory yobs in the House of Commons grunt, yak and snarl their satisfaction over the radio airwaves, baying in tune with the press like the lynch mob they are.

If it goes any further they'll be doing victory dances in Whitehall.

And well they might – if the miners go down to defeat. They see the prospect of the break up of the NUM.

Beyond that they see the end of effective trade unionism in Britain for a long time to come.

If they are right that they have won, then they have good reason to crow.

Listen, trade unionists, to this howling ruling class lynch mob which thinks it has the miners at its mercy! If they bring down the miners, it will be your turn next.

NUR, ASLEF, AUEW, TGWU – no trade union, no workplace, no group of workers who dare to say "no" to Tory plans will be safe from the bovver boot and knuckle duster treatment.

They conduct their semi-militarised police operations against the miners under the slogan of guaranteeing the right

Continued on page 2

# Rally to the NUM

Photos: John Harris

**6 February 1985. Mass pickets in Yorkshire at the start of February are the miners' answer to the Tory propaganda offensive. More strikers are giving up, but the big majority are still out.**

# 150 CLASS WAR PRISONERS

No. 216. February 13 1985 25p (Claimants and strikers 10p)

# Free the jailed miners!

*Police arrest picket at Silverwood Colliery, Yorks. Photo: John Harris. Terry French, Kent NUM, jailed for five years. Photo: Stefano Cagnoni, IFL*

AS MANY as 150 miners are in jail because they are good trade unionists. Because they stood up for their jobs, their families, their communities and for their union.

Because they refused to roll over and play dead when the Tories sent semi-militarised scab-herding police to occupy the coalfields.

Because they fought back – against the Coal Board, against the government and against the Police.

Because they told Mrs Thatcher and her pit butcher MacGregor: "No, you don't. You've caused enough damage [illegible] many working class communities – the miners aren't having it. We'll stop you."

These men are in jail because they are the best trade unionists in Britain. Because they are working class heroes.

**BY JOHN O'MAHONY**

They are men the labour movement should be proud to call its own. Proud to stand by. Proud to fight for. Proud to defend by every means at our disposal.

In fact, the labour movement is ignoring them!

Neil Kinnock denounced miners for resisting police thuggery in the coalfields, but he is shamefully silent about the jailed miners. Most of the labour movement is silent and seemingly indifferent.

Now at last the movement to defend the jailed miners is getting under way.

The Mineworkers Defence Committee conference last Saturday, 9th, voted to launch a campaign for the class war prisoners.

The proposal for a prisoners' campaign was moved on behalf of Socialist Organiser by Lol Duffy, one of the Cammell Lairds shipyard workers jailed last year when they occupied a gas rig to save jobs.

"We got off lightly", he said. "We were in jail for three weeks. But there are miners in jail for the same thing as us – fighting for their jobs – and they have sentences of several years.

"It's important for the whole labour movement that we get those miners out of jail. Otherwise the threat of jail will be a factor in every trade union struggle in future.

"I know it has been a factor in the shipyards. Yards which had been thought of as militant have not taken action because they expected no support from the official leadership and workers feared that any action would end up with them in jail."

### Tide

The tide in the country is turning against Thatcher and her brutal bovver-boot politics. The plight of the jailed 150 (and of the 650 miners who have been sacked) must be brought to the attention of the labour movement. The movement must rally in their defence to demand that the jailed be released and the sacked be reinstated.

We must build a broad and powerful class war prisoners defence campaign.

# A blow against the Tories – By Tony Benn

"THIS is a historic acquittal, comparable to the acquittal of John Lilburne in the seventeenth century, of Wilkes the radical in the eighteenth century, or the acquittal of various people charged with sheep stealing when that was a capital offence.

The jury asserted that it would not accept the use of the State power to crush people of conscience. Considering that it was a positively vetted jury that's a highly significant development.

The verdict also destroys once and for all, Section 2 of the Official Secrets Act and gives a fresh impetus to the campaign for a genuine Freedom of Information Act. That Section is now dead and everybody knows it is dead.

The judge's summing up revealed his concept of the role of the State and the Law in a way which is exceptionally clear. He said the interests of the State are the policy of the government.

Now when you reflect on it, that is an incredible statement. Once you elect a government, that government's own policy – whether approved by Parliament, reported to Parliament – defines the total interests of the State.

The government's response needs to be watched very carefully. They have various options.

One is to pass new legislation which is more restrictive, given their anger at the defeat of the prosecution. They might adopt Diplock Courts as in Northern Ireland where there would be no jury.

One must watch out for this being made the occasion for a more repressive legal system.

Clive Ponting's offence, and this is what it was all about, is that he told the public and Parliament that the government had been lying about the Belgrano and indeed about the Falklands War.

### Torpedoes

This information should force us all to go back and look at the whole Falklands operation. We now know that on almost every matter we were grossly misled.

So this in fact torpedoes the Falklands War.

Finally, in practical terms, any civil servant, in the Department of Energy, for example, who believes it to be in the national interest to inform Members of Parliament about the truth of the government handling of the miners' strike in a sense has had a carte blanche to do it. There is a risk but at the same time, that jury felt it was in the public interest to tell Parliament the truth of what is happening, so we have a green light to do so."

**LAST Monday, 11th, the hand-picked and politically vetted jury selected to try Clive Ponting under the Official Secrets Act defied the judge and found him not guilty.**

**He admitted that he had done what he was accused of – passing to an MP a secret government document about the sinking of the Argentine ship Belgrano during the Falklands War. Ponting pleaded that he was right to do it. The not guilty verdict is an endorsement of Ponting's action and judgement.**

**The jury rejected the judge's ruling that the interests of the state are identical with the interests of the government, and that it is automatically what the government of the day says it is. The jury endorsed Ponting's judgement that Parliament has the right to know and that the government had no right to misinform Parliament. This is a major blow to the government. Tony Benn comments:**

**13 February 1985. 150 miners are locked up, and 650 sacked. A campaign to defend these miners is now developing.**

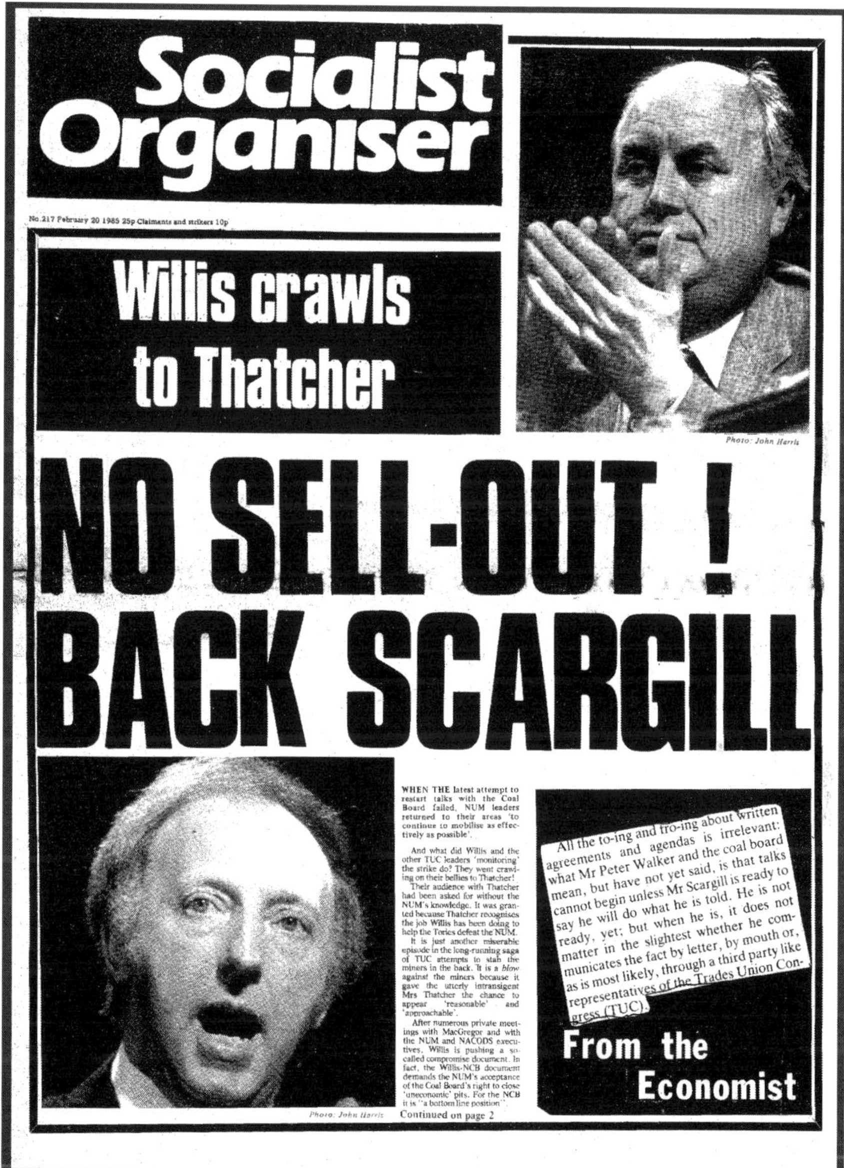

Socialist Organiser

No.217 February 20 1985 25p Claimants and strikers 10p

Willis crawls to Thatcher

Photo: John Harris

NO SELL-OUT! BACK SCARGILL

Photo: John Harris

WHEN THE latest attempt to restart talks with the Coal Board failed, NUM leaders returned to their areas 'to continue to mobilise as effectively as possible'.

And what did Willis and the other TUC leaders 'monitoring' the strike do? They went crawling on their bellies to Thatcher!

Their audience with Thatcher had been asked for without the NUM's knowledge. It was granted because Thatcher recognises the job Willis has been doing to help the Tories defeat the NUM.

It is just another miserable episode in the long-running saga of TUC attempts to stab the miners in the back. It is a *blow* against the miners because it gave the utterly intransigent Mrs Thatcher the chance to appear 'reasonable' and 'approachable'.

After numerous private meetings with MacGregor and with the NUM and NACODS executives, Willis is pushing a so-called compromise document. In fact, the Willis-NCB document demands the NUM's acceptance of the Coal Board's right to close 'uneconomic' pits. For the NCB it is "a bottom line position".

Continued on page 2

All the to-ing and fro-ing about written agreements and agendas is irrelevant: what Mr Peter Walker and the coal board mean, but have not yet said, is that talks cannot begin unless Mr Scargill is ready to say he will do what he is told. He is not ready, yet; but when he is, it does not matter in the slightest whether he communicates the fact by letter, by mouth or, as is most likely, through a third party like representatives of the Trades Union Congress (TUC).

From the Economist

**20 February 1985. Seven TUC leaders visit Downing Street. They emerge to tell the NUM to give up the fight. The NUM contemptuously rejects this. Norman Willis is pushing a so-called compromise document which says the NUM must accept the right of the Coal Board to close "uneconomic" pits.**

# Socialist Organiser

No. 218. February 27 1985. 25p (Claimants and strikers 10p)

# SCRAP MI5

**FORMER MI5 agent Cathy Massiter has blown the whistle on widespread illegal surveillance by the state of labour movement leaders and peace campaigners. Their activities are legal, constitutional and the very stuff that politics and public life in a democratic society is supposed to be about. Nevertheless they are spied upon, recorded and sometimes have their homes broken into — as did TASS leader Ken Gill.**

In a blatant act of political censorship, the IBA banned the TV programme in which Cathy Massiter told of her experiences as an MI5 officer.

MI5 keeps files on political activists, taps their phones and passes information about them to the government — thus contravening its own charter.

Bruce Kent and Joan Ruddock of CND, Arthur Scargill, and Harriet Harman MP when she worked for the National Council for Civil Liberties were all victims of MI5's illegal activities.

Cathy Massiter spent 14 years with MI5, but she was sent to a psychiatrist when she voiced criticisms of such operations. She explained to the Observer last week how MI5 expanded its surveillance in the 1970s to cover solicitors, barristers, journalists and pressure groups.

Initially, her job had been to monitor 'known Communists' to check on their work in peace groups. She objected when the likes of Joan Ruddock came to be included in the targets. Joan Ruddock was able to be categorised as a 'potential subversive' following an interview she did with a Soviet journalist who — unknown to Ms Ruddock — was a KGB agent.

In its monitoring of CND, it is quite clear, MI5 broke its own rules, stretching its own definitions to allow itself greater powers.

MI5's own rules permit it to keep a check on 'subversives' — defined as those who threaten the safety of the state, and seek to undermine parliamentary democracy. Clearly, their perception of who would fall into this definition would be very wide indeed. It certainly includes the ommunist Party.

These revelations point to two conclusions. The Official Secrets Act is being used here yet again to stifle the democratic flow of information — in this case without even being used: its mere existence has proved enough to make the IBA run.

And organisations like MI5 are there to defend 'the State' from us — from labour movement activists. They are undemocratic and anti-working class, and should be scrapped.



*The solidarity demonstration on Sunday 24th. Photo: Stefano Cagnoni*

# STRIKE ON MARCH 6th

On March 6 the miners' strike will be one year old. It has been a year that has shaken Britain and remodelled the political landscape.

Class conflict, class bitterness, and naked class hatred, at a level not seen here for a very long time, have been brought into the centre of British politics.

Stark class hatred is the only description that fits the savage, relentless, conscienceless baiting to which the miners and their leaders have been subjected from day one of the strike.

Nothing has been too low or too dirty for the ruling class in the bitter war they are waging to defeat the miners.

They starve men, women and children for a year, and then their press gloats and crows indecently when thousands of miners break under the pressure of hungry homes and prolonged isolation, and go back to work – to scab on their more resilient brothers and sisters.

These events are storing up memories and hatreds that the ruling class will live to regret.

Tens of thousands of new militants have learned to hate the capitalist system and those who run it.

The men now going back to work are not like the Notts and other hard-core scabs: they are broken men being driven back to work against their will – still convinced that the NUM is right, but unable to stand the tremendous pressures.

They go back to work with the bitterness of defeat in their hearts and the foul taste of betraying their comrades in their mouths

Yet despite it all, as Arthur Scargill says, 64 per cent of the miners are still on strike

On March 6 other workers will strike in protest at rate-capping and in a gesture of support and solidarity towards the heroic miners.

Join them! Make March 6 the day the labour movement began to tell the Tories that we will not let them break the NUM!

Victory to the miners!

## INSIDE

**Build a class war prisoners' campaign!** — centre pages

**Police violence from the coalfields comes to Whitehall: eye-witness accounts.** — page 3

**Yalta 1945: the counter-revolutionary alliance to carve up Europe** — page 8

**Strike diary from Paul Whetton, secretary of the Notts strikers (in a personal capacity)**

**27 February 1985. A local government workers strike is set for 6 March. Before then an NUM conference narrowly votes to return to work without an agreement.**

## ISSUES AND EXPERIENCES

# Women: the heart of the resistance

"At a time of unrest and strike action, the proletarian woman, downtrodden, timid, without rights, suddenly grows and learns to stand tall and straight. The self-centred, narrow-minded and politically backward 'female' becomes an equal, a fighter, a comrade. The transformation is unconscious and spontaneous, but it is important and significant because it reveals the way in which participation in the workers' movement brings the woman worker towards her liberation, not only as the seller of labour power, but also as a woman, a wife, a mother and a housekeeper."

Alexandra Kollontai wrote that in 1920, yet it could be about today. Alexandra was writing a history of working-class Russian women with whom she fought, as a socialist and sister, against the Tsarist tyranny. The development and organisation of those women then is comparable to the spirit of the women today, organising in Women Against Pit Closures groups.

The Russian women Kollontai writes of were struggling for basic rights of bread, peace and land. They fought alongside their male counterparts but fought also for their self-liberation as women.

Women Against Pit Closures was much more than a support group of women fighting for the jobs of their husbands, sons, brothers, lovers.

At first, women responded to the strike by providing essential services — organising food distribution, soup kitchens, etc.

Within weeks, women were not just staffing the soup kitchens but organising pickets, rallies, demonstrations, collections and public speaking.

"On early pickets, 2.30 am and 4.30 am, too early to go back to bed. Back in an hour or two or three. Stay up to see the kids up and breakfast. Food parcels to go out 11 am-3 pm. Back for the kids coming home. Tea time. Meeting, social security problems to sort out. Someone needs shoes for the picket line. Someone is depressed. Fundraising needs organising. Provisions need buying for the food parcels, and parcels need making up, 500 of them."

The list of tasks is endless and gruelling. Most women doing this have kids, some like Ann from Kiveton Park have jobs to do as well. Some like Mary from Wales have to stop a husband and son going back to work.

Clearly the strike could not have got as far as it did if it were not for the dynamic, forceful organisation of women in the pit villages. The level of solidarity they provided has been unrivalled by any other section of the organised labour movement.

Crusty socialists still maintain that the self-organisation of women is by nature divisive and, what is more, working-class women just don't do it. Really?

Women Against Pit Closures have turned such arguments on their head.

"It was as though women had been asleep for hundreds of years. We awoke to a new awareness, a realisation of what we as women could do. It is only comparable to the suffragettes. Do you know, I believe we are a part of history being made" (from South Yorkshire).

The aspirations raised by women involved in the strike can only take us forward.

Women have gained much by breaking their isolation, having childcare more available and collective eating. We must now organise around such demands as 24 hour free nurseries, a woman's right to choose, and collective facilities.

"After the strike we will keep ourselves together and do you know what we'll do first? We'll have a campaign against low pay because it hits women — and we'll start with the women in the canteen and bar staff — get them

## Miners at Greenham peace camp

Three striking Notts miners visited Greenham Common peace camp on 26 June. Afterwards they spoke to Angela Fraser.

**Why did you ask me to take you to Greenham?**

To see how the women were struggling. It was an experience. I was really frightened, but I enjoyed the visit.

**Why were you frightened?**

Because of what the media have said about them. They are not really like that... It's like the miners. Everybody's expecting the miners to start trouble and it's the same with the women there. They are made out to be right freaks.

**Do you see any link between the miners' strike and the Greenham women's struggle?**

They're fighting for what they believe in, aren't they... They're fighting for loads of things, aren't they? They're fighting for equal rights tor women. We're supposed to have that. Well, what can I say? It is supposed to be equal rights for women but it's always been the same — men always seem to be the most dominant. I think they're fighting to do something on their own. They need to keep men out of it because of that.

**When you go back home, will you encourage women to go and stay at Greenham?**

I don't really know — I'm not so sure.

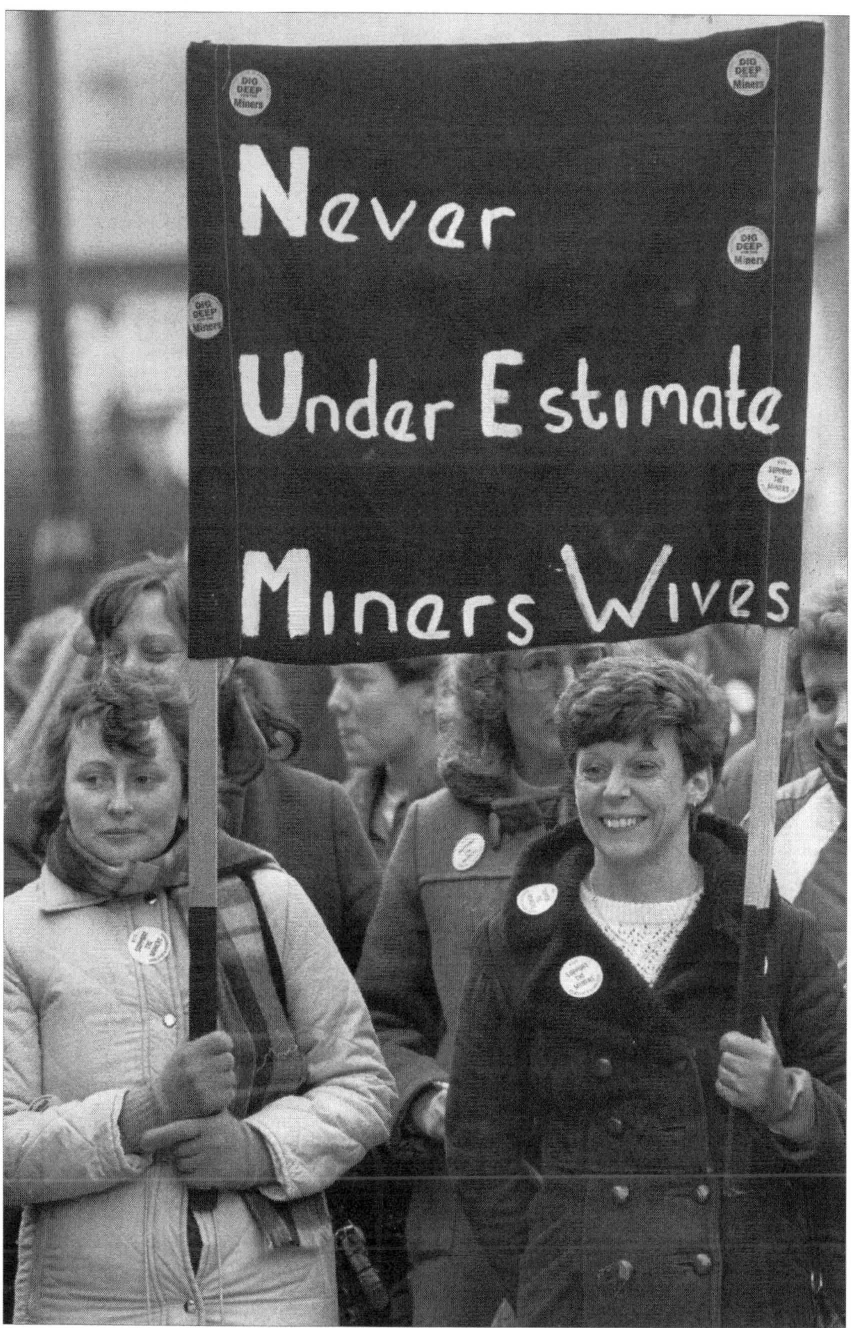


WAPC day of action protest in support of miners, Barnsley, Yorkshire. February 1985.
John Harris/reportdigital.co.uk

a pay rise, something the NUM should have done" (women from South Yorkshire).

In a traditionally male dominated set-up, many men are acknowledging the contribution of women and respecting their need for independence. A sense of equality has been reached far greater than at any other time of our working class history.

At the same time, women have witnessed in themselves changing consciousness and political awareness which makes them say: "We cannot go back to the status quo". Kids have eaten better in the collective soup kitchens, shopping has a whole new meaning — it's collective or nonexistent because it's distributed, shared and some days you don't have to do it at all.

Women get out more, go off in flying pickets, go to meetings or even get away to parties organised by support groups.

Women meet other women in struggle, from Greenham Common, from Barking and South London Hospitals, from Namibia, from Ireland.

Women do not want to return to the status quo. That means we have to take up women's demands and fight for them here and now. Women have fought alongside their men in the NUM because they realise that if the NUM is smashed then our hopes of equality and liberation will be that much harder to fight-for.

Working-class women, normally isolated and alienated in the home, have come out, got together and organised with determination to win.

Though circumstances are the most materially severe and repressive they have ever experienced, there has been a sense of freedom gained. It has cut across much of the mythology of women's "natural" role, leading them to question their former selves.

## Build a working-class women's movement!

In 1981 12 million workers were members of a trade union, of whom 30% were women.

When you look at the people in the leadership of the trade unions and of the TUC, how many women do you see?

And that's at a national level. At a local level of areas and branches, it is just as bad if not worse. In unions where the majority of members are women, the people in the decision-making positions tend to be men.

What are the reasons for this? Many men are convinced that it's because women aren't interested: we only work for pin money anyway — it's the men who earn the family wage.

Actually the reasons are more practical than that: meetings tend to be held at times women with families can't attend, creche facilities are not provided at meetings, and because the issues that affect women both at home, at work, their conditions, etc., are not taken seriously, or even seen as trade union issues.

Over the last few years, women have organised in the trade unions to change this situation, and the issues we have been taking up are those that enable women to attend — meeting times, creches, and positive discrimination.

Positive discrimination means encouraging women to take up positions and get involved in the union; it means that a certain number of positions in the union will be reserved for women only, to ensure that women are encouraged to be in the decision making and playing an active role in their union.

A lot of people both on the left and right argue against positive discrimination, saying that we should vote people into positions on the basis of their politics.

In fact, most of the time, men get re-elected year after year on personal likes and dislikes, making the movement quite stale and not moving forward with new people or bringing in new and younger people into union activity. So positive discrimination is actually a democratic thing in that it opens it out to new people.

Secondly, such is the oppression of women in society that prevents us getting involved that we have to make special attention and arrangements to allow women to get involved.

It is not just meeting times and creches but also sexist attitudes we face every day which make coming to meetings and getting involved very intimidating. At union conferences you're whistled at as you walk to the rostrum; or in local branches they sneer at women and make comments about our breasts.

## "If we'd been organised before..."

We were saying last week how if the women in the village had been organised a couple of years ago the way we are now they would never have got those schools shut. Never.

We had some problems with one of the blokes at the pit here, he really is a male chauvinist pig... He comes out with "Oh, the one with big tits".

I mean, it was really insulting, so we had him about it, and we said we didn't like it... we said things like "how would you like it we described you as the one with the little bulge in your trousers?" He just went bright red. He couldn't handle it at all, so we said, "Well, that's how we feel"...

Coal mining is swamped in tradition, and the tradition is that it is a men's job and it's no place for a women. But the attitudes have changed very much during the strike.

Sylvia Jackson, from Keresley (Coventry) Miners' Wives' Committee.

*Socialist Organiser* 14 June 1984.

That is one of the issues that women organising in the union must and do take up — sexual harassment. Not only at work by management (in the typing pool, etc.), but also by the union — for example, nudie calendars.

Women are organising in the Labour Party and forcing it to change its politics and structure in a very small way. But there is still a long way to go.

For example, every year there is a national women's conference in the Labour Party and quite often it is a section of the Labour Party which takes up more militant positions than the rest of the party. It was, for example, the only section which opposed the sending of the Task Force to the Falklands. They supported Tony Benn for deputy leader, they have a position of troops out of Ireland and they were one of the sections to back the moves to democratise the way the leader and deputy leader of the party are elected.

But women's conference does not have a right to put to Labour Party conference as a whole any policies that it adopts, so it's more like a lobby than an active section of the Party.

Also, the women's conference does not have the right to vote women onto the Labour Party National Executive Committee.

## The women's movement

Meanwhile, the women's movement, from the 1960s to the present, has tended to be a middle class movement. It does take up issues that should concern all working-class women, such as the right to abortion, control over our own bodies, the questions of sexuality and gay and lesbian liberation, the right to walk the streets without fear of attack, against the portrayal by the police and courts of victims of rape as if they asked for it, etc.

But to a large extent the movement has organised in a way which does not attract working-class women. Women's movement meetings tend to be consciousness-raising groups, and many elements in the women's movement refuse to have anything to do with the Labour Party or the unions, because they see them as male-dominated.

Consciousness-raising is all right. It is necessary for every woman to be able to meet other women and discuss their oppression and talk about how they are isolated in the home and how the law discriminates against them. But if you stop at just talking about it and don't put those ideas into action and force the labour movement to take them up, it becomes a futile exercise.

The miners' strike, opens up the possibility of breaking down this division between a male-dominated labour movement and a middle-class women's movement — of building a working-class based women's movement.

The miners' strike and particularly the women's involvement in it, forces the labour movement to see women as political, active, militant people who don't just sit at home and soak in the media, or just work for pin money or can be treated as mere sex objects. It really does challenge all those attitudes which the male labour movement has lived by for years.

We need to discuss how that challenge to men's attitudes can be sustained after the strike has been won. How do we make sure that these lessons learned during the strike, like the men who now tell other men to shut up when they come out with, "Get your tits out", and the men in the labour movement who can no longer say "women aren't interested in politics, they just organise get back to work movements" and things like that, aren't forgotten but become a way of changing the labour movement into one which includes women and seriously takes up women's issues?

And also how do we use the lessons to make the women's movement a movement for working class women rather than middle class consciousness-raising groups?

## Women in the labour movement

The growth of women's support groups since the start of the miners' strike has been a tremendous boost to the women's movement in Britain. The Tory government have not been able to buy them all off, or use them as propaganda against the NUM.

Their courageous stand has given confidence to working class women everywhere who, over the years, have been attacked by the policies of cuts, redundancies, extra police powers and media lies.

All the women involved in WAPC are determined that their groups will not just disappear when the miners' strike is over, because there are still so many battles to be taught.

The only way that this can be ensured is it all working class women in struggle join together and fight together — not just against the Tories' attacks which throw us out of work and treat us as second class citizens, but also to force the labour movement to take our battles seriously and to give us equal voice.

The militant action of working-class women can only strengthen the labour movement and democratise it.

*Socialist Organiser*, 9 January 1985

# Nottinghamshire: the eye of the storm

## 1. The importance of Nottinghamshire

Throughout the strike, Arthur Scargill argued that it could be won without getting the whole of the Notts coalfield out — it would just be more difficult and take longer.

His assessment is basically right. However, the job of attempting to get the coalfield out was a major consideration for the NUM for the first four months of the strike.

Indeed, many militants have argued that too much was put into it, especially after the second month and the firm consolidation of a semi-police state in Nottinghamshire, at the expense of sending pickets to steel works and power stations.

Whatever the tactical assessment, Notts was important. At stake was the unity of the NUM. All coal production would have been stopped if they had brought out the second largest coalfield in the country. In fact, the government and NCB kept the coalfield working.

How important was this? Coal was certainly produced throughout the strike's 12 months, but it was a blatant lie — if effective propaganda — to say that there was "normal working". The overtime ban started in October 1983 remained in force and was generally observed, cutting normal production figures by up to 20%.

The strike also cut production. The NCB itself reported a 52% decline during the May peak for the strike. For most of the time the impact was less than that, but even with the great majority of Notts scabbing it was still disproportionate because faceworkers remained the backbone of the strike.

Distribution was affected too. Despite the difficulty of organising a boycott in a coalfield where the majority were scabbing there were sufficient railworkers prepared to take solidarity action to disrupt the rail "merry-go-round" (pit-power station-pit) linking the pits to the long and crucial chain of Trent Valley power stations.

At the end of August, Rob Dawber, secretary of the Sheffield and Chesterfield NUR District Council, reported in *Socialist Organiser* that "all movements of coal by rail are now more or less stopped."

But production was continued — at the rate of 300,000 tonnes per week for most of the strike, claimed the NCB. And the coal produced was transported to the power stations in massive convoys of scab lorries. The overwhelming majority of power station workers accepted the coal, and were little troubled by the feeble campaign run by the TGWU and GMBU in support of the TUC guidelines.

Most of Notts coal goes to power stations — in 1983, 70% of the total production of the coalfield, and 100% of the production of six of the 25 pits. With the Central Electricity Generating Board withholding detailed information, it is impossible to assess how important Notts coal production was during the strike in helping the government to avoid power cuts, as compared to the massive shift to oil-burn and the increased nuclear output. But the government obviously thought the Notts output had more than propaganda value. As they showed by their frightened reaction to the threat of a national NACODS strike in October and the immediate possibility of Notts being shut down.

Throughout the strike, the Notts coalfield was commonly referred to as the "jewel in Thatcher's crown". Whatever the precise importance of the coal produced, the propaganda, organisational and political value of the Notts scabbing was immense. It was a very large fifth column for the NUM for the whole 12 months, helping the NCB and government, and also acting as a beacon and organising centre for scabs in other coalfields. It tied down and demoralised large numbers of pickets, it made more difficult the job of convincing other workers to take solidarity action. It helped bureaucrats throughout the trade union and labour movement evade their responsibility to organise support for the NUM. It gave leverage to the Tory-sponsored use of "democracy" as an ideological bludgeon against the miners.

## 2. Why did Nottinghamshire scab?

For most miners, the Notts coalfield is synonymous with conservatism and right wing domination. At the last election, Sherwood constituency, with the largest number of pits of any constituency in the country, elected a Tory MP. There have been militant struggles in the coalfield — notably at Harworth, to break the "Spencer" union in 1936-7 — but the reputation is made by different events.

The first coalfield to return to work in 1926; the home of "Spencerism"; the main supporters of the introduction of an incentive scheme in 1977; the base of George Spencer and Ray Chadburn.

Conditions in the coalfield — thick straight seams, and relatively good wages and conditions — helped. Notts is not the only area with a right wing tradition but, unlike neighbouring Yorkshire (also right wing until the late 1960s), it has had little history of militant rank and file organisation and strikes.

The Notts coalfield came out in 1972 and 1974, following national ballots, but the issue in both cases was wages, and the area had suffered particularly badly with the introduction of the National Power Loading Agreement (NPLA) in 1966. Following the introduction of the incentive scheme in 1977 which the Notts Area had championed, the divisions reduced by the NPLA reasserted themselves with a vengeance.

On the issue of pit closures — on which the Notts coalfield was relatively unscathed and had the promise of a secure future — the area was always going to be a hard nut to crack. In the March 1983 national ballot, only 19% of Notts miners voted for action in support of the South Wales strike.

The Notts Area did abide by the national overtime ban, from its beginning in October 1983 until the very last days of the strike in March 1985, but an overtime ban is very different from a strike.

Was the national ballot issue crucial?

Even late in the strike, after nearly a year of strike-breaking, leading Notts scabs would proclaim that, if only there had been a ballot with a yes vote, they would have been out too. Coming from people who had refused to abide by the national ballot decision against a bonus incentive scheme in 1977, and who in early 1985 refused an area ballot on their decision effectively to break away from the NUM, this was disgusting hypocrisy. Most scabs, however, were not as cynical as that. Rather the ballot was a convenient excuse for their unwillingness to come out.

The flimsiness of the argument was underlined in April 1984, when the Notts Area voted against the simple democratic proposal to reduce the majority needed in a national ballot from 55% to 50%. The only justification could be that they didn't want a majority for strike action, never mind the democratic principles.

But the issue still remains. If there had been a national ballot with a majority for strike action, would this have changed the situation in Notts? The answer must be a qualified yes.

Yes, a few rank and file scabs did regard the issue as one of principle, and saw the failure to have a ballot as a denial of their democratic rights. Yes, many more saw the ballot issue as a rationalisation for their unwillingness to come out. Stripped of it, they might not have felt strong enough to hold back. These people could have been won to the strike, at least in the short term.

Yes, the issue of the ballot certainly did give the leading scabs an ideal campaigning weapon to use with waverers against the strike — though even if there had been a national ballot many in Notts would have simply ignored it, and it would have been preceded and followed by a legal campaign to declare it invalid.

Few people doubt that a successful ballot vote would have made some difference, but that was never the basic question. The key issue was whether a ballot would (as the Notts Area hoped) demobilise and go against the strike action. The strike against pit closures was the central thing, the ballot issue a secondary tactical point; it could never be used to jeopardise the struggle.

# 3. The attempt to picket out Nottinghamshire

The alternative tactic in the fight to unify the NUM was to spread the area strikes through picketing. The main responsibility for picketing the Notts Coalfield was taken by the Yorkshire Area. Originally the Area leadership tried to stop pickets crossing the border into Notts, but they were rapidly forced to change their position after rank and file strikers from a number of South Yorkshire pits seized the initiative and started picketing from Monday 12 March.

Many have since wrongly blamed those men, and the officially organised picketing later on, for polarising the majority of Notts miners against the strike.

On Monday 12 March, and Tuesday 13th, the Yorkshire pickets adopted a domino strategy — first picket out one pit, then move onto the next. They were initially successful.

On Monday Harworth was closed by "the weight of the pickets and persuasive argument" as the scarcely sympathetic *Guardian* labour correspondent reported. On the Tuesday and Wednesday, they moved from Bevercotes to Ollerton and Thoresby.

On Thursday 15th David Jones was killed outside Ollerton pit entrance.

This event, and subsequent clashes, received a lot of publicity and were used to back up the picture of violent Yorkshire pickets. But what was the real picture?

Frank Slater, Maltby NUM delegate, who was involved in the picketing from the beginning, explained in *Socialist Organiser*:

"...when Ray Chadburn said that the Notts miners would ballot but he expected them not to cross picket lines when they were formed, the rank and file of the South Yorkshire miners not unreasonably took this as a go-ahead for flying pickets... the mood on most picket lines has remained generally cordial, with Notts miners joining pickets and miners' wives supporting..." (*SO* 171).

There was also clearly hostility. Frank Slater reckoned that the disgraceful role of most local and Area officials was decisive. More concerned with getting re-elected in June than with the fight against pit closures, branch officials either equivocated or openly encouraged strike-breaking.

And: "...Chadburn gave us practically no support. He's not issued any clear instructions to his members. As far as I'm concerned, with the death of Davy Jones, he's got blood on his hands." (Frank Slater, *SO* 171)

The other basic cause was the role of the police. Speaking later in the strike, at a *Socialist Organiser* meeting in the Rhodesia Miners' Welfare, Frank Slater described what happened.

Initially, the pickets were having considerable success. Standing on one picket line, they told the local Chief Constable: "We've come down here to peacefully persuade our fellow members not to go to work. Fair enough, he said, pick out six men and I'll stop everything that comes in so you can talk to them. He did exactly that. I think there were three men went into work that night.

"On the morning shift exactly the same thing happened again. Then a riot van rolls up, and another one...I've never seen a provocation like it. That was the start of it, because we were having success..." (*SO* 200)

Soon the whole of the Notts coalfield was flooded with police. On Thursday 15 March, they waded into pickets outside Thoresby.

Roadblocks were set up at every junction, in and out of the county. On Sunday 18 March, Kent pickets were turned back at the Dartford tunnel. Police on picket lines made no secret of their orders — to keep the Notts pits open "at any cost". They succeeded in stopping the great majority of flying pickets, and walling off most of the Notts miners.

In April, South Wales miners from Cwm were arrested and charged after trying to leaflet houses in Blidworth. The May and June police riots in the same village were principally aimed at driving out Yorkshire pickets who were staying with local strikers.

Could the arguments have been got across to the Notts miners? Certainly, much more could and should have been done before the strike in getting the propaganda across to the rank and file. The need for it was crystal-clear after the derisory yes votes from Notts in the national ballots. Indeed when the pickets did get through in the first two weeks, a number reported that the Notts miners were hearing the arguments for the first time. But by then, police organisation, brutality and national media propaganda ensured that it was probably for the last time.

## 4. The responsibility of the area leaders

After the 19 April special delegate conference had put the dispute in the hands of the national officials, there was a concerted attempt by the NUM nationally — right through May — to convince the majority of Notts miners. On 27 April Arthur Scargill spoke to a packed meeting in the Ollerton miners' welfare, and then led the strikers and their families onto the Ollerton picket line. A number of similar meetings were held. The campaign culminated in a national solidarity demonstration in Mansfield on 14 May attended by 20,000 from every coalfield in the country.

But few, if any scabs came to the meetings, and the Mansfield demonstration had no noticeable effect on the scabs. The campaign was a very important morale-booster for the strikers in the coalfield, but it didn't change many scabs' minds.

The number of Notts strikers did increase significantly at two points — at the end of the first week of the strike, and during most of May. On 10 March a number of Notts pits were completely closed down for the only time during the strike. In May the number of strikers approached 50% of the coalfield. In a number of North Notts pits over 50% were out. The NUM claimed a high point of 12,000 on strike; local strike leaders estimated up to 16,000. Around twice the 7,285 Notts miners who had voted for action in the area ballot on 16 March were on strike.

The actions of the Area leadership were decisive for both periods of advance. In March they called an official strike while the area ballot took place, and as a bargaining ploy to get the Yorkshire pickets withdrawn. At the end of April, strike action was declared official in the Area and remained so throughout most of May.

Following the national delegate conference on 19 April the Notts Area Council met on the 20th and officially called for strike action. On 26 April Area Secretary Henry Richardson issued a circular insisting that the official picket lines should be respected and assisted by local branch officials. Only after this policy was declared invalid by the High Court on Friday 25 May, following legal action by leading scabs in the area, did the number of strikers begin to decline. By the end of July, the number still on strike had dropped by at least 50 per cent, to five or six thousand.

The advances in mid-March and in May indicate what would have been possible given a clear lead by the Area officials. So do countless other examples in different NUM Areas. In the neighbouring North Derbyshire coalfield, an area ballot showed a tiny majority for not taking action. But the Area leadership still called the coalfield out and with the help of picketing (almost all peaceful), shut all the pits with a strike that remained virtually 100% for eight months.

Despite votes against action, the importance of a decisive lead from the Area (together with picketing) was also underlined in South Wales and North Staffs. Such a lead never came in the Notts coalfield, and that is why there were never more than a minority of miners in the Area prepared to join the other 80% of NUM members on strike.

On Sunday 11 March, the Notts Area Council met and voted for no strike action without a ballot. During the following week and in response to the flying pickets, a number of miners came out but the Area and local officials — including Area Secretary Henry Richardson, who had been elected on a left ticket — while sometimes mumbling about not crossing picket lines — attacked the Yorkshire pickets and said the coalfield should be working until there was a ballot.

When the ballot was held mainly on 16 March the vote was 3:1 (20,188-7,285) against the strike, with no single pit recording a majority. The 27% who voted in favour did represent an improvement on the 19% who had voted to strike in the previous national ballot, but in the atmosphere, and with the issues posed sharply, it was not a very significant increase.

On Sunday 18 March the Area Council met again and declared that Notts wouldn't be coming out unless and until there was a national ballot vote in favour. For Henry Richardson, the area ballot had given them "their marching orders". Only two delegates spoke out against crossing picket lines.

For the crucial next three and a half weeks the main demand of the Area officials was for a national ballot. Ray Chadburn was centrally involved in the right wing's attempt to get one. It wasn't until after the 12 April National Executive Committee meeting — the heavily lobbied meeting that ruled the call for a national ballot out of order — that Chadburn and Richardson called on Notts miners not to cross picket lines. Right-winger Chadburn declared: "Get off your knees and support the strike".

Paul Whetton, at the time Bevercotes branch secretary, said that these statements gave "a hell of a lift to a lot of men".

12 April was the first time that the two main officials clearly and publicly supported the strike. Just over a week before, after the transport unions had voted to boycott coal movements, the Area executive (on an 8-5 vote) called on Notts miners to respect picket lines. But this was overturned two days later by the full Area Council.

# 5. The rank and file strike committee

The Notts strikers were thus the most exposed targets of the whole state offensive against the NUM. Unlike in 1926 they were always a minority — for a brief period in May nearly 50%, but for most of the time 20% or less.

In some of the pits only a small handful were on strike throughout — 16 out of 600 at Pye Hill. In no pit was the hard core much more than 100.

As in 1926 they were victims of relentless police harassment and violence, open occupation of their villages and blatant victimisation by the courts.

Pit villages in other coalfields suffered similarly at a later stage, but without the strikers having the double burden of being a perpetual minority in a sea of scabs and the violence that often entailed. The Notts strikers also had to contend with at best apathetic local Labour councils and local government organisations in which the scabs were a significant influence.

From the 25 pits in the area, the only miners' welfare the strikers had regular use of was at Ollerton. In Welbeck, the Women's Action Group had to occupy the village hall in September to ensure that they had a soup kitchen for the second half of the strike.

Despite the odds, though, as Alasdair Jamison wrote in *Socialist Organiser* following a solidarity visit to Ollerton in August (and every visitor agreed), "The fighting spirit among the striking miners in Notts is irrepressible." (*SO* 192).

Whenever the Notts strikers' banners appeared during the course of the strike, there was enthusiastic applause. Tribute was paid to them from countless platforms. They were, as Peter Heathfield said in February 1985, "the foundation of the NUM."

Defiant and militant, they were still an embattled minority.

Largely because of the special situation faced by Notts strikers they threw up a unique rank and file organisation. But in other coalfields where strikers became minorities, for example, in North Staffs, similar organisations were not set up.

The Notts Miners' Rank and File Strike Committee was formed in April. Pete Radcliff explained:

"In the early stages of the strike the lack of an organised left in the NUM outside the official bodies of the union presented Notts strikers with many problems.

"The right wing of the Notts Area NUM based themselves on the parochialism resulting from the productivity scheme. They had control of most branches in the Notts Area and held sway over the Area executive and Area Council.

"Those refusing to cross picket lines at the beginning of the dispute often found themselves supported neither by their branch, nor the Area executive nor the Area Council. Some also had no contact with strikers in neighbouring pits.

"There was real confusion. 400 of the 1100 miners from Cotgrave pit, for example, who were on strike from 30 March to 6 April, eventually went back to work in order to campaign for a strike vote in the national ballot they thought inevitable.

"With Yorkshire and other pickets unable to reach every pit because of the police, many miners were forced back to work.

"When a North Notts (later all Notts) Rank and File Strike Committee was formed it was a turning point. Experienced branch officials on strike in the more militant North Notts pits organised a meeting on 10 April at Ollerton Miners' Welfare.

"About 100 miners from four pits attended. They decided to join forces and organise their own flying pickets.

"One striker declared at the meeting, 'We need our own area leadership for those supporting this strike. The scabs have got theirs in Chadburn.'

"Before that the only coordination of the left had been the Notts Miners' Forum, a small though influential grouping primarily designed to mobilise the left vote in union elections. It had produced a leaflet early on in the strike, but it was clearly inadequate.

"The second meeting of the Strike Committee, on 17 April, attracted 500 striking miners, including representatives from 17 of the 25 Notts pits. For the first time strikers from pits such as Hucknall and Cotgrave saw the possibility of a planned campaign to stop the Notts coalfield.

"The Strike Committee was also an important pressure on area leaders Ray Chadburn and Henry Richardson, counteracting the right-wing majority in the NUM branches. Chadburn and Richardson came out in favour of the strike.

"The Strike Committee has also spurred on miners in the weaker pits and encouraged them to form strike committees and strengthen their picketing." (*SO* 174 and 177)

Paul Whetton, secretary of the new committee, said in *SO* 175, "The prime objective of the committee we have set up is to organise the picketing in Notts — to get the Notts coalfield to identify itself with the National Union of Mineworkers, and to bring the coalfield to a standstill.

"The second objective is to raise finance to achieve that, with petrol for the pickets and hardship money for the single lads who have been out on strike for five weeks and haven't received a penny from anywhere."

Some strikers still refer to the 500-strong meeting on 17 April as the beginning of the strike for them — it gave them confidence, showed what was possible. The picketing that the committee organised was crucial in backing up the official strike call at the end of April, and getting a significant section of the coalfield out. After the strike, Paul Whetton said:

"If it hadn't been for the formation of the Rank and File Strike Committee... the strike in Notts would have crumbled very quickly; and we would have had the whole of the Notts coalfield churning out its full quota of coal. In fact, the Rank and File Strike Committee made a very valuable contribution in keeping the police away from other areas; keeping production down and raising the political debate, the political arguments."

The single Notts strike committee covering the whole coalfield was soon split up into North and South Notts Committees, linked together by a small coordinating committee. It remained in existence right until the end of the strike.

Given the balance of forces, the history and what had happened in the first weeks of the strike in the Area, the Committee was never going to bring all of Notts to a halt — and therefore cannot be blamed for not doing that. Its main — invaluable — job was to hold the strike together in extremely difficult circumstances.

## 6. The scabs organise

Meanwhile, the main strike-breakers began to organise openly.

On 1 May about 7000 scabs assembled in a mass demonstration outside the Area headquarters at Berry Hill, Mansfield.

Although a number were bussed in from other coalfields. and they had the full cooperation of both the police and the NCB (buses were laid on, paid leave granted), it was still an impressive demonstration. They outnumbered the strikers who managed to get through the police roadblocks and harassment to demonstrate their support for the Area Council's pro-strike decision.

Later in the month, the "Notts Working Miners' Committee" was officially launched, although even earlier a letter appealing for funds had been sent to local Labour Parties (and to Tories, Liberals, businessmen). At the same time leading members of the committee won the legal action against the Area's official support for the strike.

The Working Miners' Committee's links with the NCB and government were clear right from the beginning, with open cooperation from the police and direct use of Coal Board facilities. The chair of the committee, Bevercotes COSA member Mick Smith, was quoted at the time as saying "...the police want us to carry on". Later, starting with Paul Foot's exposé in the *Daily Mirror*, the full extent of the links came out. MacGregor had put them in touch with lawyers; and one of his (and Thatcher's) advisers had sat in on and helped to organise the early meetings.

This Tory/NCB assistance helped the scab committee, though they also had a real base amongst the rank and file scabs.

The Committee presented an anti-strike slate for the June branch elections. With the police harassing strikers who wanted to vote, the scab committee swept the board. They gained control of all the branch committees. Before he had even taken up his position, the secretary-elect at Bolsover wrote to all the strikers: "In your best interests I ask you to start work as soon as possible." The scabs also gained overwhelming control of the Area Council.

After this capture of the official machinery, the need for the scab committee receded, and it became only a platform for some of the individuals involved. By December, the main scab organisers felt quite able to repudiate the Committee — it had become an embarrassment, particularly after publicity about its links with the Tories and the NCB.

Scab control of the official machinery also brought closer the formation of a breakaway union in the Area. Given their open strike-breaking drive, the possibility of them co-existing inside one union with the NUM majority became less likely (and less desirable for the scabs) the longer the strike went on.

Unlike in 1926, some of them probably had a breakaway perspective from the beginning. They couldn't move more quickly than they did because their base among the scabs was for strike-breaking, not for leaving the NUM and setting up a company union. Indeed, most of those who went back to work, and some who never came out, were hostile to any breakaway.

They had to be lined up and manoeuvred slowly. In the meantime, and using bodies like the "National Working Miners' Committee", the leading scabs tried to help organise strike-breaking in other Areas.

## 7. The move towards a breakaway

Inside Notts the scab leaders had to wait for the normal rule-change meetings at the end of the year to widen the breach. With a series of detailed constitutional amendments, drawn up by friendly lawyers, they cut loose from the NUM at an Area Council meeting on 20 December. Later they first suspended and finally sacked Area Secretary Henry Richardson (and the staff that had supported him at Area HQ) in retaliation for the clear stand in favour of the strike he had taken from mid-April onwards. In February they organised for and won a vote to unilaterally break the national overtime ban. From 20 December, they effectively had a breakaway union, and all their actions since then underline their determination to bring back a company union into the coalfield, similar to the one organised by George Spencer after the 1926 strike.

That they want to dress up their actions by denying the intention, by putting it in terms of defending themselves, by keeping the name NUM but gutting the substance, by — at worst — provoking their expulsion, doesn't change what they're doing — it just shows the problems they have in taking a lot of rank and file scabs with them.

The growth of this openly "Spencerite" movement during the strike presented the national union leadership with major problems. It threatened the future unity and strength of the NUM. Under extremely difficult conditions they endeavoured to prevent a breakaway. Perhaps what they did — some threats against the scabs and some organisation, but mainly no action while the strike was on, and, at the end, attempted conciliation — was imposed on them by force of difficult circumstances. But whatever the reason, these moves actually helped the scabs more than anybody else.

In July and August the national union leadership introduced the long-prepared and scheduled new disciplinary rule 51, and then immediately insisted that it wasn't intended to be used against scabs.

Because it was never used, the rule was never a positive weapon against the scab-herders. But the existence of the rule and the way it was brought in, gave the scab leaders another "democratic" issue to campaign around. So it wasn't used? Most scabs believed the accusation that the national leadership had been forced to back off, but would come back with the rule as soon as they could.

The proposals to change the composition of the NEC, making for a fairer and more accurate representation of the membership, equally backfired. Again, these proposals had been promised and prepared for before the strike. But again, they were proceeded with during the strike in a way that was bound to be interpreted as an attempted blow against the scabs. And an ineffectual blow — the proposal was dropped in January 1985, before it came to a NEC meeting, in a last ditch attempt to conciliate the South Derbyshire Area and prevent them joining the Notts breakaway.

Dropping the proposal did not undo the effects of the scabs' campaign against it — it probably confused and demoralised some strikers, and certainly it encouraged the scab leaders, who interpreted it as a sign of weakness.

The national NUM's whole policy was based on the correct idea of trying to avoid driving the rank and file scabs into the arms of the scab leaders: that is why they proceeded cautiously. But the basic polarisations in the strike had lined up most of the scabs behind the scab leaders. and the longer these leaders were left untouched the greater their chance of consolidating their links.

In the end, the national leadership was forced to take some action because of the blatant breakaway moves at the Notts Area Council on 20 December. But again it was indecisive.

On 10 January 1985, the NEC began proceedings to expel the Notts Area. At the same time, with the Notts strikers, it began a "Keep Notts National" campaign, aimed at re-recruiting rank and file scabs to the NUM. By putting the issues sharply, and positively organising amongst the rank and file, the campaign rapidly gained support among the scabs. But it just as rapidly ground to a halt when the expulsion threat was not proceeded with.

Silence throughout February, followed by a meeting between the national officials and the Notts scab leaders, indicated that the expulsion had been dropped in favour of attempted conciliation. Scab leader Lynk and his friends simply interpreted this as a further sign of weakness. They lifted the overtime ban immediately and sacked Henry Richardson just after the strike for the "crime" of supporting national NUM policy. The *Financial Times* reported that the scabs were pressurising both the NCB and the government to maintain their intransigence, and not to settle too soon — they wanted time to consolidate their organisation.

With the end of the strike there remains a de facto breakaway union in the Notts Area, which is part of the NUM in name only.

# 8. The strikers beleaguered

After the scabs' successful court action at the end of May, and the declaration that the strike action was no longer official in the Area, the numbers on strike declined during June and July. It wasn't a wholesale and rapid collapse, but a steady decline. By August the NUM accepted that 80% of the coalfield were scabbing. Bevercotes striker Stan Crawford accepted that "a low point has been reached in Nottinghamshire" (*SO* 193) and Paul Whetton reported that "Notts has reached a levelling-off point". (*SO* 194).

Between late May and August, more than 6,000 Notts miners started scabbing (many for the second time). In the next seven months — the most difficult in the strike — a further 4000 at most went back. When the strike was called off, 1,500-2,000 Notts strikers were still out.

By August the storm centre of the strike had shifted decisively to other areas, above all South Yorkshire. It was clear that the strike was going to have to be fought with the majority of Notts scabbing. The struggle in Notts became a clogged, defensive one.

Notts strikers continued to make their presence felt nationally, lobbying the TUC Congress and NEC meetings; speaking throughout the country; sending pickets to help their comrades in South Yorkshire, but their basic activities were fund-raising and maintaining the pickets.

With few if any of the NUM Area and branch resources available to them for most of the strike, getting substantially less picketing pay than most other areas, and with little help from local councils and other organisations, fund-raising was critical.

Picketing was maintained throughout, mostly at strikers' own pits. There were also, regularly, at least until December, surprise mass pickets — "big hits" — which helped to tie up the police and maintain the strikers' morale. There were debates among the strikers on picketing strategy. Wasn't it demoralising and a waste of resources to keep standing outside pits with little if any hope of turning back scab miners or transport? But then wasn't it necessary to keep a presence there and prevent other strikers returning? As early as May in *Socialist Organiser*, Bevercotes striker Stan Crawford argued forcefully to "go flying" outside the county. "We're just banging our heads against a brick wall here. The police presence here is so much, we can't do anything. We can't peacefully picket the pits now. So we might as well go on flying pickets." (*SO* 180).

The Notts strike committee did manage to send pickets on an occasional basis to the long chain of key power stations in the Trent Valley. Despite these power stations' central importance, direct national assistance was not given until the end of November to help the strike committees cover them on a regular basis. By early January, Paul Whetton reported, "We're attempting to ensure that power stations are now covered by pickets virtually 24 hours a day, seven days a week." (*SO* 211).

The strikers also debated what to do about the scabs. In early August, Paul Whetton wrote: "I know that the vast majority of the rank and file on strike in Notts are saying they want to see something definite done about the scabs. At least the leadership has got to be disciplined. And not after Christmas, but now." (*SO* 191). By Christmas, when the scabs had taken their decisive moves to break away, the strikers were unanimously for the expulsion of the Area. The only issue was how, and under what conditions the rank and file scabs should be readmitted into the NUM. The overwhelming majority accepted that they had to be won back, to stop Lynk's break-away company union and to rebuild the strength of the NUM in the Notts Coalfield.

## 9. Women in Nottinghamshire

The women also organised. In one of the scenes in Ken Loach's TV film, "Which side are you on?", a woman in Durham reads out a poem written by Pat Davison from the Whittal Miners' Support Group. It was dedicated

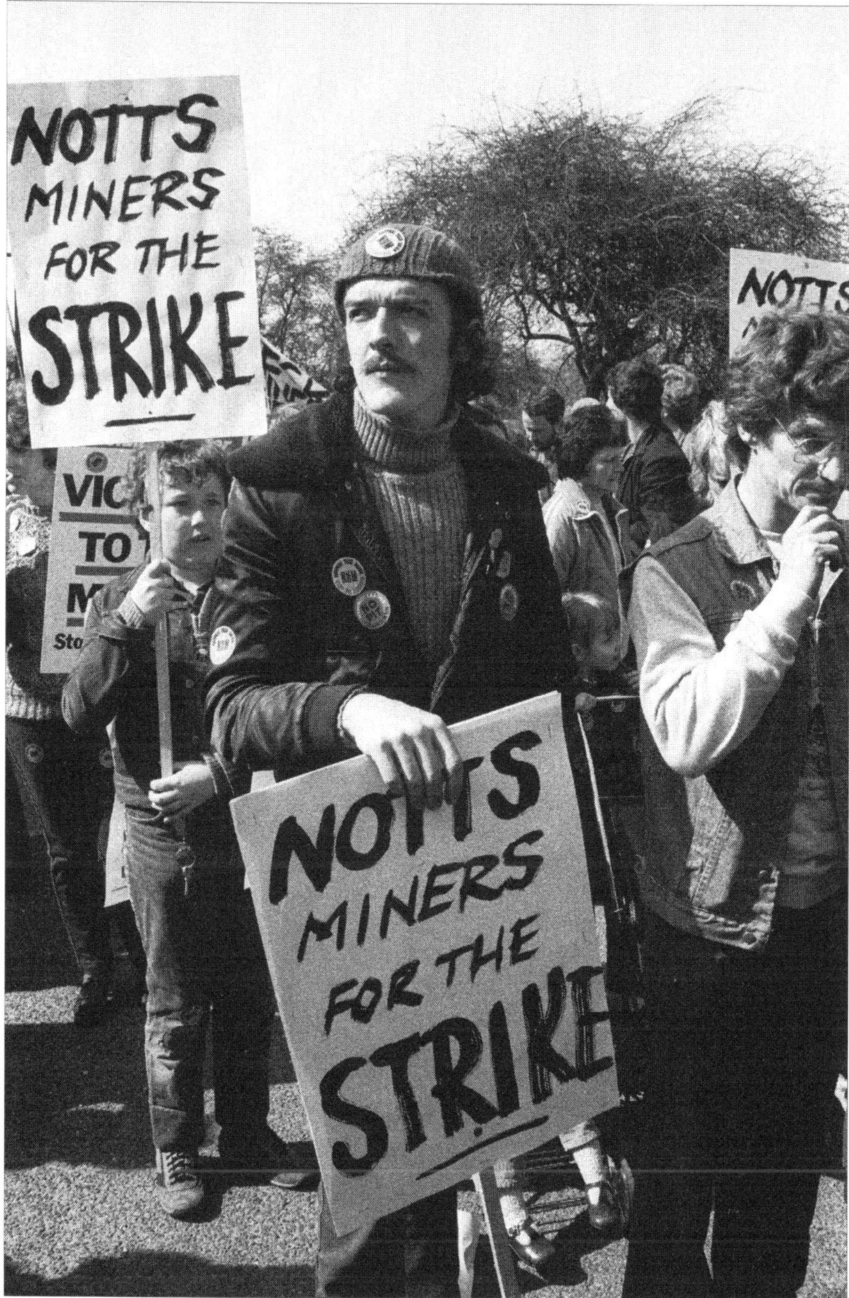


Striking Nottinghamshire miner at a demonstration in Nottingham to welcome Kent miners who had marched from Kent to try and persuade Nottinghamshire NUM members to stop working, April 1984.

John Harris/reportdigital.co.uk

to the Notts strikers' wives who "have had a hell of a time".

Now here's a tale for all to hear,
As wives of the striking miner,
Search the country far and wide,
But you will never meet none finer.

Not for them the mopish life,
Staying home and crying,
Or sitting back while others fight,
Their part in the battle denying.

As living gets tougher we tighten our belts,
And despair the work to be done,
We remember your courage, our sisters in Notts,
And you give us the will to go on.

No mercy was shown you, no peace ever given,
Your lives must be one living hell,
But always remember, though distance may part us,
Our thoughts are with you, hearts as well.

When the years have rolled by and we'll sit and remember,
The struggle our jobs to protect,
We'll tell them with pride how the Nottingham wives
Wholeheartedly earned our respect.

Husbands and wives hold up your heads,
Walk tall, look all straight in the eye,
For the tale of your courage through these bitter times,
Will live on and shall never die.

The women lived with the day-to-day effects of police brutality and the occupation of the villages; of being a minority in a "sea of scabs", and of having few if any official union resources or other facilities. In Welbeck women organised and undertook an occupation of the village hall in September so that they could continue to have a soup kitchen.

The women organised groups in every pit village from very early in the strike; these were soon linked through an all-Notts Women's Support Group, which later produced an information bulletin "Here We Go!"

They also got onto the picket line, with women from other areas (particularly Yorkshire), as part of the national campaign to stop the coalfield. *SO* 177 carried a report by Ann Crowder of the first such picket outside Thoresby colliery on Monday 30 April.

"It was the first attempt, and a very successful one, at getting Notts miners' wives, women trade unionists and women activists out picketing together, showing the great solidarity that is growing...

"They felt it necessary to organise a woman's picket to fight against the image that women are strike-breakers, to fight against the image that they are just fundraisers, and to fight against being kept in the background, quietly working away.

"We also have to fight against the sexism of some of our brothers. The slogan "Maggie Thatcher's got one, lan Mac Gregor is one" has been widely used during this dispute. But we challenged the miners and at the picket the men present dropped the use of it.

"...We were physically jabbed back by the police who seemed shocked that we were fighting back. The solidarity seemed to shake some of the men and take them by surprise — it certainly shook the police!"

*Women's Fightback* carried a report of Yorkshire women from Thurnscoe going to Ollerton on 24 April to help the women set up a soup kitchen, and also to put the case for the strike across to the women in the village. When they had been there before they had got a good response: "some of the women wanted to hear our side of the story". On the second visit the police stopped their coach. "After a couple of hours...we decided that if the police were going to treat us like flying pickets, we might as well be flying pickets". They then walked three miles to picket Harworth, turning five lorries back.

The women suffered police obscenities and brutality. One woman from Ollerton, Brenda Greenwood, was thrown in prison for seven days last November. But the women went through a long and liberating experience of self-organisation and political activity. They are committed to continuing their organisation and their growing political involvement after the strike.

# 10. The Labour Party

Because of the close links between the NUM and Labour, it was inevitable that the battle in the coalfield would spill over, to an extent at least, into the local Labour Parties.

Traditionally they were solidly right wing.

The core of the "Notts Working Miners' Committee" were right wing Labour branch officials. Many other leading scabs are active in the Party. In Sherwood CLP in September, four of the five NUM members on the EC were scabs. Don Concannon, the NUM-sponsored MP for Mansfield, was reported to have complained at the beginning of the dispute about local rail workers taking solidarity action. At the end of the dispute, he addressed the scab-dominated Notts Area Council and assured them that they wouldn't be expelled from the Labour Party. There were persistent reports of striking miners being vetted when they applied to join the Party. In the first weeks of the strike, the County Council police committee, with a Labour chair, passed a unanimous vote of confidence in police chief McLoughlin's handling of the dispute!

But the right's control has been challenged. Newark CLP, in the north of the county, solidly supported the strikers from day one; it also submitted and got carried the strongest resolution against the police at the 1984 Labour Party conference. Paul Whetton spoke as the Newark CLP delegate.

Most of the strike leaders in Notts are active in the Party. The County Labour Party strongly attacked the police's actions and passed a resolution demanding not a penny for the extra policing, the withdrawal of outside police forces and a public enquiry into McLoughlin's behaviour.

Many strikers and strikers' wives joined the Party — as an arena for political activity; to help in the battle to defeat the right wing and the scabs; and to turn local Party organisations into instruments for the working class. In September Sherwood CLP processed more than 50 new membership applications, mainly from strikers. 45 came from the Ollerton branch. In the village of Blidworth alone there were 27 new applications.

Despite the right wing Labour Party links of many scabs, some of the scabs clearly want to use the sharpening conflict to cut union links with the Party. The "Notts Working Miners' Committee" held a fringe meeting at the SDP conference and some scabs have been organising a campaign to withdraw from the political levy. Reports of the number who have withdrawn vary from 2,000 to 5,000, so clearly the main body of scabs have not withdrawn.

The County Labour Party blocked three scabs going forward to the panel for the county council elections. The three then appealed to the Regional Executive. Following an initiative by *Socialist Organiser* supporters, strikers responded with a statement about why they thought the appeal should be rejected.

The signatories to this statement included strike committee members Paul Whetton and Jimmy Hood, and the statement was also supported by Betty Heathfield.

"...The Labour Party, through the financial and political support of its membership for the miners, has gained considerable credibility in the eyes of the NUM membership. Hundreds of miners locally and many thousands nationally are joining the Labour Party as a result. This work would be seriously undermined if the Labour Party were now to allow scabs to go forward to secure positions of responsibility in its name..."

The Regional Executive supported the scabs. But the issue is coming up again at the 1985 East Midlands Labour Party Conference, with a resolution modelled on the strikers' statement (again originating from a *Socialist Organiser* supporter).

# 11. The fight goes on

The battle in the local Labour Parties is just one aspect of the continuation of the fight for the Notts striking miners, their wives and supporters. It is by no means the only one.

On Tuesday 5 March, they went back to work en bloc after the delegate conference decision to call the strike off. Management reaction varied between pits, but all the strikers have to organise as best they can against harassment and possible victimisations — with a union structure dominated by scab-herders and company-union men.

They have the immediate campaign to reinstate the 26 Notts strikers sacked by the Coal Board. They have to continue the "Keep Notts National" campaign, and fight to stop the development of the breakaway union. And they are also considering how to involve those politicised during the strike and organise a left within Notts NUM that is not just a machine to get left wingers elected to positions but is based on rank and file struggles. Such an organisation is a precondition for a campaign to transform the area union, and prevent a recurrence of what happened in the 1984-5 strike.

The core of it will come from the strikers who carried on the fight for a whole year against tremendous odds. They have tremendous assets — militancy and fighting spirit, a wealth of organisational and political experiences.

Something happened right at the end of the strike that illustrates this better than anything else. On the Friday before the last delegate conference, four representative of the Rank and File Strike Committee went to France with £1,000. The money had been raised from a levy on the picketing pay — 50p from £2, over two days. For some strikers this picket pay was their only income.

The £1000 was for the relatives of the 22 French miners slaughtered in an underground explosion at the Simon mine near Forbach. The delegation of four Notts strikers went to the funeral as a mark of respect and of international working class solidarity.

# The critics of the NUM leadership

Even competent and dedicated leaders can make mistakes. Did the NUM leaders? Many questions have been raised against their tactics. Some are scurrilous, some deserve serious consideration.

The chief charge against the NUM leaders during the strike from the Neil Kinnock wing of the labour movement is essentially that they were too militant.

Their demands were too extreme. To oppose all economic pit closures was to seem to fly in the face of iron laws: some more moderate formula should have been found. They didn't address themselves sufficiently to broad public opinion, and instead narrowed their appeal to the dwindling ranks of traditional industrial trade unionism.

Moreover — so the argument goes — the miners were too violent, and their leaders were at fault in not condemning the miners' violence. Besides, their picketing was too heavy-handed: it antagonised the Notts miners.

The whole argument is scurrilous. No doubt in the coming months the universities will resound with the din of typewriters, as academics fill expensive volumes and glossy magazines with attempts to render this drivel more profound and deck it out with quotations from Antonio Gramsci: scurrilous it is nonetheless.

The miners' defiance of the "iron laws" of Profit First actually broadened their appeal. By arguing the issue head-on, they rallied Professors of Accountancy, editors of scientific journals, pop stars and bishops to come out against the Coal Board — and, more importantly, they helped to generate a mass working-class support movement.

Compare the oh-so-moderate, ever-so-humble approach of the steel unions, who have constantly argued in terms of the "viability" of this or that plant. They get campaign meetings with Tory MPs and Chambers of Commerce, but these meetings, much though they warm the hearts of Popular Front enthusiasts, build nothing at all. The result is a degrading business of different plants vying to be the one to be spared, narrow-minded competition to promote "Welsh steel" or "Scottish steel", and defeat after defeat.

The class politics put across by the NUM leaders built a broader popular movement (and not only among "traditional" sectors of the working class) than "moderation" ever could. Indeed, if a valid criticism can be made of the NUM leaders, it is the opposite one to the Kinnockites — that they laced their class message with phrases about the "national interest" and did not talk about a workers' plan for energy.

On 18 July NUM-NCB talks broke down over the Coal Board's insistence that pits must be closed unless they can be developed "beneficially". It would have been good if the NUM could have countered by asking, beneficial for whom, and by spelling out a definition of "beneficial" in terms of human need, not profit — instead of just saying no.

Nevertheless, the distinctive fact about the miners was the class content that came through the phrases imposed on Scargill and McGahey by their Stalinist and syndicalist training.

Violence? How could the miners maintain effective picket lines against massive police assault without self-defensive violence? How would it have helped if Arthur Scargill had condemned miners' violence? Who would it have helped? It would have been about as useful to the miners as nightly appearances on TV by Margaret Thatcher to denounce police violence would have been to the Tories!

Again, any valid criticism would be in quite the opposite direction: that the NUM did not manage sufficiently to organise its self-defence, nor to press home the arguments about police accountability and so on.

It does seem that some Yorkshire miners started off with a distrustful attitude towards Notts miners, and that didn't help on the picket lines. But the answer is not the sort of numb indifference that the TGWU leaders, for example, showed towards non-striking or weak ports during the dock strikes — but more pickets, better organised, better trained, better primed with the arguments.

# The question of a ballot

On the same level was the argument that the NUM leaders were "undemocratic" because they did not have a national ballot.

The argument is disqualified by sheer hypocrisy. Nobody balloted on the Coal Board's closure plan or the massive police operation. No-one elected Ian MacGregor. None of the born-again "democrats" complained in 1977-8 when Joe Gormley manoeuvred the NUM into area incentive schemes in direct defiance of a national ballot.

In October, when the pit deputies were set to implement their 82.5% ballot vote for a strike, those same newspapers which had been howling at the NUM for not calling a ballot were encouraging deputies to defy the ballot mandate.

The strike was called according to NUM rules and endorsed during the strike by seven national conferences of elected NUM delegates. Not many things in Britain are done as democratically as that.

In any case — this should be said plainly — it would not alter the fundamental rights and wrongs even if the strike were called undemocratically. The course of history is not determined by meditations upon the concept of democracy, but by class struggle. The NUM, and through the NUM the trade union movement as a whole, faced an assault which had to be resisted democracy or no democracy.

There was not much point in the NUM seeking the most exquisitely democratic ways to decide whether to resist or not: for not resisting would mean no effective NUM, and therefore no NUM democracy of any sort worth having.

Obviously a national strike sanctioned by a ballot would have been better than an area by area strike. It would have strengthened the NUM and deprived its enemies of valuable weapons in the propaganda war.

Would there have been a majority for a strike if a ballot had been called? It is difficult to know. Opinion polls taken from 9 March onwards showed a steady 60% majority for a strike. The area ballots in March showed some shift towards strike action by comparison with the 1982 and 1983 ballots. NACODS had a majority for a strike. But the question is complex.

Consider South Wales. In March 1984 it voted two to one against a strike. Nevertheless, the pits agreed not to cross picket lines. Pickets were quickly put on — as the miners knew they would be — and South Wales became the most solid area of the whole strike. John Lloyd reported in the *Financial Times*:

"Mineworkers at the South Celynen colliery voted once against striking and twice for a national ballot; yet these same men later went off to picket pits in Staffordshire and Leicestershire. 'Well, I'm against a strike, I just can't afford it, but once we're into it, well, it's a different matter then', said Mr

John Harrison, one of the flying pickets. He has one son aged 22, who has not been able to get a job since he left school. 'I'm going to Leicester for him'." (*FT* 17 March).

Although North Staffs crumbled during the summer of 1984 it had the same experience at the start of the strike: a vote against a strike but a vote for not crossing picket lines which was bound to mean the same thing.

Notts voted 73% against a strike in an area ballot: yet it was very difficult to find a scabbing miner in Notts who would not say that he personally had voted for a strike!

So don't miners know their own minds? Or what? When a worker votes for or against a strike, it is not the same sort of thing as a comfortable middle class person choosing whether to put their cross opposite Tory, Alliance or Labour. The worker is not expressing a preference about something relatively remote; he or she is deciding whether to undergo risks and hardships (very large ones in the case of the miners' strike) for the sake of a principle. (Very rarely, and certainly for no miner during the 1984-5 strike, do the immediately foreseeable material benefits from a strike exceed the immediately foreseeable material costs).

The South Wales and North Staffs votes are thus perfectly plain: the miners preferred not to have a strike, but felt that if other miners picketed to demand solidarity, then on principle they must respond. Many Notts scabs felt the same: but they didn't do what on principle they saw as their duty. Therefore they pretended they had been in favour of a strike and hid behind the pseudo-principle of a ballot.

All that means two things. First, that there is nothing sacrosanct about the individual ballot as a form of democracy. The mass meeting, where the fear of hardship can be tempered by the confidence of solidarity, is generally a better form for decisions on strikes. And "voting with their feet" in response to picketing, as the miners did, is by no means inferior to a ballot. In fact the opinion polls actually showed a 57% majority of miners against a ballot.

Second: it is not certain that the responses given to an opinion poll (which didn't immediately commit the miners who responded to anything, and which may have been coloured by a desire to stick by the union as against alien pollsters) would translate into the same figures in a ballot. Yet not calling a ballot may have been a tactical error. If a ballot would have produced a majority, then it should have been called. But the decision whether to call a ballot — say, in April at the time of the first national delegate conference — was a matter of judgement which the leaders of the NUM were best placed to make.

## Price worth paying

A ballot majority would not have guaranteed a 100% solid strike, but it would have reduced the initial number of scabs drastically. The tactic of picketing out collieries — which was the only possible one without a ballot — did not work fully, and its partial failure seriously weakened the strike from the start. Given the length of the strike, the fact that solidarity from other unions would be crucial, and the high profile role of political accusation and counter-accusation in the strike (all of which were partly foreseeable from the start), any temporary loss of momentum through a ballot would have been a price worth paying.

*Socialist Organiser* supported and publicly defended the NUM leadership in March and April when they rejected a national ballot, though by April we also felt that we should not criticise them if they went for a ballot: it was a matter of judgement and assessment, and they were better placed to know than we. (According to Peter Heathfield, speaking in Crewe on 19 February, 1985, Arthur Scargill personally favoured a ballot at that stage (*SO* 218).) In hindsight, the choice not to ballot may have been a mistake, but it is still not certain.

In March many miners were open-minded about a ballot, though many also were against one because of the bad experience over Lewis Merthyr. In mid-March two Kent miners told *Socialist Organiser*: "I don't blame Scargill for not wanting to put himself out on a limb again after being let down in ballots twice before"; and, "we'll have a national ballot in our own time, not when the *Sun* tells us to".

Alex Hogg, delegate from Cardowan NUM Scotland, told us: "The national ballot is a difficult question. But the normal custom and practice in mining means that — rule 1. you assist your neighbours if they are in trouble and ask you to; and, rule 2. you don't cross picket lines.

"These unwritten rules supersede the parliamentarians' laws." (*SO* 171). By April opinions were hardening, as the right wing and the media intensified their clamour.

Kent Area NUM executive member John Moyle told a meeting in Birmingham that week: "At Baddesley pit there is a pond, and I am told that even the ducks there swim around quacking, 'ballot, ballot'."

Steve Shukla (Armthorpe NUM) said: "The call for a national ballot now is a strike-breaking effort" (*SO* 174).

After 19 April the ballot was a dead issue — except for the Tories, the media, the right wing and the scabs.

# A general strike could have beaten the Tories

Were the calls for a general strike just empty words? Given the inability of the labour movement to deliver some of the most minimal forms of solidarity, wasn't talk about a general strike an exercise in futile wishful thinking?

*Socialist Organiser* campaigned for a general strike all through the struggle. Tony Benn, Dennis Skinner, Ken Livingstone and Jim Slater all called for a general strike at various times. South Wales NUM president Emlyn Williams appealed for a general strike when his area's funds were seized. The initial NUM proposal to the September TUC congress ("industrial action involving all trade unions") and Arthur Scargill's demand after the receiver was sent in on 30 November ("the most massive mobilisation of industrial action our movement has ever seen") were the same thing in different words. The "big bang" of industrial solidarity which Ron Todd talked about in August could only have been something near a general strike.

But nothing happened. There was no general strike. And, as always, in hindsight it all looks inevitable.

But suppose the NUM leaders had been as half-hearted and fumbling as the major trade union leaders. There would never have been a miners' strike. And in hindsight, wouldn't appeals from Cortonwood and Polmaise miners for such a national strike have looked as utopian as the calls for a general strike now appear?

## General strike?

These are the times when the political soul of everybody in the British labour movement is being probed and tested — especially of those who claim to be on the left. Anybody in the labour movement who is no good in the miners' strike will never be good for anything. The titanic battle between the miners and the Tory government is moving into its sixth week. Nobody but a political child or a political idiot can now argue that this is not a stand-up political fight between the Tories and the entire labour movement... We are strong enough to beat them. That's why we must fight in the labour movement for a general strike.

*Socialist Organiser*, 19 April 1984

The failure, in many areas, of elementary solidarity, does not necessarily mean that a general strike would have failed. Even the steelworkers scared into using scab coal by the threats to shut their plants, could have been rallied by the prospect of an all-out struggle in which they as a particular group would not run the same risk of being picked off.

Fear weighed heavily on the steel workers. But that does not mean that they had all become Tories. Far from it. Their treatment since 1980 had left a lot of resentment.

Working class history is full of examples of workers previously unwilling to mobilise on a minimal level joining advanced struggles. Take France in 1968: only three million workers had been willing to join trade unions. Ten million joined a general strike.

The miners' strike itself had an example of that pattern. In Scotland, the Polmaise miners had been campaigning in vain for an area strike to back their fight against closure. Then Yorkshire's initiative changed everything: within days Scotland's miners were solid in a strike against all economic closures.

Such a domino effect could have happened in the wider working class if, for example, the TGWU leadership had prosecuted the docks strikes more seriously. If it had stood up boldly against the law over the Austin Rover strike. If the rail unions had struck over pay and job cuts, instead of twice doing a Grand Old Duke of York.

The issues were there to rally the whole labour movement: a halt to cuts

## Linking other workers with the miners

If the TUC had leaders like Arthur Scargill instead of the sub-grade office boys it does have, the TUC would organise now for a general strike. But most of the leaders won't lead, so the rank and file must do it themselves. We need a general strike right now. What we ourselves can do is agitate, organise and prepare for it.

We must demand that the TUC calls a general strike. These people will only do that under great pressure, and then they would take the first chance to sell us out. But they are at the head of our movement. In practice the way to a general strike is through the growth and escalation of solidarity action with the miners, and through other workers linking their light to the miners. Right now the Tories are weaker to resist working class action than at any time in the last five years.

One way to help the miners is to fight for your own claim. We know that Thatcher was mortally afraid of a rail strike coming together with the miners, and intervened in buy off the rail unions.

*Socialist Organiser*, 28 June 1984

and closures; trade union rights; civil liberties. The Labour Party and the TUC refused to campaign on these issues. Labour leaders did not question fundamentally what the police were doing; they only asked for it to be done more softly: their most vigorous phrases were reserved for the condemnation of "violent" pickets.

Labour's economic policy does not even promise to repeal all the Tory cuts — it is little more than an unconvincing plea for the possible good effects of more state borrowing. The TUC chose the September 1984 congress as its time to drop its commitment to industrial action in defiance of unions struck down by the Tory laws. These failures of leadership explain well enough why a general strike did not happen. But they don't mean that the leadership could not be challenged, or that we were wrong to try to do that.

A general strike was necessary, so we made propaganda for it. It would have been wrong if, during the greatest British working class battle for half a century, we had made a cold a priori assessment in our heads that the working class could not rise to the level of action its objective interests demanded — and, on the basis of that assessment, given up on the job of propaganda for what was necessary.

That would have been to let the setbacks and defeats the movement has suffered in the last five years so oppress our spirits that we could no longer do the proper work of a socialist newspaper — advocate whatever the logic of the class struggle indicates and working class interest demands. Some workers reading *Socialist Organiser* thought our talk of a general strike was crazy. But most didn't. Most were sympathetic. They didn't think that a general strike would happen, but they thought it was right and proper that

## Agitating for a general strike

The call for a general strike is winning more and more support in the labour movement. But "general strike" is not a slogan that should be used lightly.

As Leon Trotsky put it in 1935: "But is the general strike possible in the immediate future? To a question of this sort there is no a priori answer possible, that is to say, none ready made. To obtain an answer it is necessary to know how to question. Whom? The masses. How question them? By means of agitation.

"Agitation is not only the means of communicating to the masses this or that slogan, calling the masses to action, etc. For a party agitation is also a means of lending an ear to the masses, of sounding out their moods and thoughts and reaching this or another decision in accordance with results."

*Socialist Organiser*, 10 May 1984

activists like ourselves should argue for one. They could see that we were in a fundamental showdown between the Tories and the labour movement, and that therefore the labour movement should be mobilised 100%. Only, they had no confidence about getting that mobilisation, and therefore they put very little pressure on the trade union leaders.

What could socialists do? We had to fight to raise confidence, to stress again that the issues were urgent and could not be dodged or postponed. Should we have followed the example of *Socialist Worker*, who explained that only collections could be argued for, not a general strike, or the example of Socialist Action, which campaigned for a national demonstration in London "led by Neil Kinnock" instead of a general strike? Should we have copied Socialist Action in theorising that socialist revolutions are impossible in the advanced capitalist countries now, and for the next period ahead can happen only in the Third World?

If we did that we would make ourselves part of the problem rather than part of the solution. There was no general strike. But even that does not mean that our arguments were wasted effort. Remember that the general strike of 1926 came just four years after the apparently crushing defeats of 1921-22.

## "We need your support!"

"The time has come to say to other unions: Yes, we want your support, but not only financial contributions. When we are faced with Thatcher, McGregor, the CBI, the Institute of Directors, we're entitled to say to colleagues in other unions: Join us, come out with us in dispute."

Arthur Scargill, 28 April 1984

"I think it should be a general strike. Other workers should be supporting us. Why are TGWU drivers still crossing the line? Their union hasn't been doing its job properly. MacGregor's doing to us what he did to — the steel industry. I only wish we had supported the steel workers then."

Sheila Jow, South Yorkshire miners' wives' organiser

"If we go under, than the trade union movement goes under. We want their support, but we also want positive action, including strike action. Eventually, it's got to come to a general strike to get rid of Thatcher's monetarist policies".

Roy Barsley, chair of South Yorkshire NUM panel

# The use of civil law and the state

The civil law was used against the miners to an unprecedented extent. A trickle of actions ended as an avalanche. The unfavourable balance of economic forces, the divisions within the unions, the lack of solidarity action, the consequent lack of any perspective for victory, and of course the deadening cumulative deprivation: these were the real reasons for defeat. Nonetheless, the legal apparatus — it is increasingly less useful to talk separately of the civil and the criminal law — played an important ancillary role in maintaining divisions, in obstructing the resonance of the union's case, in underpinning the Tory ideological offensive of "law and order", "democracy", and "the right to work".

It was clear at all points in this heroic strike, to Thatcher if not to those who over- estimate the potency of her ideology, that her ideas, no matter how imaginatively and forcefully constructed and argued, could not win the day. It was the use of the law, not as confidence trick but as coercion, whether through police truncheons or through the state taking possession of the NUM's funds. that was in the end crucial to the strategy of capital and its captains.

## Picketing

Mass mobile picketing won big strikes in the past. It could do so again. The dispute has seen the state assault on this basic civil liberty and essential tactic of class struggle — an assault developed through Grunwick, the steel strike, and Warrington — reach a new zenith. If the right to work was to be utilised to throw thousands of miners on the dole, the right to picket had to be rendered meaningless. A powerful stereotype of picketing, as inherently violent in all its forms, had to be constructed and propagated. The police must be seen to be acting to maintain a public order which was in the interest of all citizens by upholding the law.

The reactions of pickets to the police attempts to control law-breaking could be placed at the start of the reconstituted instant replay, so that the pickets' reaction appeared to come before the police action, not the police action before the response. The pickets, not the police, were the problem, the ignition key to the violence. "Pickets attack police upholding law" replaced "police attack pickets attempting to exercise a basic human right essential to save jobs and safeguard communities".

Thus the law acted to close mines.

Kinnock and Willis joined hands with Chief Constables, magistrates, judges and Cabinet ministers to remake reality and add another warhead to the missile aimed at working-class communities. The role of the state in guaranteeing capitalist political economy is illuminated in the interplay of police, criminal law, and the civil courts.

Chief Superintendent Holford stated in an affidavit to Mr Justice Lane: "I have yet to attend a mass picket where violence and intimidation of working miners has not been the sole intention of those present".

Taking the point, the Lord Chief Justice ruled that any mass picket is a criminal offence. "Any suggestion of peaceful picketing was a colourable pretence ... it was a question of picketing by intimidation and threats. It must have been obvious to all those participating in the picketing that their presence in large numbers was part of the intimidation and threat".

These observations are then codified in the civil law. In February 1985 Mr Justice Scott issued an injunction banning mass picketing at five South Wales pits. The judgment was later extended to eleven Yorkshire collieries. Sheer weight of numbers, said Scott, echoing Lane and Holford, was intimidatory even if pickets stood silent and inactive. The suggestion of the Department of Employment, in the Code of Practice, that six pickets might be a reasonable figure was thus translated by Mr Justice Scott into a legal requirement.

## Civil and criminal

And no distinction could be made between "pickets" at the entrance and "demonstrators" standing in the background. The appearance of more than six pickets constituted a civil wrong. The union was to act as a "support unit" and police these rules, ensuring ineffective picketing, making sure they were complied with. The police would arrest those who resisted enforcement of the rules under the criminal law. Breach of the rules would attract an injunction against the union under the civil law. Refusal to comply with the court's order would lead inevitably to sequestration.

Yet if the court directives were to be complied with, it would be impossible to try to win the dispute. More broadly, the denial of the right to demonstrate by the courts cruelly undercuts working-class self-activity in capitalist society. "Thus", the *Guardian* commented, "do judges make our laws". Home Secretary Leon Brittan, they went on to report, had remarked on the very satisfactory state of the law on picketing. No change was required.

If throughout the dispute the main burden of obliterating effective picketing lay on the police, backed by the criminal courts, the civil law was always with us. The Coal Board felt that its use by the direct employer would be counter-productive. Its objectives could be met by other, better, means.

But the sequestration proceedings taken against the South Wales area by Reads Haulage in August can be seen as ending the first phase of the strike. The fact that union assets could be efficiently appropriated without any industrial action from other workers convinced the government that the strike was and would remain isolated. It also convinced scabs and their advisers that there was a way for hyenas to make a kill. The civil law process, if pushed to the limit, could (they now saw) constitute a powerful weapon against the national union and bring the organisation of the strike to its knees.

## Contract actions

Unions have unfortunately long accepted that the courts should have the final right to adjudicate in disputes between members. This idea not only erects a firm bulwark against union autonomy and democracy; it is a product of and a potent reinforcement of the conception that the state is neutral and the judiciary is objective and impartial, above class conflict.

In essence, the right of dissidents to sue the union is an attempt to decollectivise trade unionism and to press its collectivised, active democracy into the individualised mould of the law of contract. As such it represents for Thatcherism the best possible mode of legal intervention. If MacGregor suing the NUM might just have had the smack of partiality, who could object to action taken against a powerful union by miners themselves, the victims of intimidation by their powerful and unaccountable leaders? Thatcher and MacGregor would just stand on the sidelines. Of course, there was another way of looking at it, a way which saw rule-making by an unelected, unaccountable judiciary, independent of the people but not of the state and capital, as an undemocratic means of thwarting the will of the majority of NUM members.

The repeated decision of the courts that the strike in Scotland was democratic and legal led to not a peep of approbation from a state which had made "democracy" its basic touchstone. That it dealt in counterfeit coin, that the role of the judiciary was in essence strike-breaking, not democracy-creating, was highlighted in February when action was taken against the National Union of Seafarers, whose members were refusing to transport coal.

The judge refused resort to coercion. He would not grant the employers an injunction. Why, he pondered, didn't the union hold a ballot? They did. It was overwhelmingly in favour of a continued boycott. The judge swiftly issued an injunction ordering the union to do all in its power to make its members handle coal and scab on the strike.

In the early days of the strike the law was used by scabs to have the strike declared unlawful in area after area; to have the new disciplinary code declared inoperable, to have the special delegate conference outlawed. It was used to legitimise scabbing, build the confidence of Thatcher's fifth column. and construct the image of the hireling as hero.

By the late summer the second phase of the strike was opened via an intensive Cabinet propaganda offensive accompanied by a spate of individual rule-book actions by several scabs. The link between the two lay with people such as David Hart, adviser to Thatcher, MacGregor and the National Working Miners' Committee, and Tory lawyer David Negus.

It was Negus's masterminding of the impulse of the scabs to break the strike which led to the order for sequestration of NUM assets on 25 October and the appointment of a receiver to take over the NUM assets on 30 November. Having first attempted to appropriate democracy, only to have its aspirations foiled by the majority of miners, Thatcher's court now appropriated the union. In a falling-back on coercion in the ultimate interests of democracy, the union was taken out of the hands of its democratically-elected leaders, who for some reason still retained the active support of the vast majority of its members, and entered as a new item in the business portfolio of a Tory solicitor who was able to declare in all truth, "I am the NUM".

## Thatcher's breakthrough

The experience of the civil law during the strike illustrates the limitations of Thatcherism as a set of ideas, and the stumbling block that state coercion constitutes for trade unionists in a period of general working-class retreat. The directive that they had no right to picket, the statement that the strike was unlawful, and the opinion delivered by the highest courts in the land that the NUM leaders were in breach of union rules — all of this had little impact on those who had committed themselves to the struggle. Its impact on those who had taken up a stance of opposition through more obvious material factors requires careful tracing. It was certainly not determinant.

One ingredient in the failure to mobilise solidarity action was (it is argued) the lack of a national ballot and the partly-legal offensive over democracy. In truth the most relevant fact was that a central NUM area was working — a situation which might have occurred even if there had been a national ballot.

But the lack of a national ballot, understandable in the light of the need for minority rights over an issue like the destruction of whole communities, or rather the inability of the national union to gain an understanding over this issue, provided the courts with an entry and with what resonance they had. This points to the need to reorganise the structure and democracy of unions. The strike also signalled an important breakthrough by Thatcher in her attempt to make her employment laws part of the fabric of industrial conflict. Initially the NUM boycotted the courts. Then they were represented. Then they appealed. Then they negotiated compromises. In February both Yorkshire and South Wales agreed to abide by High Court decisions and instructed their members to that effect. Finally, in March, South Wales area president Emlyn Williams told the court that he had purged his contempt by taking a lead in the return to work.

Whilst this process was going on we witnessed the disintegration of the Wembley strategy for opposing the anti-union laws, as union after union accepted injunctions against picketing and boycotts, held ballots on the closed shop and industrial action, and publicly declared that they would not advise their members to break the law or to ignore injunctions.

## A programme of change

It is now clear that with the coercion available no one union can resist the law — and that in today's period of defeat and retreat, there is little possibility for solidarity action, which is the only sure way to defeat state coercion. Like it or not, if we do not come to terms with this unpalatable position we will be denying the heroic effort of Britain's miners by failing to recognise the lessons of the strike.

This is not a recipe for giving up the struggle, merely an acknowledgement of its present constraints and the fact that the existing consciousness and the existing leadership of our movement are the products of decades and cannot — in today's circumstances — be changed in days.

We have to look at the question of the law in context. The strike was an important defeat, which has nonetheless created a constituency for socialist ideas and action. It showed the left to be a weak force in British society, incapable of rising by an effort of will to what was objectively needed. A study of the use of civil law in the dispute discloses the need not only to continue to press for opposition to the Tory law, but also to attempt to deepen our understanding of and opposition to the role of law and the role of the state in capitalist society.

We have to build on what thousands have learned in the past twelve months. We have to do this not merely by focusing on what workers can do now in terms of self-organisation, but also by working out a programme of change — a programme which can be carried out by a future workers' government, and which can strengthen the struggle here and now.

Recently Jim Mortimer, Labour's retiring general secretary, spoke about a future Labour government simply returning the unions to the legal position that existed in 1979. That's the legal position that allowed the NUM to be taken over. That's the legal position that has allowed the Coal Board to sack hundreds of miners and the police to cripple and jail thousands more.

We need to start discussing now how we replace the judiciary, how we transform the police, how we make magistrates' courts people's courts, how we formulate legal codes on dismissal, strikes, picketing and union membership and internal democracy.

It is time to move beyond polished critiques of the rule of law in capitalist society plus the vague statement that "new forms will emerge after the revolution". We need more concrete proposals for moving forward now.

Detailed blueprints formulated outside the struggle against Thatcherism may be elegant and arid. A socialist programme for legal change can play a role in strengthening workers' self-organisation and in deepening consciousness. We owe a responsibility to Britain's striking miners to make a start now.

# Economics — whose economics?

Capitalists produce coal for the same reason that they do anything else — to make a profit. Of course, coal production — as a source of energy — has an importance to capitalist production as a whole, too: so even if it is not directly profitable, the state may step in like it did in Britain after World War Two to keep the coal industry going for the good of capitalism as a whole (whilst paying out hefty compensation to the old owners).

But coal production in capitalist society is not based on people's needs. *The Economist* magazine put the issue quite starkly from the bosses' point of view: "Coal is an extractive industry, not a social service" (9 March 1985). The NCB's planning is all based on such considerations.

The coal industry is being drastically reorganised in order to boost its overall profitability. Between March 1981 and the start of the strike, 41,000 jobs were lost in the coal industry. A pit-closure programme — for 23 pits — was withdrawn because of a threatened national strike in February 1981; but by October of that year, half the programme had in fact been implemented.

In July 1982, the Board admitted to be undertaking a "searching financial review" of 30 or so pits; by November leaked reports suggested that 75 pits and 50,000 jobs were under threat.

In mid-1983, the Monopolies and Mergers Commission claimed that 141 of the then operating 198 pits were unprofitable; the NCB proposed to lay off 70,000 men over the next five years.

This reorganisation was in part to be achieved by the introduction of new technology — like the extremely sophisticated MINOS system. MINOS (the Mine Operating System) is a computerised system for remote control and monitoring of activities in the colliery.

The NCB announced on 6 March 1984 that 25 million tonnes of new capacity are to be introduced by March 1988. Half of this is to be the result of reorganisation of existing pits.

Half is to be produced by the high-tech development at Selby in north Yorkshire. By March 1988, Selby is to be producing 12.5 million tonnes a year, with a workforce of only 3,500.

South Wales and Scotland combined, with a workforce of 39,000, only produce 13:5 million tonnes. That's the NCB's plan in a nutshell: expand the super-pits — scrap the South Wales, Scotland and Kent pits, and let the communities around them rot! From the point of view of profit, it makes complete sense!

Throughout, the enemies of the strike condemned the NUM for the "absurd" call for no pit closures. The law of profit was not to be challenged. Jimmy Reid went so far as to condemn the whole strike as "reactionary": "In the long term this [the right to work] cannot be achieved by claiming a person's right to work at a specific job for the rest of his or her life. This would freeze the division of labour and would preclude any economic or technical progress. If jobs had been frozen two hundred years ago, we would still have thousands of stage-coach drivers in Britain today, presumably driving stage coaches... To envisage people working down the pits for evermore is not just Luddite... but thoroughly reactionary." Reid's argument is ridiculous. Closing down a pit is not like abandoning a stage coach. We will continue to need coal: but shutting a pit means abandoning presently recoverable and irreplaceable resources.

NCB policy would mean the reduction of recoverable reserves of coal in Britain from 300 years' worth to 50. Pit closures do not, as Reid suggests, lay the basis for a bright technological future.

They threaten to leave future generations without a useful source of energy. What technical progress! With different economic criteria, it is the notion of 'uneconomic' pits or of closing pits with recoverable coal, which can be seen to make no sense at all.

Oxford economist Andrew Glyn has shown how the overall costs — of

## The history of coal

The British coal industry goes back at least to the Middle Ages. Until the late 16th century, there were only very shallow mines, with a maximum of a dozen workers. By the end of the 17th century, there were many pits employing several hundred workers. Those were by far the biggest workplaces of the time. Most were in Durham and Northumberland.

Many small pits were run as cooperatives. Some pits were worked by serfs; some had wage labour of the modern type; many were worked on a labour-subcontracting basis (this continued right into the 19th century).

In 1700 there were about 15,000 to 18,000 miners. The industry grew rapidly after 1800, with the Industrial Revolution. In 1841 there were 225,000 mineworkers (of all types, not just coal). In 1881, 812,000; in 1921, 1,249,000.

In the mid 19th century Britain had been producing two-thirds of all the world's coal. After 1920 the workforce declined steadily to 711,000 wage-workers (in coalmining) in 1947. Nationalisation did not change the trend.

In 1984 there were about 200,000 workers of all sorts in the coal industry.

closing down pits, redundancies, dole, lost tax revenues, etc. — are greater than the cost of keeping "uneconomic" pits open. He and others have also shown how the NCB's accounting for its costs are extremely questionable. Costs appear higher than they really are (in no small part because they include £400 million interest payments to the government) and profits appear lower.

And pits become "uneconomic" because they have not received investment. Profitability itself is often the result of particular decisions made by the NCB.

From the standpoint of the capitalist system, based as it is on the search for profit, the NCB's pit closure programme is rational, good and necessary.

From the point of view of people's needs now and the needs of future generations, the pit closure programme is entirely irrational and disastrous. At issue are two radically different views of how society should be organised. Or, in other words, the profit system is — from the point of view of humanity as a whole — not a rational regulator of the exploitation of natural resources.

The profit system wantonly wastes natural resources. Closing coal mines is one example. Even more graphic an example is the famine in Africa now. Drought has been able to spread and have such tragic consequences because of changes in land-use. In part of Ethiopia, for example, agricultural businesses started to produce cotton for export. To do so they had to take land from the cattle-herding nomads. The nomads were forced into lower-quality grazing areas; and over-grazing led to soil erosion.

The result: cattle died, famine spread. Throughout the Third World, agriculture has been reorganised by big agribusinesses so as to leave millions of people underfed, whilst producing food for livestock in rich countries. The meat we eat is an enormous waste of food energy for Third World peoples. In many parts of the world, the basic fuel is still animal dung or wood. Often forests are chopped down to make way for export-oriented agribusiness. The wood is then just burned where they are. The poor who depend on wood-fire energy then have to take it from the hillsides — resulting in erosion and loss of soil fertility.

Partly as a result of the crazy misuse, and inequality in use, of energy on a world scale, millions of people are currently dying of starvation. Closer to home, while the Tories and the National Coal Board plan the closure of coal mines, young and old people die of hypothermia.

Capitalism also makes energy production quite often extremely unsafe for those working in the industry — coal is an obvious case. It is often reckless about pollution. The dangers posed by nuclear power are notorious; but coal leads to air pollution. Most of industry pollutes the atmosphere and the countryside. If the terrible by-products of energy production are the result of the profit system, the answer is to abolish that system and replace it with one in which different criteria — based on people's needs, and taking geological and ecological considerations into account — are the starting-point for conscious, rational planning. And to be conscious and rational, planning has to be democratic.

Also at stake in the strike were the basic prerogatives of management. In fact, the pit closure programme is part of a drive by the NCB to further dominate the work process in the pits. New technology plays a big part in this. High technology operations like MINOS reduce drastically the number of workers, replacing them with less strike-prone machines. Other systems like FIDO (Face Information Digested On-line) — dubbed the "watchdog" by face workers — is designed to monitor delays by miners working on the face. Delays of more than 20 minutes cause workers to lose some of their bonus.

But new technology need not mean a worse life for workers. If it was to go hand in hand with workers' control, it could be a liberating force.

# The case for workers' control

Democratic workers' control as the basis for developing a workers' plan for energy, could put an end to the inhuman effects of coal and other energy production. In the coal industry in Britain, there is a long tradition of fighting for workers' control.

*The Miners' Next Step* published in 1912 declared: "That our objective be to build up an organisation that will ultimately take over the mining industry, and carry it on in the interests of the workers." A sequel to this pamphlet, *Industrial Democracy for Miners*, produced by the Unofficial Movement, argued for the Miners' Federation of Great Britain (MFGB) to take control of the mines. It argued for direct control of the pit by rank and file workers.

Nationalisation, in 1947, did not bring workers' control. As South Wales miners' president Emlyn Williams has recalled, after nationalisation "it was the same management with the same aptitude for carrying out [the coal owners'] policy and not a socialist policy." Developing rank and file control over production and over the introduction of new technology is still a dire necessity. An important part of that — one of the strike's demands — is for a shorter working week. That way new technology could mean more free time — time to participate in politics as well as time for leisure.

The NUM's proposals go part of the way towards such an objective. The union's Technology Agreement calls for: a four-day, 28 hour week with no loss of pay; early retirement at 55; longer holidays; radically-improved working conditions; an end to occupational disease; a dramatic reduction in injury from accidents; retraining in new skills; and the opening up of new jobs for young people.

Workers' control in energy really needs to be international. Some countries have lots of oil or coal or hydroelectric potential, others little; but people everywhere need energy. Rational energy planning — to deal with problems like famine — would have to be international.

International planning would have to attempt to rationalise and integrate different kinds of energy production, and deal with the problems they pose now. All energy production raises a big problem. Most of our sources of energy are finite — that is, sooner or later, they will run out. To burn up energy that is not renewable therefore threatens to leave future generations with nothing but a return to the Dark Ages.

There's been a lot of scare-mongering even so. A study by a Yale University professor in the early 1970s presented the following picture of world reserves of energy resources. Recoverable coal reserves stand at six trillion tons, or enough to fill all world energy needs at today's consumption rates, for 500 years. Total recoverable petroleum reserves stand at 200 billion tons — 60 years' worth. Reserves of natural gas stand at 150 trillion cubic metres, or 150 years' worth. Largely unexploited oil shale reserves are believed to be around 200 times greater than those of conventional oil.

Nevertheless, it is important to think of the future and to find renewable sources of energy. At the moment the major source of energy being devel-

## History of the NUM

The first miners' union of any strength was in Northumberland and Durham in the early 19th century. It fought a 10-week lockout in 1831, despite marines and cavalry being drafted in. That union soon collapsed, but by 1844 a Miners' Association of Great Britain and Ireland claimed 70,000 members. A four months' strike by it in Northumberland and Durham in 1844 was eventually defeated by the eviction of the miners from their tied cottages and the recruitment of scabs.

In 1863 a National Miners' Union was formed by Alexander Macdonald. who in 1874 was the first worker to become an MP — as a Liberal. The slump of 1878-9 severely weakened both this union and the Amalgamated Association of Miners, formed in 1869.

Finally, in 1888, the Miners' Federation of Great Britain was set up, the direct forerunner of the NUM. The MFGB was not always left-wing. It refused to join the Labour Party when it was founded, backing the Liberals until 1909. But in 1912 it fought a tremendous and victorious strike which established it as by far the strongest union (or rather, federation of unions) in Britain.

In 1914 the MFGB counted more than one quarter of all TUC trade unionists: 762,000 out of 2,682,000. The MFGB reached its peak in 1920, with 945,000 members. The South Wales Miners, in July 1921, voted to affiliate to the Communist International: Lenin hailed this as maybe "the beginning of the really communist mass movement" in Britain.

But defeats in 1921 (Black Friday) and 1926 weakened the miners. When the MFGB was transformed into the NUM, on 1 January 1945, the new union was one of the bastions of the right wing in the labour movement. It had 548,000 members in 1947

The National Power Loading Agreement of 1966, making wages a national issue, was the basis for a revival of militancy shown especially by the Yorkshire strike of 1969. In 1972 and in 1974 the miners defeated the Tories over pay, and in May 1974 the right-wing regime in the Yorkshire NUM was finished off as Arthur Scargill was elected area president.

oped with the potential for indefinite production is nuclear power — which has big attendant problems.

Partly, nuclear power is being developed because it has some important political advantages for the ruling class. The Tories are deliberately developing a nuclear programme which, as one report put it, "would have the advantage of removing a substantial portion of electricity production from the dangers of industrial action by coal miners and transport workers".

In other words, nuclear power is being developed in order to weaken the NUM. The nuclear industry has a very authoritarian regime, which potentially threatens civil liberties more generally. The Atomic Energy Authority, for example, has its own police force. Safety regulations enforced from the top down can be used to discipline the workforce. It has been known for workers to be directed to work in "hot" areas, where they will be exposed to more than the "permitted" dose of radiation, and so have to be laid off. And after banning unions at GCHQ, the Tories have set the scene for banning unions (or at least severely circumscribing them) in the nuclear power industry on grounds of "national security"'.

Nuclear power is clearly not safe. There have been many cases of illness and death from radiation. The Windscale fire of 1957 undoubtedly led to cases of cancer. Areas around Sellafield and Sizewell 'A' are now showing increased rates of leukemia.

Safety precautions could, of course, be improved, and, possibly, the dangers of leaks and so on could be completely eliminated. The real problem with nuclear power is that of waste.

At present, no one knows what to do with this waste which will remain dangerous for thousands of years. Environmental and trade union groups put a stop to sea-dumping, while burial underground has met with community opposition. Possible solutions range from firing the waste into outer space (presumably extremely expensive and itself wasteful of energy), to burying the waste in gold containers, which do not corrode and also hold in radiation.

Present Labour Party policy does not deal with the issues at all. It is committed to the British-produced Advanced Gas-Cooled Reactor (AGR), condemning pressurised water reactors (PWRs) for being American! AGRs have been years late in completion and have barely managed more than a few months of continuous operation. And the Labour Party has little to say on the scandal of Britain's uranium imports from Namibia, never mind the appalling conditions that uranium miners work under. It may or may not prove possible to make nuclear power safe: it presently seems very unlikely. For sure, a government committed to capitalism could not be trusted to make it safe. It is possible that nuclear fusion, if it is developed, might be safer (it has no comparable waste problem). But for now it has not been developed and many argue it will have its own problems.

Apart from nuclear power, there are many other actual or potential sources of renewable energy. Wind is already being harnessed as energy — in some cases as big business. Hydro-electric power has been developed in many parts of the world. Further ideas for renewable energy sources include solar energy, geo-thermal energy and wave power..

Coal was one of capitalism's earliest sources of energy. It has been displaced by oil and gas (and nuclear power) more recently as the main source of energy; but as its reserves are greater it is likely to make a comeback. Various techniques that would both increase the present reserves of exploitable coal (coal gasification in situ, i.e. underground), and reduce air pollution, are not being developed because of cost. In fact more money is being spent on researching nuclear power.

Some people — not always hostile to the miners' strike — have argued that coal production should be brought to an end. Renewable sources should be used instead, they argue, and mining is such a hard and dangerous job that no one should have to — or be allowed — to do it. If the jobs lost in coal were going to be replaced by new ones; and if miners wanted those new jobs and it did not mean destroying whole communities, then there might be some sense to this argument. No such arrangement is on offer under capitalism!

And it is still not at all clear that coal would be abandoned in a rational energy plan, even if new, renewable energy sources are developed. Coal is a basic raw material which, with new technology, can be processed to replace both oil and gas ("liquefaction" and "gasification"). It contains all sorts of valuable chemicals, and is useful as an input to the petrochemical industry as well as for burning.

Various new technologies for using coal are available now but are not being developed. These have the advantage of being environmentally sound — or at least far less harmful than present techniques. "Fluidised Bed Combustion" for example could reduce pollution by 89%.

Mining can be made safer and less arduous. New technology can potentially reduce necessary face-working to a bare minimum. If this does not lead to job loss, its advantages are obvious. Workers' control is therefore the key to providing for the rational use of our energy resources. Workers' control over energy, but based on fundamentally different criteria to those of the profit system.

In his book *The Energy Crisis* Michael Tanzer put the basic issue very well: "Within the capitalist world, not only is there vast inequality of income, but basic mechanisms exist to ensure that the gap between needs and resources, between poverty and opulence, both within and among countries, will never be budged. Only a genuine social revolution within each country can make possible the rational use of its own economic and energy resources. And only a genuine social revolution in every country can make possible the rational use of all resources on a worldwide basis."

Linking together workers throughout the energy industry on an international basis would be an important step. We need to develop basic forms of organisation and solidarity to make it possible for the working class to take on the energy monopolies, defeat them, and set about reorganising the world's energy.

## To those who condemn the miners' "violence"

Those people who condemn miners for violence — they want to realise what they are doing. They are condemning the finest class fighters this movement has seen for many a year. All they are appealing to, all they are fawning to, is scabs, blacklegs and strike-breakers. That's who they are appealing to.

If you want to back us, show this by firm commitment — the resolution has that firm commitment. "This conference condemns the police violence used against the miners".

That is clear. unequivocal, out-and-out commitment to the miners, not walking past the bucket, dropping a fiver in and saying "we like the miners".

Paul Whetton speaking at Labour Party conference, *Socialist Organiser*, 3 October 1984.

# Rule of law? Whose law?

During the miners' strike, all sorts of existing laws — dating from 1361, or dating from 1982 — were interpreted with great ruthlessness against the miners. Shouting "scab" became threatening behaviour; a foot on the road became obstruction; presence at a mass picket became a breach of the peace.

Old laws on "riot", "unlawful assembly" and conspiracy — carrying five year sentences or more — were dug up from legal graveyards.

Civil laws and guidelines enacted in Tory trade union legislation were treated like criminal law as grounds for police action. New "laws" were created by the police, supported by an uncritical judiciary and government, without any parliamentary debate or consultation.

A national anti-picket police operation was coordinated at the National Reporting Centre (NRC) at Scotland Yard by the Association of Chief Police Officers (ACPO) — despite the fact that neither this centre nor the ACPO had any legal status. The police in Britain are supposed to be regionally controlled, but local police authorities that tried to restrain or curtail their local force's participation in this national operation discovered that they had no power to do so. While the NRC collaborated closely with officials from the Home Office and with the Home Secretary, their secret deliberations were subject to no Parliamentary or public scrutiny.

## A class-war government

There has been a great deal of hypocrisy about the government not intervening. They are deeply involved. The police are preventing peaceful picketing. They have set up road blocks, introduced curfews in the villages and provoked on the picket lines. There have been cavalry charges against unarmed pickets. That is a disgrace to the British police for which the government are responsible. (...)

The magistrates have come in and introduced bail conditions that amount to a sentence — a sort of exclusion zone — for those who have been convicted of nothing.

Much has been made of the crudity of the way in which the government have turned off every source of funds, including social security, to starve the miners back to work. They have "deemed" that the miners have been getting strike pay when in fact they have not. They have cut maternity grants and excluded from strike pay workers who have been only indirectly involved and were never employees of the NCB.

Tony Benn, speaking in the House of Commons, 7 June 1984

Roadblocks were set up, turning Nottinghamshire in particular into a no-go area for striking miners and many other citizens, especially in the early weeks of the strike.

A total of 290,000 picketing miners (in England and Wales) were turned back on legally far-fetched grounds, mainly that if they continued they might cause a breach of the peace. Most miners who refused to return were harassed, roughed up, or arrested. By September, 4,000 miners had been barred from picketing away from their own pit, or sometimes even curfewed, through bail conditions. They would be arrested — mainly on small charges on which a police officer's word is almost always enough to secure conviction — and then served with these "standard" bail conditions.

In other words, the courts, in conjunction with the police, took the power to put a curfew or semi-curfew on any miner whom they chose to single out.

## Arbitrary

Arrests at picket lines and demonstrations were often plainly arbitrary by legal standards. Snatch squads would plunge into the miners' lines to seize selected individuals — who could then be sacked by the NCB on the grounds of their arrest. Once arrested, miners were forced to give fingerprints, be photographed, and face questions about their politics. They were not given the chance to refuse, though legally they had every right to do so. Their only redress would be an official complaint which is entirely useless, or a civil suit, which might give them satisfaction at a hearing in some months' time or more likely might not, since it would often be their word against the police.

The police used great violence on the picket lines and in pit villages. Frequently when they went into action their first concern was to drive away photographers sympathetic to the miners — by force if necessary.

## Squads

The police were organised into militaristic riot squads, grouped around special police support units, backed by a cavalry and given a go-ahead by the courts and the government for the exercise of force. Numerous cases of assault on strikers have been documented. Many were severely injured. At all levels the police and the courts revealed strong and often explicit partiality in favour of those exercising "the right to work" (i.e. to break the strike) against those exercising a right to picket (i.e. wave good-bye behind a mass of police to a speeding coach or lorry). Chief Constables likened pickets to terrorism. On the ground, no police cited "breach of the peace" to prevent a small minority of non-strikers walking through the pickets of the vast majority.

## Criminalisation

Taken together these measures meant a virtual criminalisation of pickets and a deep erosion of the hard-won liberty of workers to display their collective strength and persuade peacefully others to join them. A series of other events during the strike brought the whole state machine, not just the police and courts, into question.

Sarah Tisdall was jailed for leaking to the *Guardian* documents about the government's political management of the installation of Cruise missiles at Greenham Common. At Molesworth 1500 Royal Engineers went in, with military police, to clear a peace camp. Clive Ponting, a civil servant who leaked documents that embarrassed the Tories over the Belgrano affair, was saved only by a courageous jury from a vindictive government and judge. Ex-agent Cathy Massiter revealed that M15 was watching CND and trade union activists: and the authorities banned these revelations from television.

## No power over the police

The official view at the police is that they serve the interests of the community as a whole. In both theory and practice, however, democratic accountability of the police is restricted in the extreme. The general rule is that the more democratic the body to which the police are accountable, the fewer powers that body has.

To put the matter bluntly, real power over the police is kept well away from ordinary citizens or their elected representatives. Democracy and the police are at opposite poles of social life.

*Socialist Organiser*, 2 August, 1984

# State power: who rules?

Britain appears to be democratic. Everyone has a vote and all major decisions are taken by our elected representatives. But appearances are deceptive.

Whoever voted for the police operation against the miners, and the long process of planning going back at least twelve years to 1972? Whoever elected the chief constables who directed this operation?

Parliament is only one face of the system by which we are ruled. The body of that system is the permanent state machinery — civil service, armed forces, police, prisons, courts. This machinery shapes the decisions of parliamentary governments far more than those governments shape it. And it takes many decisions and does many things with no reference to Parliament at all. The police build-up for anti-strike operations — which continued steadily under both Tory and Labour governments, with never any parliamentary decisions — is one example.

Some state forces, like M15, are not even in theory accountable to Parliament. It is likely that during the last Labour government (1974-79) M15 was actually spying on some ministers. But the state machine is not a completely independent force. It rules in the interest of the capitalist class — the top five per cent or so who own and control industry, commerce and finance.

This is for three reasons.

The top ranks of the state machine are closely tied to the capitalist class personally. Four judges out of five, for example, went to public schools. 90% of army officers of the rank of Lieutenant-General and above, and two-thirds of civil servants of the rank of under-secretary or above, went to public schools.

Police chiefs are generally less upper-crust in their backgrounds. But none of them could get where they are without being firm supporters of the present social system — or without becoming fairly well-off.

In 1984 the Chief Constable of Derbyshire was suspended for having spent tens of thousands of pounds improperly on his "executive suite". That tells us something about the style in which they live.

The bankers and bosses, having immense power directly through their economic position, are much better able to influence the state machine than any other group.

Even apart from the personal background of the top people, and the influence of big business on them — and these things vary from country to country — the state machine is a machine for administering, stabilising and reconciling society as it is. Its most basic structures and rules of functioning tie it to the defence of private property and of the "good" — that is, profitable — functioning of the economy. So the state is not neutral. It serves the ruling class. How it serves the ruling class — through what forms and procedures — varies. The Tories' regime is not a fascist system, or a police state — not like Nazi Germany, where even the Kinnocks, Murrays and Willises were thrown into jail, or Argentina where tens of thousands of trade unionists disappeared without trace. A more accurate description of what has been happening is that the Tories are shifting Britain towards the capitalist norm of violent class battles.

In other countries — even the prosperous USA — bloodshed and even gun fights on the picket lines have long been routine. But the police operation against the miners did exceed anything seen in Britain for a long while by its brutality, and by the openness with which it was proclaimed that the state, the umpire in the class struggle, was in fact on the side of the scab against militant trade unionism.

On the side of the scab meant, in fact, on the side of the bosses whom those scabs serve.

What is the ruling class? A hundred different definitions could be given of the "top people", by different aspects of their privilege and power, but underlying all those aspects is their wealth. Although the inequality of wealth in Britain has decreased somewhat this century, the top 1% of the population still own 23% of all private wealth and the top 5%, 45%. At the other end of the scale, 75% of the population owns only 16% of the wealth.

These figures, however, understate the real inequalities between classes. The top 5% have not only more wealth than the bottom 75% but a different sort of wealth.

The top 5% account for 96% of all personally-owned shares (according to the most recent overall figures: the British Telecom sale will have altered this percentage, but not much). They also own all the "family firms" except the tiniest. Now compare 1000 people who each own, say, a house, some household equipment, and a car, totalling £30,000 each, and on the other hand ten people each with a wealth of £1 million.

The ten people — the top 1% — own "only" 25% of the total wealth, but they own all of the sort of wealth that gives power and access to further wealth. The top 5% monopolise the means of production.

The division between the bottom 75% and the top 5% is not just a division between less wealthy and more wealthy. It is a division between those who live by selling their labour power, and those who live off their ownership of the means of production. It is a division between the worker and the boss.

# The question of violence

The miners were right to defend themselves against the police violence. The Labour Party conference in October 1984 was right to condemn police violence and not to condemn violence by picketing miners. The miners faced a national riot police, organised outside the control of Parliament or the local authorities. making up the law as it went along. Through road-blocks, arbitrary arrest by snatch squads and bail conditions, the police hit against the miners without any due process of law. The police are trained, highly paid, heavily equipped and tightly organised.

The miners tried to defend themselves as best they could. Were they right to do so?

Not if you believe that the working class should not resist whatever is decreed by a government in office.

Yes, if you believe working class livelihoods should stand above profits and the profit system. Yes, if you believe we have a right to resist the government and its scab-herding police force.

If rash or inappropriate tactics were used in the struggle, then that's a problem that the miners — who are sober, serious, responsible people — will sort out among themselves. Pious even-handedness, condemning "violence on both sides", is a sneaky way of helping the Tories. Usually it is quite hypocritical.

Neil Kinnock said that he was against all violence "without fear or favour". If he seriously meant that then he would propose to scrap all armed forces and police. For armed forces and police are certainly no use unless they employ violence.

In fact Neil Kinnock wants more conventional armed forces. He supports British troops in Ireland. He supports NATO. He supports the police. He accepts violence for British national defence or defence of the established order. All he doesn't accept is violence in defence of working class interests. No ruling class and no police force was ever won over by speeches against

## Scab-herding money men

"An appeal to more than 100 leading British businessmen has raised over £30,000 in the past three weeks in support of a fund for miners who want to go back to work...

A written appeal for money to help the anti-strike miners is being circulated among chairmen, chief executives and managing directors of major companies."

*Financial Times*, August 1984.

violence. They are bold, confident and immovable in their use of violence to defend the rights of property.

The only effect of preaching against "all" violence can be to weaken the self-confidence of working people who are already pushed towards submission, subordination and deference by thousands of pressures.

Rule of law? Yes! But whose law? All law, ultimately, is class law. And

## The millionaires' media

The mass-circulation press used the vilest distortions against the miners. The "heavier" papers and the TV backed them up with more subtle twists.

Papers like the *Sun* repeatedly tried to portray Scargill as a dictator, as a threat to democracy. Almost all the media joined in portraying the strike as a matter of one individual, even though Scargill was only carrying out union policy. Alleged incidents of strikers' violence against scabs and police were highlighted. Where the violence was later found to be nothing to do with strikers, that was usually not mentioned. The most horrific violence against the strikers was not newsworthy.

TV news, less crude than the mass-circulation press, nonetheless constantly portrayed the strike as a "problem" for the nation created by the miners — violence as a problem created by the pickets.

"Balance" often meant that a hard hitting Tory or NCB representative was matched by a mealy-mouthed Labour front-bencher or TUC bureaucrat. The scab miners got massive publicity.

*Sun* printworkers twice struck blows at the Fleet Street millionaires by refusing to print issues which insulted Arthur Scargill and the miners: one of them portrayed Arthur Scargill seemingly giving the Hitler salute and the other called striking miners "the scum of the earth".

Inside the media unions, a campaign has developed for an established Right of Reply for defamed trade unionists and others.

That campaign needs to be boosted. Another campaign should be for a labour movement daily paper. A lot is said about financial difficulties. But the real reason that we do not have such a paper is that the leaders of the labour movement have nothing much to say. The style and editorial line of a paper geared to their politics would be so bland, so evasive that no-one would be interested, so they don't want to take the risk!

To change the media fundamentally we will have to change society. We will have to take the presses and the TV transmitters out of the hands of the millionaires and share them out among political or other groups having a minimum of proven support. That way we could really have a free press, not just an array of millionaires' mouthpieces.

there is no force standing above classes to administer law impartially or to settle disputes by giving prizes for good behaviour.

Democracy? What sort of democracy? Democracy for the Tories means a cross on a piece of paper every five years for most of us, and between times rule by "the people who know best" — the judges, police chiefs, bankers and top civil servants who run the state machine while Parliament talks.

The rule of law, in the Tory version, means that the only people permitted to use violence are the police and the armed forces — special forces, separated off from the community, and trained in unquestioning allegiance to the established order.

For the Tories, when Ian MacGregor tries to take away the livelihoods of thousands of miners without any voting or even consultation, it is quite democratic. It is "the right of management to manage".

The miners' strike was a head-on clash between the rights of property and the rights of labour. The police upheld the "right to work" of scabs by violence. The miners defend the right of every worker to a livelihood, as something more important than the claims of profit. And between equal rights, as Karl Marx, put it, force decides.

# Workers' self-defence

The pity is that the miners' force was not more organised. *The Miner* advised (30 June) that because of "increasing concern at the spectacle of heavily armed police confronting unprotected miners in tee-shirts and jeans... miners at risk should take a leaf out of the police book and take elementary precautions by wearing headgear such as pit helmets to protect themselves from truncheons. Arm and leg padding is also recommended and cricket boxes."

However, mostly this was not done. A few groups of miners did get themselves more organised on an ad hoc basis, but mostly the pickets faced the police with nothing more than their bare hands, native wit and individual initiative.

In the US, where industrial disputes have long been more violent than in Britain, a tremendous example was set by Minneapolis coal yard and warehouse workers and truck drivers during a strike in 1934. They organised hundreds of strikers — trained, disciplined, and armed with clubs — to defend themselves. They took on the police and "in less than an hour after the battle started there wasn't a cop to be seen in the market and pickets were directing traffic in the now peaceful district."

British trade unionists will have to think about organising in this sort of way if picketing is to be effective in future strikes.

## Violence initiated by the police

People should stop to examine exactly what they mean by violence on the picket line. Nobody can convince me that four miners sat in a car are being violent to such an extent that coppers have got to take truncheons out and smash the windows and drag them out the car in order to stop violence.

It seems to me that when we're talking about violence, we need to be very careful and say where that violence is coming from. When we sum up the question of violence on the picket line, the score is Police 2 Pickets 0. We've had two of our comrades die on the picket line and I don't see how you can get much more violent than that.

A certain amount of violence has always been there and it is bound to be there in a situation like this. But the violence is initiated by people who carry sticks and organise themselves in such a fashion as to intimidate. And by that I mean the police and not the pickets.

From Paul Whetton's Diary, *Socialist Organiser*, 30 August 1984

**Silverwood colliery near Rotherham, August 1984.**
John Harris/reportdigital.co.uk

# Police versus democracy

By the end of the strike, tens of thousands of people in the pit communities, previously conservative on such questions, were saying that they hated and feared the police and distrusted the courts. Many people started thinking critically about the state machine as a whole for the first time.

During the strike we saw the emergence of a new type of police, dismissive of democratic inhibitions, arrogant in its assumption of power, politically charged against the labour movement. The roots of this policy preceded the strike itself; there is little chance that with the end of the strike this new police will simply disappear from sight.

Self-defence against the police is a first step. But obviously it is not enough. What policies can we propose for a future Labour government? What should we demand of Labour representatives on police committees?

We cannot be indifferent to the forms in which the state machine serves the capitalist class: centralised or decentralised, arbitrary or accountable, secret or open to scrutiny, militaristic or civil. Such apparent ultra-radicalism would leave the state machine untouched until the revolutionary day when we can sweep it all away anyway — and thus save the Chief Constables, the judges and their colleagues from any immediate challenges.

Millions of workers still think that the police are more or less impartial. That is why the Tories were able to get away with their scab-herding operation. Reform campaigns can help convince them otherwise.

## Mealy-mouthed

During the strike, most of the labour movement was shamefully mealy-mouthed and evasive on the issue of the police. Neil Kinnock, who denounced picketing miners for "violence", took it for granted that the police had the right to use whatever tactics they thought necessary and to employ as much force as "keeping order" — quelling the miners' pickets — required them to.

At most, Labour leaders would advocate milder police methods, while stressing that they did not question the fundamental command structure and objectives of the police. They did not argue for an "alternative" law and order, but simply for softer enforcement of established law and order. To many people those Labour leaders must have seemed simply soft-headed.

The police are supposed to represent the general interest of society as a whole, as against the individual criminal. But the very fact of establishing a hierarchical force, carefully kept separate from the community around it, reveals a contradiction. The police are supposed to serve the public interest, but the ordinary public are forbidden to interfere or inquire too closely into the police! The public interest becomes the police force's own private domain.

For "society as a whole" was and is a fiction. In a society torn by class conflict the police, like the state machine as a whole, serves the ruling class. It represents the "general interest of society" as constructed and interpreted by that ruling class. We should not be deluded by the claim of the police that they represent the public interest and stand above politics.

A democratic programme of reform would need to increase massively the powers of local police committees and Parliament to oversee police policies and operations. This would entail, for example, opening the Home Office to effective parliamentary scrutiny and giving police committees real power to hire and fire chief constables.

*Operational* control of the police should be put in the hands of elected bodies.

Judges and magistrates should be elected. Access to the law for ordinary people, not backed by the kind of wealthy pressure groups behind scab miners, should become cheaper and simpler. The arcane mysteries of courtroom procedure should be democratised. The power of the police to interfere in the labour movement should be minimised.

Elected tribunals, completely independent of the police, should hear complaints against the police and possess effective sanction against them.

The police should have the right to unionise in real unions committed to accountability and demilitarisation, not the yellow management "union" called the Police Federation. They should have the right to negotiate for their members and to take industrial action, as they did in 1919. The democratic police union in Italy has fought on these issues since the war; it expressed solidarity with the British miners!

Similar reform demands should be developed for other sectors of the state machine: election of top civil servants, freedom of information, trade union rights for troops, disbandment of M15, etc.

Reforms — or pseudo-reforms — can lead to incorporation. Instead of subordinating the police to the will of the people, the will of the people finds itself subordinated to the police. This is the current danger associated with the establishment of toothless liaison committees between the police and unrepresentative members of the community; or with Neighbourhood Watch Schemes, which perform surveillance functions on behalf of and under the direction of the police; or Multi-Agency Liaison which, under the guise of co-operation between the police and other state agencies, enables the police to secure a foothold on their own terms in schools, social work institutions and the like.

Reforms may be subordinated to ideals of improving relations between the police and the community which in effect gives the police a veto over changes which it does not favour.

The answer to this danger is to couple the fight for reforms with a fight for self-organisation and with a battle for socialist ideas.

The 1984 Labour Party conference passed a resolution moved by a Notts striking miner, Paul Whetton, to demand no police intervention in industrial disputes. In Nottingham itself, where support for the strike was difficult to mobilise, 7,000 people turned out on 14 April to demonstrate for "Police out of the coalfields". (The initiative for the demonstration had come from *Socialist Organiser.*)

Such moves present a challenge to the labour movement: how to "police" ourselves, how to develop our own "law and order". While policing — in

## How Labour should have campaigned

It is miners who are standing up to the massed ranks of semi-militarised police. But it is the entire labour movement which is now being probed and tested. The brutally candid Lord Denning, former Master of the Rolls, put the issue squarely: "The trade unions are on trial". The trial is a trial of strength, which the Tories and the police are turning into a trial of naked force.

Neither the Tories nor their centralised gendarmerie are invincible. They are seemingly strong only because of the divisions in the ranks of the NUM and because of the general depression in the labour movement. They are strong only because of the miserable quality of the TUC leadership, who do nothing to mobilise support for the miners and their picket lines.

No coal should pass the ports or travel on rail.

No miners' picket should be left isolated to face the police. Rally to the picket lines!

Trade union branches should demand that the TUC organise a general strike against Tory anti-union laws, against cuts, and in support of the miners.

The Labour Party should come off the fence. Neil Kinnock's weaseling in the middle of the road is a disgrace to the Labour Party. Kinnock should do like the Labour Party chair Eric Heffer, and stand on the line with the miners.

Labour councils should follow Sheffield's lead and object on Police Committees to the deployment of local police on Tory police-state duty in the coalfields. They should refuse to pay them.

The Labour Party should take the issue to the country. The Tories are creating a centralised national police force, and without any popular mandate or popular licence to do so. It is part of the same drive as the abolition of major areas of local government.

If the labour movement throws itself into this fight, the miners can win.

*Socialist Organiser*, 10 May 1984

the sense of internal regulation — is a function of every social organisation, the police as a particular institution is not. Hierarchy, bureaucracy, authoritarianism and unaccountability are not inevitable. There are many ways in which the function of policing can be performed.

The community patrols of "no-go" areas in Northern Ireland in the late 60s and early 70s are one recent example near at hand.

Likewise, defence is necessary, so long as different states exist: but it need not be by a nuclear-armed standing army rather than a people's militia. Courts are necessary: they need not be presided over by unelected, ageing, wealthy, male, white Tories.

Administration is necessary: it need not be done in secret by highly-paid officials who shuttle to and fro between civil service jobs and top posts in industry and banking.

An elected legislative assembly is necessary: it need not be capped by a Monarch and a House of Lords, deadened by medieval mumbo-jumbo, dominated by a strong separate executive, and insulated from popular accountability by elections only once every five years with the choice of polling day in the hands of the government.

It could be superseded by a "workers' parliament" based on delegate democracy, right of recall, elections not just of the legislature, but also of the executive, workers' wages for state officials and a massive education programme to empower workers with the same knowledge possessed by their leaders.

# A peaceful road to socialism?

The top leaders of the labour movement look with horror at the notion of trade unions organising their own defence squads or working class communities setting up their own street patrols. They would say that this leads to chaos and violence.

But the miners' strike showed that we already have chaos and violence — only it is chaos and violence in uniform and is directed against us! Leon Trotsky put it like this: "The reformists systematically implant in the minds of the workers the notion that the sacredness of democracy is best guaranteed when the bourgeoisie is armed to the teeth and the workers are unarmed."

## Blind faith

But working class self-defence, and a fight for democratic controls over the existing state machine, are necessary. Otherwise the police will simply ride over us more and more roughshod. It would be good if the present state machine could be gradually, quietly transformed into a system really serving the majority. It would be good if all industrial disputes could be satisfactorily resolved without strikes and conflict. But only blind faith can cling to such pleasant dreams.

All the experience of history tells us that no ruling class ever leaves the stage peacefully, to slink quietly away into its historical grave. A threatened ruling class fights. Look how the Tories fought the miners, and they weren't threatened with losing everything. A ruling class facing the threat of socialist takeover would fight without rules and without scruple.

Yet not only the mainstream reformists like Neil Kinnock — who do not want to replace capitalism with socialism — but also the Communist Party and Militant, preach the dogma that the ruling class can be persuaded to peacefully let the workers overthrow capitalism.

After the experience of the miners' strike anyone who thinks that should think about it a bit more! There can be no peaceful road to socialism!

If the labour movement is going to fight for something more than a softer administration of capitalism, then we must be prepared for violent resistance from the ruling class. The miners' strike is only the latest addition to a mass of historical evidence confirming this conclusion. The miners' strike was a limited challenge to the ruling class. They could have agreed to leave pits open without a disaster to themselves. Yet they met even that limited challenge with brutal force and during the strike Thatcher (in a speech on 12 November ) made it clear that as much extra force would be used as was necessary to win. "We shall introduce measures to give [the police] what they need."

Justice, democracy and moderation fly out of the window when the ruling class feel that important interests are at stake. After the October 1984 Labour Party conference voted to condemn police violence against the miners and for reforms to restrain the police, Police Federation chief Leslie Curtis said that the police might feel unable to serve a future Labour government. In 1974, during the big upsurge of strikes that brought down Edward Heath's government (so former army chief Lord Carver has revealed), "fairly senior officers were ill-advised enough to make suggestions that perhaps, if things got terribly bad, the army would have to do something about it...".

When Tony Benn declared that Labour was seriously going to implement its policy of abolishing the House of Lords, Lord Denning said that the courts should intervene to rule such abolition unconstitutional.

Now, Curtis was slapped down by senior policemen. Carver had told his officers who talked about a military coup — some of whom are probably today at the top of the military hierarchy — that they were "ill-advised". Other judges have deplored Denning's attitudes. So long as the class strug-

## "The same methods as Ireland"

**Tony, you were in the army. Do you think the police have learned any lessons from Ireland?**

Tony: I was In the first regiment that went into Northern Ireland in 1969 and we trained what were then the B Specials in riot control. And the police here now are using the same methods that we trained the B special police in Northern Ireland for.

The only thing missing is the gas masks, and I don't think they're far behind — I bet they're parked at the back in the wagons somewhere.

I don't know about rubber bullets, but they'll certainly bring in tear gas.

In Ireland, kids used to taunt us to fire rubber bullets at them because they hate the Brits. They're brought up to hate the Brits. They've seen what the soldiers do and it's natural they're against them. They have seen them arresting their fathers they have seen them flooding the villages. So kids are bound to turn against the police.

Tony Thewlis, Keresley Colliery, interviewed in *Socialist Organiser*, 7 June 1984. Tony later cracked under the pressure and started scabbing but the truth of what he said about the police still stands.

gle remains low-key, moderates win out within the ruling class. But will they always?

Only blind faith could say yes, especially in view of the recent terrible lesson of Chile. All the people who say that a peaceful road to socialism is possible in Britain (and therefore we should leave the monopoly of violence in the hands of the ruling class) said that Chile proved their point. It had long democratic traditions. Allende would bring about socialism peacefully, in a parliamentary way.

Yet the facts spoke otherwise. As soon as the Chilean ruling class (in collaboration with the CIA) decided that the workers' and peasants' mobilisation encouraged by the Allende government had gone too far, they forgot all about the long democratic traditions and went for a bloody military coup.

After the miners' strike, the labour movement must gear itself up to the fact that we face a violent, ruthless enemy — and there is no umpire standing above the classes.

## LESSONS OF THE STRIKE

# Yes, they should have fought!

A major event like the miners' strike can have the effect of propelling the labour movement and the left forward, as it has politicised many miners and their families. But it can also throw political people backwards depending on what conclusions they draw. A defeated strike is likely to do that. Faint-hearts and quitters are going to say: "They shouldn't have fought" or "They shouldn't have fought in that way".

What lessons has the left learned from the miners' strike? What are its conclusions for the future?

*Tribune* has concluded from the strike that mass picketing is an outdated tactic.

"It is no longer enough to beat manly hewers' chests and expect governments to quake in their boots".

The Communist Party has taken a similar view.

There is a glimmer of truth behind these arguments. Mass picketing was not enough. Mass picketing is very difficult when workers are wary about

## The problem in 1974

Sean Matgamna, editor of *Socialist Organiser*, asked the miners in the meeting to consider why it was after their crushing victory over the Heath government in 1974 they were having to fight Thatcher under such difficult circumstances ten years later.

"The problem was that in 1974 there was nothing effective to replace the Tory government with. The bitter experience of the Wilson/Callaghan government which resulted from the miners' victory brought *Socialist Organiser* into being a part of the fight to take control of the entire labour movement by and for the working class."

Although Britain's workers' movement is tremendously strong, it does not have the politics it needs to make it capable of taking power in society. *Socialist Organiser* fights for the necessary socialist politics in the mass movement, and for the widest unity in action among those who commit themselves to that fight.

*Socialist Organiser*, 14 June, 1984

responding because of the threat of the dole queue, and when thousands of specially-trained police are mounting a big operation against you.

But then the whole strike was difficult. Struggle is difficult when you face a ruthless, entrenched enemy. But there is no substitute for struggle.

Without mass pickets the strike would never have got off the ground. Without mass pickets it would never have got the support it did outside the main coalfields hit by closures. Without mass picketing the government's scab-herding operation would have cracked the strike long before March 1985. Without mass pickets the coke from Orgreave would not have been stopped even for one day — and with more mass pickets steel production might have been seriously brought down.

The difficulties actually made mass pickets more important than before. When workers' confidence is high and solidarity is easy, a few people with a union placard may be enough for an effective picket. When confidence is not so high, the strength of numbers is more important.

The answer is not to scrap mass pickets but to make them better-organised and to supplement them with other activities.

The CP's alternative to mass pickets seems to be an appeal to broad public opinion. Thus, CP industrial organiser Pete Carter sums up the lesson of the strike like this:

"In the present political and economic crisis, even the best organised and most militant sections will face considerable difficulties if they cannot present their demands in terms capable of winning wide support." (*Focus*, 7 March 1985).

Asked about solidarity for the miners (*Focus*, 7 February), George Bolton, chair of the CP and vice-president of the Scottish miners, devoted one column inch to trade union action and collections, two and a half inches to how difficult trade union solidarity is, and six inches to the churches!

"We have had Liberals on our platforms and the SNP, obviously... We recognised the need to approach the churches very early on. We leafletted the General Assembly of the Church of Scotland in June, and we got the response..."

But "broad democratic alliances" of (as they put it) "bishops and brickies" are no answer to the problems of mass picketing. They mean that CPers being ultra-moderate in order to win over their Liberals, SNPers, bishops or Chambers of Commerce thus fail to give a fighting lead to the working class.

The Ravenscraig workers' notion that their survival depended on proving "viability" had been fostered by months of CP-dominated campaigning to get an alliance of Scots of all classes to oppose closure of the works. And for all the leaflets the Scottish NUM put out to Church Assemblies, they did not do a leaflet to the workers of Ravenscraig with the message that Arthur Scargill spelled out in the *Miner* of 30 June:

"Join with us. Do not be misled. Once the pits have been butchered, attention will once again be turned to your own industry, creating more dole queue fodder. And when that day dawns, who will be left to fight together with you?"

The opposite pole to the CP and *Tribune* is the Socialist Workers' Party. The SWP's line throughout the strike was to call for "much more picketing". The cause of the defeat was too few mass pickets.

"Much more picketing?" Up to a point it is hard to disagree. We can always benefit from more militancy and more activity. For sure this message is better than the CP's and *Tribune's*.

But there is something very peculiar in the sight of the SWP standing on the fringes of Britain's most tremendous workers' struggle ever, shouting monotonously, "Not militant enough! Not militant enough!"

The SWP do not get to the roots of the problem about mass picketing and solidarity. The other side of this coin is that the SWP completely missed out on the political issues of the strike.

Issues of democratic control over the police; links between the police operation against the miners and state violence in black communities and in Ireland; civil liberties issues; the four-day week and the economics of human need versus the economics of profit; workers' control versus NCB dictatorship — all these issues through which workers might have been convinced of a link between their concerns and the miners' strike, and the basis could have been laid for broader action, were scarcely mentioned by the SWP. Instead they repeated their message again and again: "Not nearly enough has been done to organise the picketing..."

Firstly, the facts. *Socialist Worker* argued that far fewer miners were involved in picketing than in 1972. But that is probably not true.

It is estimated that in 1972 some 8,000 miners were involved in picketing in the first week and 40,000 altogether.

Various figures give us a rough idea of how many pickets were involved in 1984-5. Over 11,000 miners were arrested. So if one picket in four was arrested, that makes over 40,000 pickets. On 290,000 occasions miners were stopped at police roadblocks (up to September, in England and Wales alone). If each picket was stopped an average of ten times at roadblocks, that makes about 30,000 pickets.

In 1972 there were about 3,000 miners at Saltley and about 1,000 on the other big mass pickets in East Anglia. In 1984-5 there were dozens of pickets of that size.

Overall there were probably at least as many regular pickets in 1984-5 as in 1972. The difference is that in 1984-5 a lot of miners had to picket pits instead of power stations and coke depots; and that in 1984-5 it was much more difficult. The 1972 pickets in East Anglia and at Saltley shut their targets within a few days. The mass pickets in 1984-5 often failed to shut their targets.

More pickets would have helped. And though *Socialist Worker*'s claim that the area NUM leaders were "sabotaging mass picketing" and "more worried about preserving their [union] machine than winning the strike" (*SW*, 21 July) is overstated, doubtless the CP influence among NUM officials did hinder mobilisation.

The *Miner* on 9 May said: "The NUM position is clear: the [steel] plant[s] should tick over, but not produce any steel" — yet NUM area officials allowed massive supplies of coal and coke. Arthur Scargill often seemed to be on his own in appealing for miners to turn out to mass pickets, as at Orgreave. Scotland was notably sluggish about picketing.

But why could sluggish officials get away with it? (The NUM official structure was a lot more conservative in 1972 than in 1984.) Why did officials who were militant picket organisers in 1972 become cautious and sceptical in 1984?

The repeated message, "Be more militant", is not much of an answer to these questions. Doubly so, because the SWP rejects (as "integration into the bureaucracy") any struggle to transform the official structures and replace conservative leaders. *Socialist Worker* lambasted the "militants' mistaken belief that betrayals can be avoided by winning control of the union machine. The reality is very different. Once in office, one-time rank and file leaders become prisoners of the machine they supposedly control" (*SW*, 21 July).

Of course militant rank-and-filers do often become conservative once in union office. Just fighting for an "alternative leadership" is not enough: we need to fight for clear policies and to democratise the whole structure. But the SWP's view replaces any strategy to transform the labour movement by an iron law of bureaucracy. Any organised official leadership will always be conservative; therefore overall political strategy for the labour movement is always empty talk, and all socialists can do is champion rank and file revolts — urge the rank and file to be more militant or (as more often with *SW* these days) complain that it is not militant enough.

Political links with steel and power workers; political arguments about workers' self-defence which could have helped the pickets more effectively to counter the police — these were more useful contributions from socialists than just the cry "More picketing! More picketing! More picketing!"

And they could have helped to make more picketing possible, by getting to the roots of the problems with picketing.

There were problems with mass picketing: but both the CP/*Tribune*, and the SWP got them wrong. The CP/*Tribune* find direct-action militancy inadequate, and look vainly for something else to take its place; the SWP find it inadequate, and stridently and rather peevishly call for more of it. The real job is to unite direct-action militancy with a working class strategy.

We need to build a rank and file movement, uniting workers in different unions round socialist policies, and to commit the labour movement to workers' self-defence.

## Neil Kinnock and Margaret Thatcher

Mrs Thatcher is tough, nasty, brutal, spiteful, single-minded and very hostile to the labour movement — but a good, tough, committed fighter for her own cause and capable of being an inspiring leader for her own side. Mrs Thatcher knows how to lead.

There is no double-talk from Thatcher about the miners' strike. She is out to beat us down and crush the NUM. She leaves her supporters in no doubt about it.

When Thatcher denounced "violence" she doesn't feel obliged to be "impartial" and denounce the police as well as the pickets who stand up to them. She denounces us — she praises, lauds and defends the army of police thugs she sends to beat us down. She knows a bitter class war is being fought — and she knows which side she is on.

The contrast between Thatcher's conduct during the miners' strike and yours, Neil Kinnock, is a devastating one.

You have rightly blamed the Tories for the strike. But your backing for the NUM has been vague and equivocal at best. You have added your voice to the vile chorus of Tory-=orchestrated propaganda against the picketing miners who are, in fact, victims of police thuggery. You denounce us for defending ourselves against the police and for trying to stop the police herding scabs to break our strike.

Whatever your intentions you thereby help Thatcher and MacGregor in their war to beat us down. You boost the Tory propaganda campaign which is designed to stop other workers giving miners the solidarity action that would make such a difference to our strike.

Thatcher is a Tory pig, but I find it impossible to compare Thatcher's performance on her side with yours on ours, without feeling a deep disappointment in you.

One reason why Thatcher knows how to lead is that she does know which side she is on.

From an open letter to Neil Kinnock by Paul Whetton, a delegate to Labour Party conference, September 1984

# Build a rank and file movement!

Students of British labour history will compare 1984-5 with 1926. The comparison will serve up to a point, as long as the aftermath of 1926 is studied soberly and accurately. It was not so unrelievedly black as is sometimes painted. Nor was everything lost when the General Strike failed — militancy continued into 1927. By 1934 trade union membership increased again; in 1936 there were more strikes than in any year since 1920.

The damage, moreover, would have been much less if not for the fact that the most advanced element in the labour movement then — the Communist Party, at that time still a revolutionary party — went on a self-isolating, self-destructive, ultra-left binge after 1928, emerging from it in 1934-5 only to swing towards reformism. What the organised, active, socialist minority does can make a huge difference to the effect of defeats on the whole working class.

In the wake of their victory in 1926, the ruling class strategy was to push through a policy, started years earlier, of splitting the militants and socialists from the rest of the movement, while embracing the trade union leaders and building up their positions against the shop floor.

The anti-union law of the day — the Trade Disputes Act — had as its guiding principle to "demand support of the great mass of public opinion, including moderate trade unionists". Just a few months after the end of the strike, top government ministers were proposing talks with labour movement leaders, using "reliable men" from the TUC and Labour Party.

This conciliatory attitude was also reflected in the press. Yesterday's Bolshevik agitator became today's responsible trade union leader.

Inside the velvet glove was the iron fist. The shop floor worker was on the receiving end. Blacklists, sackings, speed-ups, settling of "old scores" by management were the reality for the workers.

The Tory government could not have pursued their policy without the support of the Labour leadership. Just as these people had rushed to betray the strike so they fell over themselves, too, in their scramble to support the government's policy.

At the 1927 TUC Congress the former 'left winger' George Hicks declared: "We should not be deterred by allegations that in entering into such discussions we are surrendering some essential principle of trade unionism". The "new realists" of the 20s were pushing through their policy of open class collaboration.

The "new realists", in their turn, got away with it because the lessons

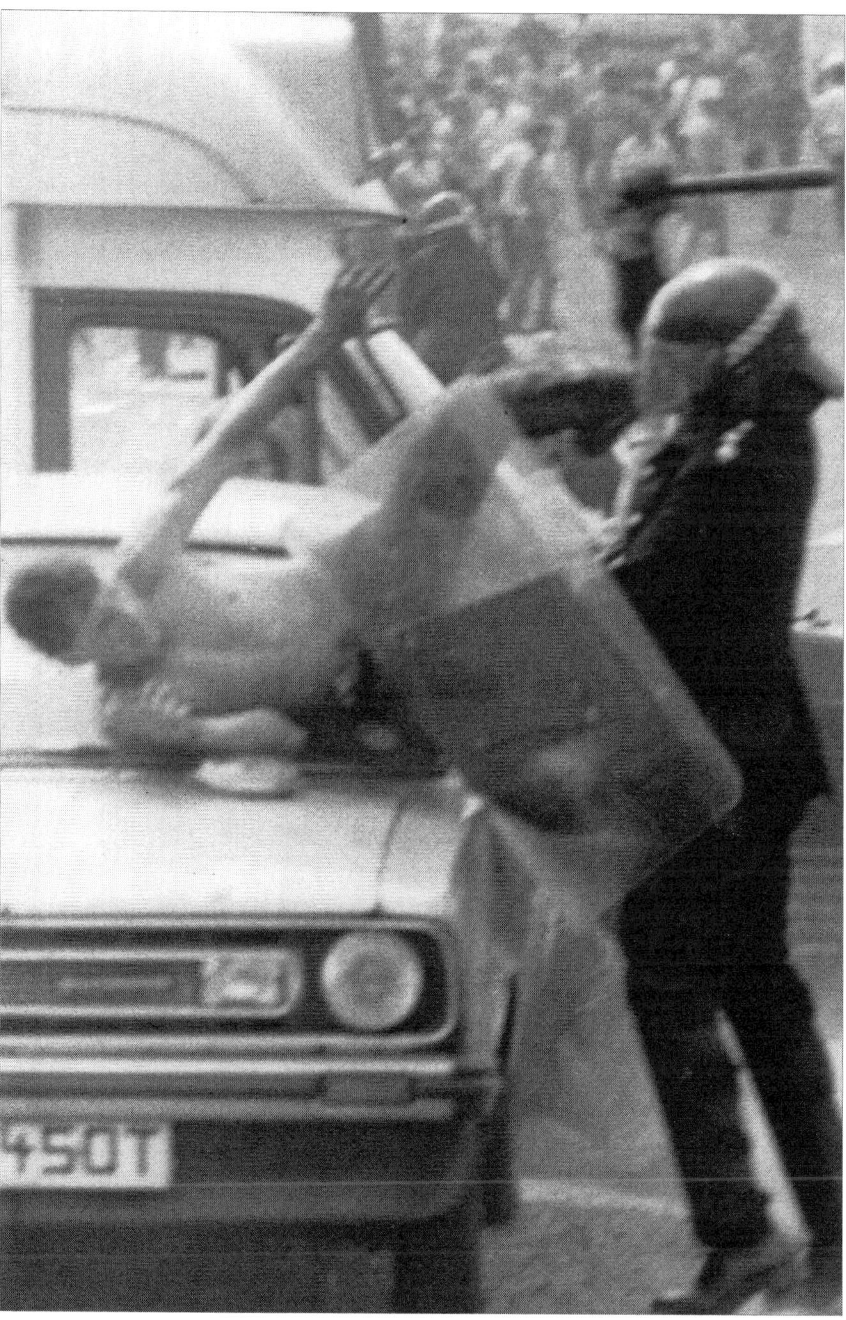

Orgreave coke works. A senior police officer attacking a miner guarding his car. The attempt to prosecute the miner for riot collapsed.

John Harris/reportdigital.co.uk

which many thousands of workers had learnt from the strike were squandered.

The best militants of the day were in the Communist Party. Between 1926 and 1928, derailed by the misguidance of Stalin, the party moved from a rather "soft" attitude to the TUC leaders to one of self-isolation, forming breakaway unions and reserving their most vehement criticism for the most left wing leaders, whom they called social fascists, such as the miners' leader A J Cook (the Arthur Scargill of the 1920s).

So the chance of building a political opposition was lost. The way was

## When TUC general secretary Len Murray announced his retirement

Forget for one moment the miners' strike, the local council elections, Liverpool, even the future of the TUC. There is something far more important: the future of Len Murray. After all, Len has given more than a decade of selfless service leading the trade union movement. For much of that time he's been forced to eke out some existence on a miserable pittance of £30,000. Now is the time for all of us to show our gratitude; now is the time to give Len some real gravy. He should go to the House of Lords.

Lord Len of Warrington? Earl Murray of Cheltenham? They both have a firm ring about them. In fact, we could hold a secret postal ballot to decide what we should call Len, as some will have other, perhaps cruder, suggestions.

But I want to go further. I want to propose that Len should not be created a Lord for life, those are ten a penny, but a Hereditary Peer. This would have tremendous benefits for workers from Lands End to John O'Groats, and far further afield. It would show them that socialist statisticians are damned liars: social mobility is not dead, but even in this day and age the humble scion of the proletariat can still reach the very top.

All workers would feel that little bit better, clocking on at eight on cold mornings, knowing the Shropshire lad, still comfortably in bed, would soon be donning his mink and ermine underwear, hobnobbing with the toffs.

Most important of all, Len's entry into Debrett would show him in his true colours, the bend sinister, with a yellow stripe, crowned with a grovelling cart-horse: the colours for betraying his movement and being a traitor to his class.

*Socialist Organiser*, 10 May, 1984. Len Murray became a life peer in the New Year Honours List of 1985

cleared for the right wing in the labour movement, and thus for the bosses and the Tories. But it was not all inevitable.

1921-2 is an instructive comparison, too.

In those years the British working class suffered defeats probably more serious than the one we have just had. The miners were locked out from 31 March 1921; the rail and transport unions, on "Black Friday", refused to honour their pledges of support; and the miners were forced to accept defeat on 1 July.

The engineers, in those days, were the second central militant section of the union movement. They had created and sustained the shop stewards' movement during World War One. From 11 March to 13 June 1922 they, too, were locked out and defeated. Militants were victimised wholesale. The shop stewards' movement was broken. From 1921 to 1926 TUC membership fell by one million — more than it was ever to fall in the aftermath of 1926.

Yet the movement managed to regroup after those defeats. In 1924 a Miners' Minority Movement was initiated by the Communist Party, and in August 1924 a cross-union National Minority Movement. The first Minority Movement conference had delegates representing 200,000 workers; by March 1926, MM conference delegates represented a total of one million trade unionists (the TUC at the time having only four million affiliates).

The Minority Movement linked together the rank and file, coordinated the battle for militant policies in different unions, and paralleled the fight of the CP for affiliation to the Labour Party. Without its work, the general strike of 1926 would probably never have happened; if it had not been derailed by the conservative Stalinist bureaucracy in Moscow into softness towards the TUC "lefts" (the 1926 equivalents of Buckton and Todd) at the crucial time in 1926, it could even have been the driving force taking that general strike to victory.

During the 1984-5 strike, the miners' leaders, for all their heroism, were hog-tied by the lack of any equivalent of the Minority Movement. They clearly found it difficult to relate to the TUC after they had coaxed the leaders in private and appealed to them in public, what else could they do? They had no mechanism for a campaign to stir up the membership of other unions, to prepare, for example, for a general strike.

This was not just an organisational oversight, but a matter of politics. The Minority Movement would never have emerged without the Communist Party, as its backbone, strategist and coordinator. The modern Communist Party, a sad caricature of the 1920s' CP but the most influential party in the miners' leadership, has abandoned projects like the Minority Movement as a matter of conscious policy. They prefer to work for niches in the bureaucracy.

To build a rank and file movement now we will need a political initiating minority — a group capable of incorporating the lessons of the miners' strike into a coherent socialist strategy. We need to build *Socialist Organiser*. Round that core we can then organise militants as broadly as possible.

Back in July Paul Whetton told a *Socialist Organiser* meeting:

"The fight has got to go on after this dispute is over, and it is vitally important that we get ties between rank and file members, from the pits to the docks to the railways and into the factories... The Triple Alliance fell flat on its face because it had been organised and conducted by full-time officials, and the rank and file did not get involved. I would hope that after this strike is over, we try to organise rank and file members in the pits, docks and factories, and take the arguments about a workers' government and workers' control and all that sort of thing forward".

That is the task now.

## Will you remember?

(for Lisa, Richard and Ross)
What I wonder will your memories be,
And the effect of the strike on you three?
When you look back at your grass roots,
Will you remember your marching boots?
The miles that you walked come rain or shine
To fight for the future that was yours and mine?
Will you remember the songs and the cheers,
Or will you remember the tension and tears?
Will you remember how you played your part,
And how with pride you filled my heart?
Will you remember how I stood on a picket line
And how you had so little of my time?
Will you grow up feeling bitter,
Because you were loft with a babysitter?
Or will you remember with affection and pride,
When mummy stood by daddy's side?
Will you remember how I felt so bad
Because I couldn't give you what others had?
Will you remember as you grow older,
How you cried upon my shoulder?
Or will you remember how we managed to laugh
Wile the Bobbies and Tories thought us daft?
Will you remember how you made me smile,
And made my struggle all the more worthwhile?
But will you remember the principles and traditions I've taught
Or in vain have I fought?

**Ann Burrell**

# Their leadership and ours

The Tories set their plans for the miners' strike as long ago as 1978 (see box on Ridley Plan). They carried out these plans ruthlessly. Some of the preparations — for example, for the police anti-picket operation — had been underway since 1972.

They did the public side of their preparations as well as the behind-the-scenes work. Week after week, from 1979 through to 1984, they banged out a clear, hard-edged message: there was No Alternative to the laws of market economies. More police and more profits were necessary to save Britain from moral and economic decay.

So the Tories prepared well. They had a leadership dedicated to their class.

And us? The top leaders of the labour movement prepared for 1984 by five years of dismal floundering.

In 1979 Labour fought a general election on the uninspiring promise of the same mixture as before.

In 1980, after the steel strike, the TUC quickly abandoned any real notion of mobilising against the Tories. From time to time TUC leaders would bluster about a fight back: they scarcely even bothered to conceal the escape clauses and provisos which made it all empty clamour.

They prepared for the miners' strike by betraying ASLEF (in 1982) and the NGA in 1983. They proclaimed the "new realism" — in other words, their eagerness to surrender to the Tories, if only the Tories would please sign a surrender treaty with them.

Meanwhile, what were the Labour leaders doing? Witch-hunting their left wing. Replying to the Tories' crisp message with vague, unconvincing waffle.

The Tories have just inflicted a serious defeat on the working class. They didn't outfight the heroic miners — they starved them back to work. But they outfought, out-generalled, intimidated and ran rings around the rest of the labour movement. In the miners' strike the Tories gave the British working class movement a bitter lesson in serious class-struggle politics. They will give us other bitter lessons, inflict other avoidable defeats on us, if we don't draw the proper conclusions from this one.

Before the strike many people argued that the young miners — with mortgages, cars, videos — would never fight. In fact, those young miners (the workforce in 1984 was younger than it had ever been before) were the vanguard of the struggle.

The same people will now tell us that the strike proved the working class no longer capable of solidarity. For sure solidarity was inadequate. But why? It was very difficult. Solidarity was possible, but only with a determined leadership that would link other issues to the miners' and show

## The Ridley Report

In an annexe to this report, Mr Ridley and some of his co-authors have been pondering how to counter any "political threat" from those they regard as "the enemies of the next Tory government". They believe that in the first or second year after the Tories' election, there might be a major challenge from a trade union either over a wage claim or over redundancies. They fear it may occur in a "vulnerable industry" such as coal, electricity or the docks and have the support of "the full force of communist disrupters". Behind the scenes, they would like a five-part strategy for countering this threat:

• Return on capital figures should be rigged so that an above-average wage claim can be paid to the "vulnerable" industries

• The eventual battle should be on ground chosen by the Tories, in a field they think could be won (railways, British Leyland, the civil service or steel)

• Every precaution should be taken against a challenge in electricity or gas. Anyway, redundancies in those industries are unlikely to be required. The group believes that the most likely battle ground will be the coal industry.

They would like a Thatcher government to:

a) build up maximum coal stocks, particularly at the power stations;

b) make contingency plans for the import of coal;

c) encourage the recruitment of non union lorry drivers by haulage companies to help move coal where necessary;

d) introduce dual coal/oil firing in all power stations as quickly as possible.

• The group believes that the greatest deterrent to any strike would be to "cut off the money supply to the strikers, and make the union finance them". But strikers in nationalised industries should not be treated differently from strikers in other industries.

• There should be a large, mobile squad of police equipped and prepared to uphold the law against violent picketing. "Good non-union drivers" should be recruited to cross picket lines with police protection.

The Tories' "Ridley report" on strategy, as reported in the *Economist*, 27 May 1978

workers a coherent strategy for class mobilisation for jobs and democratic rights. In fact the leadership was cowardly and had no strategy. The rank and file solidarity, in the circumstances, was heroic.

There has never been a golden age when workers would risk their jobs and wages for solidarity at the drop of a hat, without organisation and leadership. Before 1972, the miners had never had national agreement from rail and transport workers to boycott scab coal except in 1925-6: and in 1926, when the TUC called a general strike to support the miners, it called it off after nine days.

## Solidarity

Solidarity in 1972 and 1974 was stronger than in 1984-5, but it was also easier. For solidarity against the odds, in the face of harassment by the bosses, the action during the 1984-5 strike of Leicestershire and Notts railworkers and of many seafarers and power station workers has few parallels in British labour history.

Far from showing the impossibility of solidarity, the strike showed the tremendous potential — given leadership.

"A leadership which fights for our class like the Tories fight for theirs" — the demand is obvious, but not easy to implement.

Poor leadership does not drop from the sky. And equally an adequate leadership cannot be got just by battles to replace sluggish officials by tougher militants. Many of today's sluggish officials were tough militants in their day; lacking perspectives and strategy, they have been overwhelmed by the day-to-day business of acting as a broker between workers and bosses. And where individuals keep their combativity and dedication, even that is limited as long as they are just individuals.

It is not just a matter of fighting this or that battle harder, but of transforming the whole labour movement — or at least a sizeable enough section of it — so that it operates according to a worked-out strategy against capitalism, rather than reacting blindly.

Industrial battles should be fought according to a strategy: why did we let the Tories batter the steelworkers in 1980, then isolate the miners, and now take on Labour councils and council workers separately too?

Industrial militancy must be tied with a fight on the political front: why did we let the miners' industrial victory in 1974, forcing the Tories into an election which they lost, lead to such a wretched Labour government, with its IMF-ordered cuts and incomes policies?

Both industrial and political militancy must be reinforced with socialist ideas.

## Battle of ideas

Otherwise everything we do will be moulded by the ideas of the ruling class — the ideas which represent capitalist "normality" and are reinforced by the media every day. Throughout its history the British working class has generally let the industrial and political aspects of its struggle run without coordination, and neglected the battle of ideas almost completely. It has reacted, sometimes militantly, to the assaults of capitalism: it has never launched a coherent offensive.

Thus for 14 years — from 1969 (*In Place of Strife*) through to 1983 — the trade unions repeatedly beat back efforts to impose new legal restrictions on them. But they never did more than beat back the attacks. Each time the capitalist class had a chance to regroup and to come back more skilfully next time.

We cannot afford to continue like that. A new approach requires a new leadership, but it also requires more than that: a top-to-bottom transformation of the labour movement, both unions and Labour Party, in its ways of thinking and modes of operation.

And that, in turn, requires an instrument to carry through the transformation: a left wing that is coherent, organised, clear in its ideas but not dogmatic, and able to conduct a coordinated effort on all three fronts, industrial, political and ideological.

That is why *Socialist Organiser* exists and organises.

## Coal imports

Britain imported 9 million tonnes of coal in 1984 to try to beat the strike. Major sources were:

USA ........................................ 3 million tonnes
Australia ........................................ 2 million tonnes
Poland ........................................ 1.5 million tonnes
South Africa ........................................ 0.25 million tonnes

(*Financial Times*, February 2 1985)

# Facts and figures of the strike

## Statistics for scabherding

Bent statistics were a weapon for the Tories and the Coal Board in driving the miners back to work.

As early as 2 July the Tories claimed that 60,000 miners were working. This wild exaggeration probably did them more harm than good. But from August the Coal Board started using figures more carefully and more effectively.

Day after day, the television news would lead with apparently ultra-precise figures from the NCB on returns to work.

The NCB's own auditors refused to confirm these figures, but the media gave no prominence to that fact.

And the NCB was careful. It exaggerated, but it exaggerated within limits. When it said there had been a big return to work, in fact there had been — if not so big as the NCB said. Given the pressure put on the miners by the TUC's failure to deliver solidarity, the NCB figures thus tended to become self-confirming. If they said that there had been a big return to work, then that would help produce a big return to work.

In November, when the NCB was making a big push in North Derbyshire, they boosted their figures by including Bolsover colliery which is geographically in Derbyshire but comes under the Notts NUM.

The July figure of 60,000, it seems, was reached by including not only safety men and apprentices working with the NUM's permission, but also BACM, NACODS and APEX members.

Later figures may also have included safety men and apprentices. Miners on the sick were counted as breaking the strike. The NCB also took no account of miners who returned to work but then came back out on strike.

On top of all this, the NCB's national figures frequently clashed with its area figures. For example, in late February when the NCB was claiming 91,000 miners breaking the strike nationally, its area figures only added up to 78,000.

When all these tricks are taken into account, the NUM and the NCB figures for the strike both give the same broad picture.

The biggest number of strikers was probably on 16 March, when Notts struck briefly and the NCB only claimed 11 pits open. By the end of March the situation had settled down with the majority of Notts scabbing, but some 160,000 miners — over 80% nationally — on strike.

# Facts and figures

| Date published | NUM figures Out | Working | NCB figures Out | Working |
|---|---|---|---|---|
| 9 May | 160,000 | 25,000 | | |
| 31 July | 153,000 | | | |
| 23 August | 147,000 | | 120,000 | 49,000 |
| 13 November | | | 124,000 | 56,000 |
| 17 November | 146,000 | 49,000 | | |
| 19 November | NCB auditors' report shows 51,000 working | | | |
| 24 November | 140,000 | 48,000 | 126,000 | 63,000 |
| 9 January | | | 118,000 | 71,000 |
| 17 January | 140,000 | 56,000 | | |
| 19 January | | | 115,000 | 74,000 |
| 7 February | 138,000 | | | |
| 28 February | 116,000 | 80,000 | 91,500 | 94,500 |

There was a slight increase in strikers after the NUM conference on 19 April, and a slight decrease over the summer. The situation in early May was: Scotland, Yorkshire, North-East, South Wales, Kent: 100% solid. Notts: 12,000 striking, 18,000 working. Lancashire, Staffordshire: great majority on strike, but sizeable scabbing.

Warwickshire: mostly scabbing, but sizeable numbers on strike.

South Derbyshire and Leicestershire: great majority scabbing.

Over the six months May-October, some 14,000 miners went back to work, according to NUM figures, in dribs and drabs. Staffordshire had weakened considerably, Lancashire slightly; the numbers on strike in Notts had declined. But all the major coalfields except Notts were 100% or 99% solid.

A serious breach in the strike opened in November, though returns to work were then very slow in December and the first half of January. NUM figures show some 6,000 going back between mid-November and mid-January.

After mid-January, with the TUC openly abandoning the NUM, the return to work became worse. NUM figures show 24,000 workers lost to the strike between 17 January and 28 February.

Even then, 116,000 miners were still not working — over 70% of those who had come out at the start.

The NCB figures actually confirm this broad pattern. Underneath all the ballyhoo, the NCB's figure for strikers on 28 February was still 76% of their figure for 23 August.

One major element in the apparently huge gaps between NUM and NCB figures for particular dates is that they disagree about how many miners there were altogether, strikers, scabs, and others (off sick, apprentices, etc.).

## The cost

The cost of the strike to the government was the equivalent to the entire housing budget. The total loss of income throughout the economy was equivalent to 5% of industrial production. The extra imports of oil and coal were more than double Britain's car exports.

The cost to the government (up to the end of January) is analysed as follows:

| | |
|---|---|
| Cost in power industry (extra oil, etc.) | £719 million |
| Policing | £189 million |
| Loss of income tax which miners would have otherwise paid | £271 million |
| Social security payments to miners' families | £47 million |
| Cost of lost production in British Steel | £189 million |
| Losses to NCB | £952 million |
| Total of above items | £2,367 million |

Other costs to the government in the form of nationalised industry losses due to the miners' strike but less easily identifiable could be an additional £2,300 million *(Figures from Labour Research)*.

Even if they did agree, each would still have a choice of a number of different totals to give the striking/working figures as a percentage of.

As the table on the previous page shows, a confusing variety of totals were used — from 170,000 (the NCB's figure for the total number of miners), through 182,000 (NUM figure for total number of miners), and 186,000 (NCB figure for total NUM members including coke works, workshops, etc.), to 196,000 (NUM figure for total NUM members). The NCB claims that the difference between its total and the NUM's is accounted for by voluntary redundancies, retirements, deaths and sackings since March 1984.

## 11,000 arrested

Over 11,000 miners were arrested during the strike. Up to 15 February (1 February in Scotland) there had been 11,013 miners arrested.

Something near 1,000 other people — collectors, supporters on pickets, etc. — had also been arrested.

By 12 February, 145 miners had received jail sentences and 25 had been sent to detention centres. Other miners were jailed awaiting trial. These figures cover only England and Wales, not Scotland.

Terry French was sent to Wandsworth Prison for five years for allegedly attacking a policeman. In Derby one miner has been given three years, and eight others two and a half years, for setting fire to an (empty) scab bus; in Stoke-on-Trent four miners have got two years' jail, another two years' youth custody, for the same.

Some 2,600 miners were still awaiting trial as of 12 February (England and Wales, again). Many of these face heavy charges (including conspiracy) on which they could be jailed.

Most of the jail sentences so far handed down have been recent — over two thirds of them since 13 November. The police and civil-court offensive against the miners in the last months of the strike was matched by vindictive criminal courts.

In the earlier period of the strike the police concentrated more on minor charges (obstruction, breach of the peace, etc., on which people can be convicted on the sole evidence of a police officer). In later months, these minor charges dropped to 58% of the total (October-January), as against 79% in March to May.

The minor charges were used to intimidate miners, to drain strike funds through fines, and to impose bail conditions which prevented them from picketing.

2,424 miners got fines (up to 12 February, in England and Wales). Most were large fines: half were £82 or more.

Standard bail conditions imposed on miners stopped them picketing anywhere else than their own pit. Up to September some 1,650 people had received such bail conditions at Mansfield (Notts) magistrates court alone.

Throughout England and Wales, 3,800 miners were on bail conditions by 2 October.

Kent miners' president Malcolm Pitt was jailed in May for defying such bail conditions, even though the charge that he was bailed on drew only a fine.

Up to September (according to police figures for England and Wales), 290,000 miners had been turned back at police roadblocks (some miners, obviously, are counted twice or several times in this total). Figures for Notts show two high points: from 25 April to 25 May (after Easter and the 19 April NUM conference), when an average of 1,500 pickets were stopped each week-day; and from 25 June to 10 August (as the NCB did its first back-to-work drive) an average of 2,200 stopped daily.

(Figures from: *Labour Research*; *New Statesman*; and articles by Nick Blake and Louise Christian in *Policing the Miners' Strike*, ed. Fine and Millar).

# International solidarity

Workers in many countries showed solidarity with the British miners, by trying to stop extra coal exports to Britain or by contributing to collections.

The Polish workers' movement Solidarnosc also sent messages of solidarity, while explaining that because of the martial law it was not in a position to take industrial action. The self-proclaimedly "socialist" government of Poland sent large quantities of coal to help Thatcher defeat the British miners.

*Socialist Organiser* reported: "The slave labour of the Polish miner serves to break the resistance of the British miner. British miners... in the prevailing conditions of terror, the Polish workers' movement is at present not in a position to undertake protest actions. But you may be certain... that we are in solidarity with you."

Silesian miners, some of whose comrades were shot down when they struck in protest against the declaration of martial law in December 1981, broadcast this greeting to British miners over the underground radio in Upper Silesia on 17 June: "The Underground Provisional Co-ordinating Committee of Solidarnosc miners sends you fraternal greetings and full support and solidarity in your struggle for the right to work... we will do everything possible, including in action. The protest we have sent to the Polish government and parliament is an initial measure taken in support of your struggle."

NUM militants must see to it that the union throws its full support behind Solidarnosc and against the bureaucratic dictatorship. The NUM should back the persecuted pioneers of independent labour movements in the USSR and other Stalinist states.

The British labour movement must support other workers against police state oppression wherever it occurs, whether in Chile, South Africa and El Salvador, or in the USSR, Poland and Cuba.

Another message from Solidarnosc read:

> "For four months the British miners have been on strike against a programme of mass closures of mines for economic reasons. The miners are threatened with unemployment. The government has rejected compromise solutions and has resorted to severe police methods against the strikers. Thousands of miners have been arrested; hundreds have been hospitalised and one has been killed.
>
> "The government of the Polish Peoples' Republic, despite hypocritical condemnations of the activities of the British police in the columns of the regime's press, by the regime's pseudo-trade unionists, is profiting from the export of coal to Britain. It sells dirty, cheap coal which has been mined in scandalously neglected working conditions and with reckless

exploitation of the labour force and the coal field. The slave labour of the Polish miner serves to break the resistance of the British miner.

"British miners! The true sentiments of Polish trade unionists towards the authorities of the Polish People's Republic and their practices was shown in the recent electoral farce which was boycotted by the workers. In the prevailing conditions of terror, the Polish workers' movement is at present not in a position to undertake protest actions. But you may be certain that as you have supported and are supporting our struggle, so we are in solidarity with you.

"We strongly oppose every case where force is used against workers struggling for their rights and interests.

"Long live trade union solidarity!"

Resolution of underground Solidarnosc, Mazowsze Region, 26 June, 1984

In the past Arthur Scargill had opposed Solidarnosc (calling it "anti-socialist"), and had maintained links with the state-run official "unions" of countries like Poland. The experience during 1984, however, moved him to declare (on 5 June): "I think I owe Lech Walesa an apology".

In a letter to the Polish ambassador In November, Scargill spelled out his disgust:

"The Jaruzelski government has dramatically increased the amount of coal imported to Britain and has totally ignored repeated requests from the NUM to stop exporting coal into Britain during the period of the miners' strike.

"In doing so, the Polish government is giving direct assistance to Margaret Thatcher's government as it tries to defeat the miners' union.

"The NUM has no intention of even considering the 'offer' to receive 100 striking miners' children for a holiday in Poland because we are aware that at the same time as such an offer is made the actions of the Polish government are directly assisting the Tory government in Britain to do all in its power to smash the NUM and the miners' strike.

"Please convey to your government and trade union movement our absolute disgust and — even at this late stage — convey to them our request to stop all exports of Polish coal either directly or indirectly into Britain".

**Letter from Arthur Scargill to the Polish ambassador in Britain:**
***Socialist Organiser*, 15 November 1984.**

# The way to win

**Editorial from *Socialist Organiser* 173, 4 April 1984**

The miners' strike is a tremendously important mobilisation, the most important working class battle for many years. Although the strike was provoked by the Tories because they thought they could take out the NUM, the government has bitten off more than it can chew. This is a qualitative development in the revival of working class militancy.

Slowly but steadily the forces are building up for a full-scale working-class confrontation with the Tory government. The movement is growing and escalating. Solidarity like that taken by some National Union of Railworkers members will turn the industrial tide for the miners.

How is the government going to react? They will escalate further. MacGregor is now saying that the strike is politically inspired. The government has already used the police in a paramilitary way not seen in Britain until now. Their next step, as the struggle escalates and solidarity bites, may be to send in the troops — something not known in Britain for about a third of a century.

Once again, the miners — despite their divisions — are the shocktroops and standard bearers of the working class. Once more the miners are telling a foul anti-working class Tory government that they can't run things exactly as they like and that the miners are calling them to account. It is the most vital and direct interest of every worker in Britain to stand on the line with the miners and help them win.

The miners' strike must be put at the centre of the work of all socialists. We must put ourselves on a war footing.

## Stop all coal!

Every union must be committed to boycotting all movement of coal not licensed by the NUM — and committed to strike action in defence of any workers victimised for boycotting coal. We should demand that the TUC adopts, advocates and fights for this policy throughout industry.

## For a general strike!

We should argue for railworkers, power workers, gas workers, water workers and others to bring forward and link their claims and strike alongside the miners. We should hit the Tories with a clenched fist.

We should oppose exemptions for steelworkers and argue with steelworkers for a common working class struggle to save jobs in all industries. This is the only way to save steel jobs.

A general strike could stop MacGregor's pit closures plan and rip up the anti-union laws. It can win this struggle. And it can do more. It can make it impossible for the Tories to govern; and the level of mobilisation involved would open up big possibilities beyond that. We should call on the TUC to organise for a general strike.

## Scrap the anti-union laws!

Since the June 1983 election and especially since the September 1983 conference of the TUC, the Tories and the bosses have gone on the offensive over anti-union laws. Though the Coal Board made a tactical decision not to use the anti-union laws because it did not want to unite the miners in response to an attack from the courts, the laws are almost certain to be used later — for example, if all coalfields are out and solid. Then the tactical considerations that have restrained them so far will have disappeared.

## Police out of the coalfields!

The massive, nationally coordinated police operation in the coalfields is a gigantic step in the development of a paramilitary centralised police force. The question of police accountability is therefore now one of the most burning political questions. So is the danger that this militant class struggle Tory government will use troops against the strikes.

We should campaign in the Labour Party for Labour councils to try to deny funds for the police operation and to demand the resignation of the Chief Constables responsible for coordinating the present first stage of police-state Tory operations against striking miners.

## Against a national ballot

As the strike gathers strength it may be that soon a national ballot would produce the necessary 55% majority for a national coal strike. A recent opinion poll amongst miners says that miners are now 60% for strike action. We should still however support the NUM Executive against a national ballot because:

a. it means demobilisation now;

b. The NUM militants are right when they argue that miners in relatively prosperous areas do not have the right to veto the action of miners in areas facing closure;

c. the individual ballot is not the most democratic method (even apart from the 55% rule). Votes at mass meetings immediately after miners have heard and discussed all the issues are far more democratic and responsible.

## Build support committees

We should argue in Labour Parties, Trades Councils, etc., for building miners' support committees which organise collections in workplaces; accommodation and transport for flying pickets; solidarity delegations to physically back the miners on the picket lines against the police. South Wales NUPE has given a vital lead in doing this.

We should argue that Labour councils should offer their facilities (accommodation, communications, etc) to the strikers.

## Argue for a socialist solution!

Against the rundown of coal, steel and rail jobs, we need a socialist alternative to the vandal Toryism of Mrs Thatcher and the inadequate policies of Neil Kinnock.

• We need a sliding scale of hours. Divide available work with no loss of pay.

• We need a workers' plan for the energy industry, transport and steel. Such a plan would have to be a plan for energy, transport and steel throughout Europe. We need to fight for a Socialist United States of Europe.

• We need training and re-training under workers' control.

• We must open the books of the nationalised industries, expose the profits of the money-lenders and suppliers.

• We must nationalise the banks and financial institutions, and the supply industries without compensation.

We need to relaunch and continue the fight to transform the labour movement, to make it capable of creating a Labour government accountable to the movement and committed to such measures — a real workers' government.

## Kick out the Tories! Fight for a Labour government

We can make Britain ungovernable. In 1974 when the miners forced him to "go to the country" — which rejected him — Edward Health also had a big, stable Parliamentary majority. We must bring down this Tory government.

Labour under Kinnock cannot be relied upon to implement the working class policies we need. Nevertheless, the Labour Party is the only conceivable immediate alternative to the Tories. We must fight for a Labour government. At the same time we must fight in the labour movement to commit such a Labour government to anti-capitalist measures. That means continuing the battle in the Labour Party for democracy, accountability and for socialist policies.

Right now the miners' strike is putting the new Labour Party leadership to the test. Neil Kinnock has made sympathetic speeches generally supporting the miners. At the same time he has talked as if the miners are to blame for picket line violence and not the police. The labour movement must demand of Neil Kinnock that he stand on the line four square with the miners without weaseling and without talking out of both sides of his politician's mouth.

Right now the miners' strike is the measure of every grouping and every individual in the labour movement. Neil Kinnock will not be forgiven if he doesn't unequivocally take sides with the miners.

Victory to the miners!

# A miner's appeal to the dockers

**Text of an appeal from Paul Whetton, secretary of the Notts miners' rank and file strike committee (in a personal capacity), distributed at the TGWU docks delegate meeting on 24 September 1984.**

Dear Brothers, your dispute is, like ours, in defence of jobs. You have the sympathy, respect and support of every striking miner.

Everybody knows that the Tory government and the port employers have targeted the National Dock Labour Scheme. Indeed, one government minister has recently said so in public. The first chance they get, they will move to destroy the National Dock Labour Scheme and the job security built into it and maintained and defended for many decades by the struggles and sacrifices of port workers.

We miners know that this is why dockers are not in a mood to give them an inch or to let non-dockers do any dockers' work. You have our complete support.

We also appreciate the solidarity dockers have extended to the striking miners over the last months and are giving us now.

I want to suggest the following points for your consideration. I am secretary of the Notts miners' rank and file strike committee, and it seems to me — speaking in a personal capacity — that miners and dockers are now fighting or getting ready to fight on different fronts of the same war to resist the attacks of this Tory government, the most brutal, insensitive, unashamedly middle-class and vindictively anti-working class government which has ruled Britain since the Second World War.

We face a common enemy and therefore we need to establish the closest links.

Together with other sections of the working class, but if necessary on our own, dockers and miners can beat the government hollow.

The points and suggestions I want to ask you to consider are these.

1. If you decide today to strike, we need to coordinate the action of striking port workers and striking miners.

The best way to do this would be immediately to set up — in areas where that is practicable — action committees. We should also invite railworkers' and seafarers' representatives to join them. Rail and sea solidarity has been a great help to us in our strike.

2. We — militants, shop stewards and branch officials — should agree to argue in our respective industries for an agreement to stick together until we have both won.

3. For miners this means, first and foremost, defeating the pit closure schemes of the Coal Board and the government, and winning a shorter working week.

4. For dockers it should first and foremost mean the fight to stop anyone else doing even the smallest job that is now registered dockers' work.

But in my opinion it should mean more. It should mean a fight to extend the National Dock Labour Scheme to all the important unregistered ports.

As you know, in the last 15 years the pattern of trade has shifted to the disadvantage of ports like Liverpool and the now-closed-down Manchester Ship Canal, to ports like Felixstowe. It is this shift that has convinced the Tories that they can move, now or soon, to scrap the National Dock Labour Scheme.

So it must be one of two things. Either the Dock Labour Scheme will be extended to the ports which are growing and developing. Or the growth of those ports will mean the weakening, and ultimately risk the destruction, of the National Dock Labour Scheme.

If you were to decide to fight to extend the National Dock Labour Scheme now, I'm sure you could count on the active support of the entire community of striking miners, and of course of other workers like the railworkers.

As well as that, portworkers, like miners, and like the whole working class, face the scourge of unemployment, which imposes terrible suffering on our working class communities and undermines trade unionism. May I suggest that you need to fight for a shorter working week, immediately? This is one of the NUM's official negotiating demands in our six-months-old strike (though you'd never know it from the media coverage).

We need a joint fight for a shorter working week.

5. British Steel will try to get coal out of Hunterston. If they do it, it will not only be a blow to the miners, but also to the dockers. What can we do about it?

We can stop them. The best way to do that would be to occupy the port of Hunterston, or the ship itself. It will be far more difficult to stop the coal when they get out of the port area. Here is common activity where miners and dockers can and should immediately coordinate our efforts.

Those are my main proposals. They make seem to some of you "extreme". If they are, they are "extreme" proposals to meet extreme conditions. We miners have been on strike six months. It has been a long and bitter strike. In this industrial climate, the choice workers face is either to fight strikes seriously and all-out, or face defeat.

Isolation and only limited solidarity has made the miners' strike a prolonged and bitter ordeal for miners and their families. We must face the fact that we can't win and defend our basic interests unless we fight the many and varied attacks of this government as seriously as Mrs. Thatcher fights us, and with as much commitment.

United, dockers and miners can massively augment and increase each others' strength. We must unite. Unity will bring us victory.

Thank you, brothers, for your attention.

**Yours sincerely, Paul Whetton, Secretary, Notts miners' rank and file strike committee.**

# Magnificent miners

**Introduction to the 1985 pamphlet**

This was the greatest strike in British working class history. Its scope and duration were unique. It aroused and involved thousands of the women of the mining communities. It made a central challenge to Thatcherism and, implicitly, to capitalism itself. For the demand and rallying cry of the strike, "no 'economic' pit closures" was a demand for a system of society radically different to what we've got now. It implied a social system and an economy whose mainspring is not profit but need. It implied socialism.

The miners didn't win that demand, but their strike has educated tens of thousands of militants — and not only miners and their families — to know and hate capitalism and those who run it.

Of course the defeat of the miners is bound to depress the labour movement. It will not demoralise it. Precisely what effect the defeat of the miners will have on the labour movement is not something mechanically determined and inevitable. It is still being determined — and we can still affect it.

This was a defeat. But it was a defeat after a magnificent battle, the memory of which will inspire and instruct other workers. And workers in other unions have seen what a difference it makes to a union to have a militant fighting leadership.

Should the miners have fought in the unfavourable conditions created by mass unemployment? MacGregor and Thatcher gave them no acceptable alternative. There are far worse things than to fight and lose as the miners did. The passivity with which, after 1979, the labour movement accepted blow after blow from the Tories without fighting back — that is the sort of defeat that demoralises, enervates and destroys.

The business of the miners' strike is far from finished. There are 700 miners still sacked and about 150 still in jail. We must fight to reinstate and release these brothers. Listen to Arthur Scargill:

"Those men who have been arrested and jailed as far as I'm concerned are political prisoners. They've been jailed because they fought for this union and we should all stand up and say straightforward what we mean. Those of our young people and those in the women's support groups who were arrested in the most brutal way have been criminalised by a state that has deployed every possible tactic against the miners' union as they have sought to defend their system against the demand of a union and a movement that sought only the right to work.

"It is a stain that the next Labour government has got to wipe clean. It is a stain that they have got to take on board. And I appeal to all our Parliamentarians and to all those in the trade union movement. When this union talks about amnesty, for God's sake stop the equivocation, we want an amnesty for all our members who've been sacked during the course of this dispute. They have a right to their jobs back."

We must build a powerful campaign for the reinstatement of the sacked miners and the release of the class war prisoners taken by the Tories during the miners' strike. Such a campaign can also help rally the labour movement and counter and offset the depressing effects of the defeat on the labour movement.

There is great scope for such a campaign. There was a notable swing of public sympathy to the miners towards the end. Thatcher figured a victory over the miners would bring her the sort of political boost she got from the Falklands war. It hasn't. Many who had not previously sympathised with the miners came to resent and detest Thatcher's bloody-mindedness and vindictiveness.

An opinion poll showed that most people think that sacked miners should be restored to their jobs.

A campaign for reinstatement of the sacked and release of the jailed miners could develop into a powerful offensive to pillory the Tories for their treatment of the miners. It would be the continuation of the battle of the last year by other means and on other ground. The building of such a campaign is now the number one task facing the labour movement.

The miners' strike was a rich experience of open class struggle such as has not been seen in Britain for a very long time. The labour movement needs to study the events of the miners' strike and discuss and draw out the lessons for the future. It is as a contribution to this essential work that we publish this special double issue of *Socialist Organiser*.

# Class against class

**Foreword to original pamphlet by Paul Whetton, Secretary of the Nottinghamshire Rank and File Strike Committee. Paul died on 3 March 2006, the 21st anniversary of the miners' strike.**

We lost. There were victories, and some degree of victory in defeat at the end of the dispute, but still: we lost. The reasons why we lost are quite obvious. TUC and Labour Party support was not forthcoming, despite the promises made at TUC and Labour Party conferences. Rank and file Labour Party and trade union activists made a very valuable contribution in support work, but we needed the backing of the big battalions, in industrial action and in a political campaign to counter the Tory propaganda — and we didn't get it.

There was no political will to do it within the hierarchy of the TUC. They just didn't want to get involved with grabbing a tiger by the tail. Neither did Neil Kinnock. But, as I say, there were victories.

For example, there are live pits working now that wouldn't be if we hadn't fought. We have shown the will and ability to fight in defence of our jobs and our communities. We've shown that it can be done. The rank and file miners have shown that it can be done.

We've learned valuable lessons, and not just the miners, but women and children too, in the mining communities and support groups up and down the length and breadth of the country. Our fight has made a valuable contribution to the working class.

The end of the miners' strike is not the end of working class resistance to the Tories but the end of the beginning of the resistance.

The working class will build on the traditions we have created over the last year. The miners who have returned to work live to fight another day: the fight goes on. We are going to have to spend some time pulling back, rebuilding — but the basis is there, the skeleton's there and all we've got to do is put the meat back on it.

Ever since I started in the pits, I've been preached at, talked at and argued with about the 1926 strike by people like my grandfather and others who went through it.

We've lived with the 1926 strike. In comparison to the fight that we've just had, 1972 and 1974 were mere skirmishes. It's inevitable that the 1984/5 miners' strike will be talked about for decades too — like 1926.

The mistakes that were made, the lessons that must be learnt will be discussed and analysed over and over again. The basic underlying lesson, the message proclaimed to the Tories and the ruling class is that the working class has got the ability to organise and to fight and we will go on to make a very radical shift in the politics of this country.

Notts was the storm centre of the strike, where the decisive battles to unify the NUM and stop all coal production were fought and, tragically, lost. Right from the start, as soon as we went out on the picket lines, the police told us they were there to see to it that Notts would work normally — at all costs. I'm of the opinion that if it hadn't been for the formation of the Notts Rank and File Strike Committee, the strike in Notts would have crumbled very quickly and we would have had the whole of the Notts coalfield churning out its full quota of coal.

The rank and file strike committee kept the police occupied and away from other areas; kept production down and raised the political debate and the political arguments. That was the valuable contribution that Notts striking miners made. Right from the start, of course, we knew that even with a 100% victory we, in Notts, were going to go back in a minority. Right from the start we dared not contemplate defeat and so we had to look on the positive side. Well, we didn't win the victory that we wanted, but we didn't get smashed and wiped out, either.

Inside the Notts coalfield, one of the problems was that information was not readily available. That was partly a physical thing.

*Socialist Organiser* made a valuable contribution. It printed information and facts, not only from Notts but from other coalfields. Throughout the strike *Socialist Organiser* gave its pages to miners and miners' wives to express their own views and opinions. It advocated policies for the strike and commented on events — but it didn't try to ram it down our throats.

*Socialist Organiser* was responsible for many of the contacts that we made with Yorks miners, Kent miners — who were absolutely amazed early on in the strike when marching into Notts they found Notts miners on strike.

It brought in news about comrades having struggles in other parts of the world and understanding of their particular problems and the way they tackled them. It was a very valuable contribution.

But *Socialist Organiser*'s contribution wasn't just information. It provided political analysis and raised questions in areas and about things that many people would not have thought of questioning. Many young people, many women, and many older miners as well who had never even contemplated any sort of political argument had questions posed. The strike created a thirst for information, a thirst for knowledge and therefore a thirst for political answers. It was the same among the women's groups.

They were able to get in contact with other women's groups and see what their particular problems were and come together.

The paper helped to raise questions about the Labour Party and helped striking miners to understand what to do about it.

Despite our strong criticism of the Labour Party leaders we did not turn away from it and run to some other quarter, leaving the Kinnocks and Hattersleys in undisputed control of the working-class political party.

Many miners turned into the Labour Party to raise the arguments and highlight the issues. And I think it's a very interesting thing that happened, that people in the mining communities didn't turn their backs on the Labour Party although it could be argued that they would be entirely justified in doing so. Instead they turned into the Labour Party and said: we're going to alter it.

How far did the politicisation of striking miners and their families go? Are those lessons going to be held onto after the strike? Mining communities were highly politicised by the strike. We held some very big *Socialist Organiser* meetings at Ollerton. But there's no doubt that a lot of things will begin to fade after the dispute. It's like planting a handful of grain. Not all of them are going to take, not all the ideas, the contacts or the women's groups are going to stay. But many will, and all the issues that were raised and argued about will continue to be argued about. If just a fraction of those politicised in the strike stay in the political fight so that next time round we'll be better prepared on the industrial front to take on the Tories, then that will mean we've made great progress, and we'll be delighted.

Miners must look closely at their experiences in the strike and learn the lesson that we 've just paid so dearly for. We have faced the vile capitalist media and the whole apparatus of the state — the police, the employer and the government, united to beat the miners and grind the NUM into the ground. Don't let that lesson be wasted.

Just because we're back at work and the strike is at an end doesn't mean an end to the fight. You have to continue to battle on. Nothing is going to be achieved overnight, it's going to be a long, hard and sometimes bloody battle, but that battle has got to go on. The dispute is still there about jobs and about communities, and you cannot afford to relax for one moment.

After the 72 and 74 strikes, many mineworkers sat back and thought, we've got it cracked and we don't have to fight any more. They were very much mistaken.

Mineworkers should not repeat the error: stay in the fight — settle accounts with the Labour leaders and the back-stabbing TUC. Help us transform the labour movement so that next time round we have a labour movement — at both the political and trade union level — able to fight on our side as seriously and determinedly as the media, the employers and the police fought on Thatcher's side during the miners' strike.

# AFTERWORD 1992
# The scab Notts miners learn what Tory gratitude is

In Thomas Hardy's novel *Jude the Obscure*, there is a strange, affecting scene, in which the butchering of a hand-raised pig is described. It is told with great sympathy and empathy from the pig's point of view.

Reared close to the family, as was common in nineteen century England, the pig is well-treated, mothered like a pet and fed on tit-bits — all the better to fatten it up so that it could at the right moment be turned into as much pork and bacon as possible. The pig is happy and contented, not knowing his place in the human scheme of things.

Then one day the indignant, bewildered, screaming animal finds himself seized by the men of the household, fettered and hauled up by his hind legs, squealing and kicking air.

It is with relief that the poor, betrayed, very confused pig sees his special human friend, the woman who petted him and favoured him with tit-bits and soft words, approaching in a business-like way, a bucket in one hand and a long shiny thing in the other.

She puts the bucket on the ground, directly under the pig's head, places one hand on his upside-down chin, pressing it down so that the neck is taut in a clean line, then jabs her shiny, sharp-edged knife deep into his neck and cuts his throat. The bucket fills up with the draining life-blood of the pig, to make black pudding for human beings....

For her too, the fattening pig, who thought himself a member of the family, was just so much potential pork, bacon, blood pudding and sausage. The once-contented pig had radically misunderstood his place in the world.

And not only pigs. Consider the story of the Nottinghamshire "working miners", who scabbed on the other miners during the 13 months of the great national coal strike of 1984-5.

A sizeable majority of Nottinghamshire miners did that. Why?

The Nottinghamshire pits were very rich in coal, highly modern, and very

***Socialist Organiser*, 1992. A version of this article was made into a leaflet by Notts NUM in 1992, when Notts pits were set for closure. In October 1992, the Government announced that a further 31 pits would close, with a loss of 30,000 jobs. Three pits of the remaining 13 in Notts were to close in 1992; seven more Notts pits would close between 1993 and 2004.**

productive. The insecurities, which drove other miners to take on the Coal Board and the Thatcher Government, were no concern of theirs. So they thought. That was the real reason why they scabbed. Their dispute with the leaders of the National Union of Mineworkers about "union democracy" was merely a "good reason", the one they could most easily live with. It was a case of: "F you, Jack, I'm alright!"

Their future was secure. So they were told. So they believed. Only a minority of Nottinghamshire miners, led by Paul Whetton, struck work.

The leader of the majority, Roy Lynk, was the Scab-Herder General in Prime Minister Thatcher's war against the miners.

The scabs and their leaders had a vital part to play in the Tory war on the miners. The militarised, often mounted police, broke miners' skulls and terrorised the mining villages; they illegally stopped miners on the public highway to prevent them going on picket-duty. The press, radio and TV denounced the miners for their "violence", and a dozen other alleged faults. Lynk? Scab-Herder Lynk's role was to organise the Nottingham "working miners" to break the strike.

Lynk was an important man. So were they all, the "working miners", all, important men. Then. They were petted and feted by the press. Some of them, no doubt, were given special tit-bits too.

Mrs Thatcher called the striking miners "the enemy within", but Lynk and his friends were part of the national family, at the head of whose table sat the bourgeoisie and their Government.

As the war of attrition wore on, the government, the police, the bludgeoning press combined with deprivation to drive individuals and small groups of miners here and there back to work. For a while the scab and the Scab-Herder were the press-lustred heroes of the British national family, the emblematic, the typical, the characteristic heroes of Mrs Thatcher's brave new dog-eat-dog Britain.

The capitalist press would focus its attention on some poor fellow who went back to work because he — or his family — could no longer take what the capitalists, the press, the police and the politicians were dishing out. The demoralised, desperate, broken man, ratting on his comrades, would be given some glamorising nickname — "Silver Birch" was one — and talked up in the press as a hero.

He did what the media, the TUC leaders and the politicians — leading Labour politicians too — were screaming at him to do. So he was a man of independent mind.

He decided under pressure to give up, abandon the strike and scab on his mates. That proved him to be a man possessing great strength of character. They were all fine, independent, strong men, the scabs, great guys, special people. Prime Minister Thatcher was proud of them.

The "working miners" would be taken care of. Nottinghamshire coal had a future, they could be sure of that! The Tory Nation would not forget.

Having helped the Tory Government defeat the NUM, the Notts scab miners then founded a union of their own, the Union of Democratic Mineworkers.

Seven years passed. Seven years during which, in conditions of general mass unemployment, the majority of British coal mines were shut down.

Once the NUM had been defeated the Government was able to do as it liked. That was the point.

There were 170 collieries in Britain in March 1984. Eight years later, 97 pits had been closed. 25 pits closed in 1985, the year of the NUM's defeat.

Notts pits too. In the six years after 1985, 12 out of the 25 Notts pits were closed down. Even so, there were no compulsory redundancies. Notts miners prospered, secure and earning well. Until 1992.

Then Roy Lynk and his followers were seized with rough hands and made to learn what their real place in the world was.

The pampered, tit-bit fed, pet workers' leader, and his followers, having served their purpose, got no better treatment than Scargill and the defeated NUM miners had had.

The savage ingratitude of it, the treachery, the casual breaking of promises that had been solemnly given when the Government needed strikebreakers — it was all so gross that there was a big public outcry against the proposed pit closures. To no avail.

Thatcher, with the help of the UDM, had already destroyed the miners' power of collective resistance.

The UDM was helpless. So, in terms of effective action, was what was left of the NUM.

Roy Lynk was reduced to staging a one-man stay-down protest, skulking at the bottom of a coal pit due for closure! (NUM people said he wanted to avoid facing his dupes and fellow-scabs of 1984-5, for a while...)

He must have pondered bitterly on the changes seven years had brought.

The Notts scab miners had listened to the press, the politicians and the scab-herders, and sided with the Government against the rest of the miners. They had heard with hostility and contempt, or refused to hear at all, the great socialist truths about the capitalist world we live in, the truths, which the NUM fought for and lived by for 13 heroic, magnificent months in 1984-5.

Workers exist in the eyes of the bourgeoisie and of bourgeois governments to be exploited. The worker's right to a job, and even to life, is subordinated to that fundamental role: workers are profit or potential profit, or else those who own the means of production will not allow them to be workers at all.

Whether the capitalists and their governments pamper workers, or cut their throats — or, as with the UDM miners during the NUM strike, encourage them to cut their own throats — the general principle governing their behaviour is always the same: the workers' place at a given moment in the system designed for exploiting their labour in order to turn a profit for the bourgeoisie.

The tragedy of the Notts "Working Miners" — and of the miners they betrayed — was that they did not know what their place in the bourgeois scheme of things was, until it was too late.

They did not know that there is no such thing as a "national family", but only a society split into classes, in a condition of latent or open class war.

Refusing to recognise the class war and take their proper place in it, rejecting working class solidarity, they played the role of traitors to their own side in the war whose outcome made possible what the bourgeoisie and the Tories eventually did to them.

# No instant replays in the class struggle

In America it is illegal for employers to dismiss workers for trying to organise a trade union.

They dismiss them anyway. They use dismissal to break unionisation drives, and the threat of dismissal to terrorise workers out of even trying them.

Then what about the law? What about the worker's legal right to do what the boss sacks him for doing? That exists, but the worker must go to court to claim it.

According to Martin Walker in the *Guardian*, it takes on average four years to get a case through the legal system. Expensive years. In the struggle for unionisation the employer still has the legal right to go round with a loaded gun and use it; and the workers — if they stick at it long enough, and can pay for lawyers — have the legal right then, maybe, to have a court say that their legal rights had been violated. The judge, even if he or she wants to, cannot recreate the situation in the plant as it was when dismissal took the union organiser out of the situation.

Last week's case of the Tilbury docks shop stewards dismissed during the 1989 strike illustrates the same pattern in Britain.

The dismissal of the stewards was a great, maybe shattering, blow to the dockers' fight. A tribunal now says it was unfair dismissal. But it has happened. The tribunal cannot even force the employer to give the stewards their jobs back.

The consequences of the dismissals have already worked their debilitating effects on the dockers' movement in 1989. Those are irrevocable. The dismissals played their part for the bosses. The dockers were defeated. British tribunals, like the American judge, cannot turn the clock back, even should they want to.

Take an even worse example of the same thing: the battle of Orgreave.

In the summer of 1984 Mrs Thatcher's semi-militarised police fought miners' pickets in one of the major battles of the miners' strike, at Orgreave coke works near Sheffield.

The police, specially trained and equipped, and operating like an army, won (though not completely, at that stage). They won by sheer force.

Much that the police did during the miners' strike was illegal. They still did it. They did everything they needed to do to win, and so did the vast machine of the Government and its allies for making dirty propaganda, whose main stock-in-trade was denunciation of the miners' violence.

And they won. Orgreave was one of the turning points in the miners'

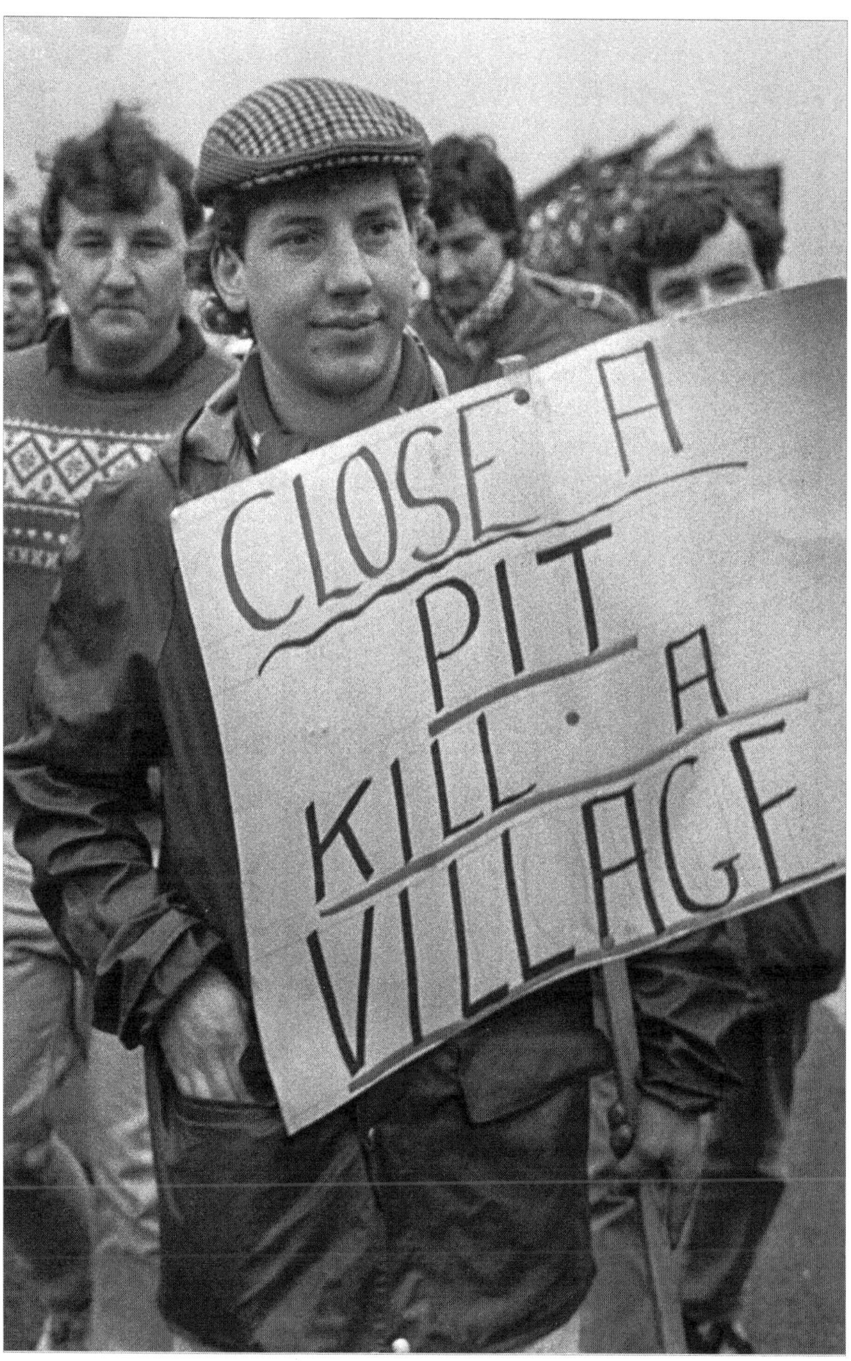


Photo: John Harris/reportdigital.co.uk

strike; the miners' strike was a turning point for the working class. The Tory victory won them seven more years in power (so far), with the opposition beaten or intimidated.

In June this year, 35 miners were paid a total of £500,000 in compensation for damage and injuries they received during the battles at Orgreave. Early in 1985 the cases against some 95 miners charged with offences at Orgreave collapsed, when police notes were found to be forged.

But no, the court cannot order a replay of the Battle of Orgreave. They cannot wipe out the still-continuing consequences of the Tory / police victory. If that were likely to follow from the ruling, the court would have reached a different verdict, or delayed giving one for a further seven years.

Force decided that battle which itself decided so much for the labour movement. The crying pity of it is that we did not manage to mobilise enough force to beat Thatcher's cossacks off the field at Orgreave.

And why didn't we? There were over 10 million trade unionists in Britain then.

We failed because the leaders of the other unions were afraid of breaking the Tory laws! Because they scabbed on the miners. Because they were committed to obeying the law at all costs — no, not the law, they were committed to obeying the police at all costs, even when the police were themselves acting outside the law and contrary to the law.

Their servility would have been wrong even had the police kept within the class law Thatcher had armed them with (and she said openly during the strike that she would pass whatever further laws were necessary to help the police win). In the circumstances it was suicidal for the labour movement.

No-guts Neil Kinnock went around denouncing the miners, not cossack-monger Thatcher and her violent semi-militarised police. He did not comment when the court criticised the police at Orgreave, any more than he commented when a police internal inquiry found the police at fault during the central London poll tax riots in March 1990, which Kinnock had blamed on the poll-tax protesters.

Kinnock was wise to keep silent. Replays are not possible. That is why serious trade unionists will do what they have to do to win in situations like Orgreave or the dockers' strike, and condemn those who counsel slavish — no, Kinnockish — obedience to class law.

*Socialist Organiser* **No. 498, 5 September 1991**

# Could the miners have won?

It is a famous picture, the one of Arthur Scargill being arrested at the "Battle of Orgreave", on 30 May 1984, where miners fought a long battle with troops of police and with police cavalry at a coke depot outside Sheffield. It was one of the turning points of the 1984-5 miners' strike.

What happened in 1984-5? Mrs Thatcher's police thugs beat down the miners with physical violence and they were able to do it because the labour movement left the miners to fight alone.

For the Tories and the police it was no holds barred. They had been planning and organising to beat down the miners since the early 1970s. They had a centralised semi-military police operation all prepared. Margaret Thatcher said, during the strike, that if the police needed any laws changed to enable them to beat the miners, then changed they would be.

As the police smashed into picket lines and became an army of occupation in many pit villages, it was, once again, the situation depicted back in 1848 in the famous *Punch* cartoon in which a government "Special Constable" tells a labour movement Chartist: "If you kill me, it's murder. If I kill you, it's nothing."

In 1984, the miners had either to fight in the unfavourable conditions they found themselves in, or let the Tories win a crushing victory over them peacefully. The Tory class warriors controlled the British state, and used it with grim resolve to make war on the labour movement.

All the patronising "sympathy" now — some of it, the *Sun*'s, for example, half-gleeful — cannot undo the effects for the last eight years of the Tory victory over the miners — communities devastated and ruined; jobs lost; and the labour movement, which had played an immense role for many decades in "civilising" British capitalism, marginalised.

There is no substitute for victory! There are no replays in the class struggle! Those who lose suffer the consequences.

Could we have beaten the Tories in 1984?

Yes, we could! Despite all the police preparations and all the Tories' determination they could have been beaten and overwhelmed in 1984 as they had been in 1972 and 1974. It could have been more difficult but it could have been done.

What, in 1984-5, would have made the difference between defeat and victory? Solidarity! General labour movement action! The leaders of the TUC and the Labour Party could, had they backed the miners instead of openly and covertly undercutting them, have rallied the industrial and other support necessary. But they are what they are — tame trade union officials and second-string Westminster politicians. That being so, only an organised network of revolutionary militants in the trade unions, trades councils and Labour Parties, pursing a common strategy, could have rallied the labour movement to a common battle together with the miners.

That was what was missing in 1984. That was what the miners needed in 1984 and no trade union alone, however heroic, could provide it.

Serious working-class politics demands, centrally, the integration and coordination of the different fronts of the class struggle — trade unions, politics, and the fight against the ideas and propaganda of the ruling class — into a coherent strategy against the common capitalist enemy, with an organised force to push through that strategy. Given the character of the entrenched leaders of the labour movement, trade unions and Labour Party alike, only an organised network of socialists can achieve this, and such a network has to be built up over years, in advance of such big confrontations as the miners' strike.

Such a network did not exist. Just as the organisations of the broad labour movement were split up into unions acting at cross purposes, refusing to synchronise their efforts, and sometimes acting against each other, and a Labour Party whose official leaders served as auxiliaries of the Tories, denouncing the "violence" of the miners in chorus with the *Sun* and Mrs Thatcher — so too is the left divided. The reasons are different, but the effect is the same.

The left is broken up into a plethora of groups, factions, and coteries, with nothing like a common strategy. It took the SWP, the biggest revolutionary group — immobilised by a deep pessimism and defeatism about a downturn in the class struggle — some six months to even being to engage in miners' support work. Never in 13 months, not until eight years later in fact, did they get round to advocating general labour movement strike action to stop the miners being ground down.

And in the conditions of 1992 it was a joke demand, called to "catch a mood" and win recruits.

They abstained on principle from activity in the trade unions' political wing, the Labour Party, though the rank and file of the Labour Party were usually active supporters of the miners, despising their own leaders.

Militant, which in 1984 controlled the local Labour Party and the council in Liverpool, and might have brought the city of Liverpool into a common struggle with the means to defeat the Tories, chose instead to do a stupid short-term deal with the Tories. The miners beaten, the Tories came back and carved up Liverpool a year later. Then Kinnock inside the Labour Party finished the job on Militant.

Many other examples could be cited. The revival of the labour movement, which has been semi-dormant since the miners' strike, shows how urgent now is the creation of an adequate network of revolutionary socialists, active in both the trade unions and the Labour Party.

The class struggle does not end. It goes on. If the working class is quelled it rises again. The class struggle is the pulse of social life under capitalism. The job of socialists is to learn from the class struggle and from history and to prepare and organise the workers' side so that we can win the major class struggle confrontations like the miners' strike.

The Alliance for Workers' Liberty, an independent revolutionary socialist organisation, exists to do this work. It groups together and coordinates trade union and Labour Party activists to fight the class struggle and works to win support for socialist politics by combatting bourgeois ideas in the labour movement. It works to overcome the chaos and disorder on the would-be revolutionary left.

That chaos is rooted in the long chain of defeats suffered by revolutionary socialism at the hands of the Stalinists and the bourgeoisie. The conditions which have reduced the would-be revolutionary movement to an archipelago of often irrational sects are only now beginning to lift.

Against the sectarians with their airtight undemocratic organisations, the Alliance for Workers' Liberty counterposes open, rational discussion, combined with proposals for practical cooperation and coordination in the class struggle — unity in action, dialogue about our differences, and recognition of the fact that revolutionary socialism in the tradition of Marx, Engels, Lenin, Trotsky and Luxemburg must be recomposed, re-elaborated and redefined for the conditions in which we live now.

***Socialist Organiser* No. 543, September 1992**

# The war we could have won

Exactly five years ago the miners' strike ground to an exhausted end after twelve bitter and glorious months.

They were glorious months, because during them the miners and their families showed again the mind and spirit that first made the labour movement.

All the courage, determination, far-sightedness and individual self-sacrifice which animated the pioneers who made a great self-bettering labour movement out of suffering and downtrodden masses of workers was shown to be still alive in the mining communities — and in great abundance. The year-long strike was like an encapsulated history of the labour movement of the previous 150 years.

The miners challenged the whole dog-eat-dog philosophy of the Tories, and put up against it a broadly socialist philosophy which rejected the rule of the profit motive in the pits, and proclaimed that people must come before profits.

In response they were hit with everything the ruling class needed to hit them with in order to beat them down.

When miners' leader Arthur Scargill said that the coal bosses planned to close half the pits in Britain — as they have since done – he was called a liar and a scaremongering agitator. The Tory government then organised a nationally controlled and coordinated army of militarised police thugs and unleashed them on the miners.

Often the police ignored the rule of law in their efforts to stop miner pickets and their supporters moving about the country. They illegally stopped people exercising their right as citizens to travel. Margaret Thatcher commented that if the law was not sufficient to cover what the police were doing, well then, the government would make new laws — as many new laws as were necessary — to win the class struggle.

Police thugs acted like armies of occupation in some of the Nottinghamshire mining villages.

The miners fought back, the women and young people with the men, in a series of pitched battles — battles like that at Orgreave, where miners were beaten down by a powerful force of highly-trained state thugs armed with the most uptodate equipment.

The glorious miners and their families held out against the harassment and violence of the state, defying all the screaming, hate mongering venom of the opinion formers in the media, whose chief stock in trade was to denounce the "violence" of the miner victims of the massive state violence, which had been planned and prepared years before.

That outcry against miners' violence alienated a lot of potential sympathy and support for the miners. It was one of the biggest frame-ups in British history.

They were 12 bitter months, too, and not only because of the suffering and hardship of the miners and their families. They bore all that without whingeing, in the hope of winning things they considered important.

The real bitterness of those months lies in this — that the miners could have won, and didn't. The working class could have won, and didn't. We could have beaten the Tories, but instead they beat us, and the Tories still rule Britain.

To do what could have been done, the miners needed the active support of other workers. We needed a labour movement led by people possessed of the normal human feeling of pride in themselves and in the movement they led, the feeling of responsibility towards it combined with the elementary courage to defend the movement and themselves.

But our movement was led by people who acted as if they had none of those things. The trade union leaders left the miners in the lurch. Some of them plainly wanted Arthur Scargill to get a beating far more than they wanted Thatcher to be beaten.

Where solidarity was needed, they gave sage advice to the union about "moderation" and "nonviolence".

When the striking miners fought for the right to picket out scabs and defended themselves against Thatcher's semi-militarised police sent to stop them, other union leaders joined in the media's condemnation of "violence" that is, the miners' violence...

The leaders of the Labour Party did that too. The miners defending themselves were condemned; the police violence was accepted as "normal" and proper by those who had just led Labour to defeat in the 1983 general election.

When the miners' strike started, Thatcher had had almost five years in office, using the state power as a weapon in the class war to grind down the labour movernent. The labour movement had had five years of slow cumulative retreat, which added up to a defeat.

Yet the leaders of the labour movement — trade union leaders, Labour Party leaders, and the Labour leaders of local councils — could have taken on and beaten the Tories in 1980 and 81, before the great mass unemployment sapped the confidence, strength, will, and fighting spirit of the labour movement.

They didn't, and the Tory juggernaut rolled over the labour movement, shackling the trade unions, beginning to dismantle the welfare state, undoing the achievements of the 1945-51 Labour government.

The miners' strike came late in the day, when the feeling of defeat had already eaten into the labour movement. But not too late.

If the trade union and Labour leaders had wanted to fight the Tories — if they had faced the Tories with a fraction of that class-war spirit with which the Tories faced us — then the miners' strike could have been the occasion for a great rallying of the forces of organised labour.

They didn't want to fight. The miners were left isolated, abandoned to a slow war of attrition which dragged on through the winter of 1984-85 until, finally, the miners went back to work.

In some places they marched back led by bands behind banners, proud and inwardly undefeated.

But it was a defeat nonetheless, an awful defeat, and all the more awful and terrible because it need not have happened like that.

Thatcher and Coal Board boss Ian MacGregor won. And they behaved like victors in a counter-revolution always do: like pigs. Many hundreds of miners were victimised.

Long-established trade union rights were ripped up. A vast programme of pit closures was commenced: in the last five years, more than half the pits in Britain have been closed.

It would be easy after such a defeat, followed by such catastrophic consequences, to find reasons to say the whole thing was a mistake, that Arthur Scargill and the other miners' leaders should have avoided open all out war with Thatcher and MacGregor. But the miners were not wrong to fight. Their defeat was not inevitable.

They were right in their guiding instinct that the Tories had either to be confronted head on and beaten, or else allowed to get on with their programme of making Britain a better place for the rich and a hell for the poor and vulnerable. The miners did not just fight for the miners: their challenge to Thatcher was not just about the running of the mines, but also about the running of the country. We all lost a great deal that day five years ago when the miners were forced back to work.

No, the miners weren't wrong to fight — the rest of the movement was wrong not to make sure they won.

Karl Marx — writing about a far bigger event, the seizure of power by the working class in Paris in 1871 (the Paris Commune) — also answered our own wiseacres who let the miners be defeated without doing anything to help them and then crowed that the defeat proved that they could not have won and should not have fought.

"World history would indeed be very easy to make if the struggle were taken up only on condition that the prospects were unmistakebly favourable". (Letter to Kugelman, April 1871).

**_Socialist Organiser_ No. 436, 1 March 1990**

# The battle for Orgreave

## By Rob Dawber

**In May and June 1984 the miners' mass pickets outside the Orgreave coking plant were attacked by riot police. One of the miners, Bernard Jackson, wrote a book, *The Battle for Orgreave*, to tell the story of the picket. Jackson was one of 15 miners charged with riot (an offence which carries a maximum sentence of life imprisonment).**

**This review of the book was written by Rob Dawber, a long-time member of Workers' Liberty. Rob died in 2001 from mesothelioma, a form of cancer which he developed through exposure to asbestos in his job as a track worker. During the miners' strike Rob — who was born into a mining family – fought to stop the movement of coal by rail.**

Bernard Jackson was one of the first group of miners to stand trial on the, charge of riot at Orgreave. The charge carries a possible life sentence.

"The Battle for Orgreave" is his account of what led up to that day — 18 June 1984 — and the trial a year later.

During that trial the prosecution's case was exposed as such blatant lying that it was abandoned after 48 days.

What I liked best about Bernard Jackson's book is the way in which many of the lessons to be learned from the strike crop up as part of the narrative rather than as part of a lecture to the reader about the nature of the state, of justice, etc. It is refreshing to see much of what we understand as Marxism expressed in everyday working class language.

Bernard Jackson begins with the prosecution's address on the opening day of the trial: "Members of the Jury, the objects I have around me here — this axe, ball bearings, nails, a wooden mallet, this metal bar..." The Prosecutor went on to paint a picture of a beleaguered and battered, but patient and constrained police force facing thousands of miners intent on doing as much damage and violence as possible: "They tore down walls and lamp posts, fences and paving stones. Spears and Molotov cocktails and nail obstacles were used..."

It was all the police could do to try to stop their lines being broken to clear the field at the top side of the plant.

Jackson comments bitterly:

"At the age of 43 I became a rioter — overnight. A bully boy, a thug, a mindless hooligan and an enemy of my own country. I wasn't really aware of the change, in fact I thought I was quite happy as a craftsman miner, as President of Wath NUM and as a governor of two schools with a fourteen year old boy to bring up."

Bernard then goes on to tell something of the strike itself, of picketing at Orgreave and the events of that day, his time in prison, and the restrictions of his bail conditions, designed to keep him from actively participating in the strike.

"The strike was three weeks old in parts of South Yorkshire before it became a national dispute. Management had tried to force changes in meal-break times in the pits that make up the Manvers complex, of which Wath is a part so as to get round the overtime ban. When they tried to implement it at Manvers the men walked out and Wath (whose coal comes out at Manvers) were sent home without pay.

"They went for support to the Panels (made up of delegates from each pit in the area) and to the pits themselves. Support was mixed with some ready to go and others hesitant.

Notably at Cortonwood the branch secretary threw them out of the canteen to stop them talking to the men! I was told many a time at Wath: 'Cortonwood didn't start this strike — but don't print it just yet. It'll all come out after.'

"Then when the NCB announced the closure of Cortonwood, which had promised nine years of life a few months earlier, no one had any doubts about the scale of pit closures threatened.

"Picketing was successful at first. At Creswell in Derbyshire they came out to a man and other teams of pickets had similar results. That was peaceful picketing. There's over a thousand men at Creswell and they were all out, persuaded not by intimidation and violence but by a twenty man picket. But once out they were subjected to the right-wing undermining of their own leadership and gradually drifted back. So we went back and explained the case again and out they came again."

So the police put a stop to it.

"No one will ever know how many police were drafted into the Coalfields but the official figure is about fourteen thousand. If anyone has ever had any doubt about the real role of the police the fact that, at the drop of a hat, so many could be removed from their normal duties should have answered them.

"Fourteen thousand police taken away from preventing crime and detecting criminals. A striking miner was considered a greater threat to the state than the most ruthless villain. But whose state."

Picketing became better organised to get round the police roadblocks. The police became more and more vicious.

"The nastiest incident I recall was at Creswell and it will live with me for a long time. Police lifted a very slightly built young lad and searched him. They found what little money he had on him and tore the notes up in front of his face, the small change was flung away into the fields. They then set about him.

"An oldish lady immediately came running out of a nearby house shouting at the top of her voice: 'Leave him alone, he's done nowt.' She had her hand inside her coat and was holding something which looked like a camera. There was no hesitation. She received a fist straight in the face and went flying backwards over a privet hedge. What she had tried to make look like a camera was a tin of food. She picked herself up and with tears rolling down her face ran back indoors."

On the day of the "riot" itself Bernard was with a small group who stood by a wall as the police charged forward in a three stage manoeuvre to clear the field and force all the miners over a narrow bridge.

Bernard was smashed in the face with a riot shield and then dragged by the neck back through police lines. They lashed out as he passed through. A friend was brought in with whom Bernard had been chatting, drinking lemonade and eating biscuits a few minutes earlier. "Now he was bleeding, bruised and in obvious pain."

Apart from the pain his overwhelming feeling was anger. At the media, at the state and also "anger at the men who should have been supporting us, the Kinnocks and Willises, pompously condemning picket line violence when they had never been on or near a picket line, when openly and arrogantly the state was intent on smashing working class organisations. How dare they pretend to represent, to speak for the working class. History will judge them and it will not forgive easily."

After a long and frustrating wait in police cells Bernard Jackson was remanded to Armley Jail for one week for terrifying Her Majesty's subjects — charged with riot — and breaking his bail conditions of an earlier arrest. The fact that his bail conditions did not bar him from Orgreave, which was British Steel Corporation property, was not considered relevant.

He describes the experience of jail, the treatment by the warders, the lousy food, the cold. The only people who showed any warmth on learning he was a miner were the other inmates. "It reminded me of a demonstration which had taken place outside Leicester Police Station when some of the first miners were locked up. The union area leadership asked us to stop the demonstration because of a warning they'd received that the blokes inside would be victimised by the other inmates. I found it hard to believe because the men in Armley made it clear to me that if I wanted them to 'rag-up' they would do so. It would have involved stamping, shouting and banging their mugs on the walls of their cells as a form of protest — about the only form of protest they have."

He describes the desolation, after a visit from a friend: "Although the visit itself was distressing the feeling of emptiness and solitude following it was even more so. I went back to my cell and wrote to Sue, to say the things I couldn't say in the artificial surroundings of a prison visiting room. I wrote to the lads at Wath to maintain my involvement because a realisation had dawned on me — the thing I missed most, after my family, was picketing. I was now a non-combattant. I had been removed from the fight. "

And Bernard says he learnt a few things: "I'd never met many black or Asian people before, but there were plenty of them in Armley, and they were at the bottom of the pecking order, particularly for the screws. I found them as friendly and supportive as the other men in there, and the question of prejudice took on a new perspective for me.

"The problem faced by black people, inside and outside prison, is one of class not race. The struggle against racism and the struggle for socialism are one and the same — of that I'm now convinced.

"And these are the people for whom the government is set on providing more and more prisons. As their policies increasingly produce a society of haves and have-nots, a way has to be found to control the have-nots. It is the prison which does it. For the first time in my life I saw with utter clarity the true role of prisons — they are class institutions."

Out of prison Bernard was free except for the fact that he had to report to the local police station every day before 11am, stay at home between 10pm and 8am and not set foot on NCB, BSC, British Rail or Dock Board premises.

Free?

"What these stringent conditions also meant was that I couldn't go away or take Mark on holiday, even for a weekend. We had to sit in Wombwell and watch the glorious summer slip away, not even sure that it might be the last one I would see for a few years as a free man."

He was only allowed to visit his own pit. He picketed there one night because of false reports that scabs were to be brought in. The police, however, gave everyone they could find another beating before arrest.

In the van the police had great fun:

"Then they started on me: 'Look at this old fucker. I bet your kids aren't getting nowt for Christmas. Bet you'd like £18 an hour, wouldn't you. They pulled my hair and every time I turned to look at the number of the copper next to me, the arresting oficer, I received a gloved finger in the eye, covered in coal dust.

"We were taken from there to another van: 'Don't sit on the seats, you bastards. On the floor, like dogs. That's where you belong.' The one who had arrested me rolled up his trouser leg and looked at a graze on his shin. I thought to myself 'You didn't miss that bloody tree but I'm going to cop for that one'. And I did. But I'd learnt the rules and throughout all this I said nothing.

He was released the next day and later found not guilty of obstructing the highway, assaulting a police officer and criminal damage.

Eventually the trial for riot began, three months after the miners had returned to work. And the prosecution made its case of general stories about stoning, missiles, mayhem but very little specifics relating to each defendant.

Bernard makes the point that the police had their own paid photographers present on that and every day while for their evidence the defence had to scour the country to find people who had cameras with them.

Not one photograph could be found of an injured policeman while those of police violence and injured miners were everywhere, showing the police to be liars.

Much of this wasn't shown as the trial was abandoned too soon.

What is also striking is the way the police and prosecuting barristers conducted themselves with pomp and self-importance as guardians of civilised society against "rioters" and even when shown to be lying through their teeth the mask doesn't slip.

What also emerged in the trial was the existence of the hitherto secret police manual on how precisely to incapacitate "rioters", none of this subject to public scrutiny, and the fact that statements of "arresting officers" had been dictated to them by CID officers.

There was little evidence against each of the individual defendants.

Their arresting officers (they had decided to have two for each to make them look more believable) contradicted each other, and as the charge of riot began to look more and more ludicrous the whole thing collapsed.

"Bryan Moreland, his life and health shattered. Arthur Critchlow, two weeks in prison and a further two weeks in hospital having fluid drained from his head in a most painful way through the base of his spine. Bill Greenaway, the oldest one amongst us and a man who would be honoured by any civilised society. One look at his hands is enough to tell you how he spent his life — in hard, honest labour, not as a criminal. His reward? A broken wrist and criminalisation!

"David Bell, barely twenty, but clear in his mind that if his job goes in Scotland he's on the scrap heap. These and all the others who had been beaten and abused listened to Mr Walsh in his affected accent announce that he had taken instructions.

"Had he taken instructions in how to say 'Hair we gew, hair we gew, hair we gew'? When he first said that in court I had visions of a thousand miners singing it the way he spoke. I nearly laughed out loud. But then his interests and ours were not and never will be the same. No, he had taken instructions and although the evidence was strong he asked for a verdict of not guilty to be returned."

And all of these, along with the rest of the 150 who followed and had their cases dismissed, had to suffer imprisonment, bail conditions, arrests and beatings and the anguish of a long wait with a possible life sentence at the end before being found not guilty.

Tony Wardle, at the beginning of the book, makes the point that trial by jury is a major civil liberty in this country, and one that is being seriously eroded by stealth. He ways we should defend it and the Orgreave trial shows why.

At the end he asks why the charges were brought against the Orgreave miners and who was responsible for it — noting Thatcher's statements and Home Secretary Leon Brittan's call for life sentences for riot. And how is it that not a single police officer has been charged or disciplined for acts of violence at Orgreave?

And how is it that police tactics, training and decision making for riot squads has been proceeding on a basis that is unlawful?

We know why, and we know that the capitalist state is run for the capitalists, but that doesn't mean we should ignore and not take up these issues.

***Socialist Organiser*, 24 July 1986**

# The miners and solidarity

**Clive Bradley tells the story of Lesbians and Gays Support the Miners.**

LGSM was a group that was set up of lesbians and gay men set up to support the miners' strike. It was initially mainly gay men, but more and more women got involved over the time. Practically it raised money for the miners who were on strike for a year. Mainly by standing outside lesbian and gay pubs rattling buckets, it raised quite a lot of money. This was sent to a particular mining community in south Wales, in the Dulais valley, with which connections had been made.

It was the idea of two people in particular, Mark Ashton and Mike Jackson. Both are dramatised in the movie Pride (September 2014). They put out a call at Pride in '84 and organised a meeting at "Gay's the Word" bookshop in London. At that time I was just moving to London from Manchester and was a member of Socialist Organiser [forerunner of the AWL]. It's not rocket science to see how I got involved.

I went to the second ever meeting of LGSM. I was active in supporting the miners and thought it was a brilliant initiative. It proved to have a very powerful effect on lesbian and gay men and on the miners. The NUM went on to lead the Pride demonstration in August 1985. The NUM, a traditional union, not famous for its view on matters such as lesbian and gay rights, became quite prominent in the changing policy on gay rights in the Labour Party.

The strike divided the country, divided everybody. A lot of people supported the miners and didn't need to be persuaded, but we argued that we needed the miners to win. If the miners lost then the Tory government would be going for everybody, and these lesbian and gay communities would be an easy target. People would put a lot of money into the bucket to show solidarity — presumably a lot of money they didn't have in many cases. LGSM was the first really concrete example of how an "autonomous" movement of the "specially oppressed" (as we used to say) could struggle alongside the organised working class, and transform working-class consciousness in the process.

Some members of different left groups were personally involved, even members of Militant [forerunner of the Socialist Party] and the SWP, whose organisations were more hostile to the project. Militant , for example, generally argued that any kind of autonomous organisation was necessarily divisive. LGSM and Women Against Pit Closures, etc. showed that quite the reverse was true.

I went to South Wales twice, the second time when the strike was actually finishing in March '85. That was very emotional for all of us. My own experience was that people couldn't really have been more welcoming.

The first time we went down, there was a minibus load of us, we were being put up in people's houses, that was the deal. We all went down to the miners' welfare in the evening to sing songs and get drunk. It was completely fine, no hostility at all.

The reality was we were raising money for them. The miners needed solidarity, and I'm sure if people were at first dubious about where the solidarity came from, need overcame that. And, of course, as you make contact with people you realise that you have more in common than you initially thought. Why the suspicions broke down, as I'm sure there were some, is no mystery. It was the nature of people meeting each other and the power of solidarity.

For many people it was their first time going to that sort of working-class community, though certainly not for everyone. We were a mixed group and certainly there were people from working-class backgrounds, it was not all middle class lefties. The vast majority were just people who wanted to do something.

When you have a big confrontation between a section of the working class and the government you have to take sides, more than just in your head.

There have been reunions [of LGSM] recently and many people still seem to hold broadly the same views that they used to. You can tell for many people in LGSM it was an absolutely formative experience in their lives, and very important to them.

The miners were beaten and most of them lost their jobs. Generally speaking in the class struggle, the defeat of the miners had a hugely bad effect. We're still living with the consequences of it.

I doubt miners' attitudes rolled back too much with regards lesbian and gay rights. You started to get stories of miners coming out. At reunions we get visits from miners. We often hear "it turns out my son is gay".

In the lesbian and gay community, struggle wasn't rolled back. You got growth of the lesbian and gay movement after 1985. Not long after was "Section 28" [the Tory law which prevented the "promotion of homosexual lifestyles"] against which you had enormous demonstrations. The Pride parades in the early '80s were relatively small, but by the late '80s and certainly the early '90s they were enormous.

*Solidarity*, **10 September 2014**

# APPENDIX: THE NUM, STALINISM, AND SOLIDARNOSC

## The special problem of Stalinism during the miners' strike

There was a terrible paradox, an outright absurdity, in the miners' challenge to Thatcher and Thatcherism. The NUM and its leader, Arthur Scargill openly supported the suppression of the Polish free trade union, Solidarnosc, the only legal free trade union in any Stalinist state. Founded during mass strikes involving ten million workers in August 1980, Solidarnosc was banned in December 1981.

The NUM maintained fraternal links with the official Stalinist police state "unions"; so did many other trade unions, and the TUC itself. Unlike Scargill, they did not support the suppression of Solidarnosc. The Russian and East European legal "unions" were the Stalinist version of what the German fascists in power had called "labour fronts" — organisations whose purpose was to regiment and control the working class. They were fake "unions", anti-union "unions", anti-working class "workers' organisations".

Those who tried to set up independent workers' organisations in the Stalinist states were persecuted and repressed. Workers who protested against the ban on Solidarnosc were shot down in the streets.

During the miners' strike we had the anomaly of people rightly protesting at the "police state" aspects of Tory class warfare, simultaneously backing the vastly greater police state repression of people like themselves in Poland!

The Polish state sent scab coal to Britain for a commercial price; and Solidarnosc miners sent messages of support to the NUM. Apart from a few protests — Scargill said "I owe Lech Walesa an apology" — this taught Scargill and the NUM leaders nothing: during the strike, Arthur Scargill pushed ahead towards the creation of a new international miners' federation whose main components were Stalinist police state unions — and the National Union of Mineworkers!

The first half of the eighties produced a strong surge of leftist support for Russia. After the Russian invasion of Czechoslovakia in 1968 to suppress Alexander Dubcek's "socialism with a human face", many on the left had grown very critical of the "socialist" USSR and taken to seeing it as one of the two great pillars of world reaction. With the "second cold war" triggered by the Russian invasion of Afghanistan at Christmas 1979, many leftists were thrown back to "support" for the Russian Stalinist state "against imperialism". Independent working class politics was subverted in large parts of the left. Many working-class militants who wanted to "tear the head off capitalism" were disoriented enough, and politically backward enough, to support the Russians.

Most of the Trotskyist organisations backed the Russians. Socialist Organiser was the only organisation in the entire "orthodox Trotskyist" political spectrum that condemned the Russian invasion and called for the troops to be withdrawn.

The confusion on the left about Stalinism created great difficulties for Socialist Organiser. For us the first principle was the liberty and political independence of the working class everywhere. We had to combine necessary criticism of Scargill and his friends in their capacity of Stalinists with whole-hearted support for them in their capacity of heroic fighters in Britain. We encountered considerable hostility.

To give an example from my own experience at the time, one of the rowdiest labour movement meetings I've ever attended was a debate I had in Edinburgh soon after the Russian invasion with a pro-USSR Labour MP, Ron Brown. He was an honest but politically foolish man who thought that Leonid Brezhnev and Colonel Gaddafi — and probably Saddam Hussein — were socialists. Just back from Afghanistan, he was keen to report that the Russians were doing great work there, and were very popular.

It was a Saturday afternoon at the end of some miners' gala or conference, and a big proportion of the large meeting were miners, many of them bevvied-up. The meeting was overwhelmingly pro-Russian and very hostile to those who denounced Russia's invasion of Afghanistan. Most of them would have been Labour Party people. To the loud approval of much of the meeting Brown praised the Russian leaders for sending tanks to Kabul. I attracted fierce abuse and much interruption when I argued that we should condemn the invasion and call on the Russians to get out of Afghanistan. "The Yanks are against the Russians, so is Margaret Thatcher, so is the CIA — and so are you".

I'd taken part in open-air mass meetings of dock workers in Manchester. Noisy, sometimes conflict-ridden affairs in which a more genteel outsider would have seen imminent violence where there was none. At a number of points I thought the Edinburgh meeting was about to break up in violent disorder. The supporters of the Russians in Afghanistan would certainly have won the vote had we had one.

This large Scottish labour movement meeting was not all that unrepresentative of opinion on the left then. Many people who called themselves socialists thought "defending nationalised property" more important than the right of the Polish workers' movement Solidarnosc to exist.

The most distressing thing about that Edinburgh meeting was who and what these angry supporters of Russian imperialism's colonial war in Afghanistan were, and the tragic gap between what in reality they were supporting and what they thought they were supporting by backing the Stalinist dictator Brezhnev.

These were some of the best people in our movement then. But they were hopelessly disoriented. Politically they had no future.

**Sean Matgamna, July 2014**

# 1. Solidarnosc is not dead

By the beginning of September 1980 the workers of Poland had won a victory unique in history. They had forced a ruling Stalinist bureaucracy, behind which stood the tanks of the rulers of the USSR, to concede to the working class the right to have its own free trade unions, independent of state control.

Short of calling in the Russian army to do to the Poles what it did to the Hungarians in 1956, the Polish bureaucracy had no choice but to make this concession. But in fact they only beat a tactical retreat to prepare a murderous counter-offensive.

The existence of independent working-class organisations was then and always will be incompatible with the Stalinist system. If workers can organise freely then they inevitably question the perks and privileges of the corrupt ruling bureaucrats. They begin to demand democratic control, they question and oppose the way the ruling bureaucrats run the economy. Stalinist rule and independent working-class organisations cannot coexist together for more than a short transitional period: that was the lesson of history — most recently of Czech liberalisation in 1968 which led the Russians to invade. But the leaders of Solidarnosc thought it was possible for them to carve out a new path of long-term coexistence with the bureaucracy on the basis of "moderation" and "compromise" with the Catholic church — tolerated in Poland as an independent power after 1956 — acting as honest broker between the government and Solidarnosc.

It was a fatal mistake. Why did they make it?

Because of the fear of a Russian invasion. What the striking workers in August 1980 wanted was to tear the head off the Stalinist system.

They had the power and the will to do it. What the workers at Gdansk created was a great Soviet — a workers' parliament — the most democratic ever known in Poland — which by its very existence found itself contesting with the government for power in society.

That's what the government said was happening, and essentially, they were right about that. Had the strike movement developed according to its own logic and according to the wishes of the vast majority of workers then they would have displace the government and smashed up all its apparatus of corrupt administration and repression and all the ties that bind Poland as an unfree satellite to the USSR.

They didn't do it because of the memory of the invasion of Czechoslovakia in 1968 and of the bloody repression of the Hungarians in 1956 — where the workers went on a general strike after the street fighting was over and had to be driven out of the factories by the invaders. That memory hung like a nightmare over Poland in August 1980. When the Polish bureaucrats repeatedly warned of the danger of "provoking their friends" across the border. It was no idle threat.

And so the resurgent workers' Poland which had something very close to control of Poland in August 1980 downgraded itself and tried to function as a trade union. It had spectacular success. Soon 10 million workers had joined the new union, Solidarnosc, and the official Polish state union shrivelled to an empty bureaucratic skin.

But in fact Solidarnosc was always much more than a popular mass opposition movement. Where opposition political parties were banned, it inevitably played the role of a political opposition.

Tragically it held to the perspective of indefinite coexistence with the Stalinist system. The alternative was insurrection and, as the only alternative to being isolated before an inevitable Russian invasion, an attempt to spread the movement to the other oppressed nations in Eastern Europe and to the working class in the USSR itself. And in August 1980, Solidarnosc had decided against that perspective and demobilised.

By December 1981 the Polish bureaucrats had made their preparations and then they struck. Martial law was declared. Thousands of Solidarnosc activists rounded up and interned. Strikes broke out, but the repression proved effective, partly because of the "moderating" role of the Catholic church hierarchy which, from August 1980 until today, has consistently strengthened its own position and its modus vivendi with the Stalinist bureaucracy.

And that's how the Polish bureaucrats are in a position to send scab coal to Britain to help break the miners' strike and the heroic Silesian coal miners — some of whom were shot dead in December 1981 — are too repressed by Jaruzelski's police state to do more than send messages of solidarity to British miners.

But Solidarnosc is not dead. It lives in the underground. The Polish workers movement will rise again — nothing is more certain than that. The message spelled out to the bureaucrats in the 1980 strikes is still true and clear, despite the terrible blows and setbacks our Poland has suffered: your time of lording it over the working class like bloated capitalists hasn't much longer to run. Your days are numbered.

*Socialist Organiser*, **1984**

# 2. British workers and the Stalinist state "unions"

In August 1980, the Polish working class kicked aside the police-state "unions" that had helped shackle them for a third of a century. In mass strikes and workplace sit-ins they re-created a real workers' movement in Poland, Solidarnosc.

Throughout the bitter and dangerous month-long struggle of the Polish workers to win the right to have free and self-governing trade unions, the British TUC maintained friendly contact and cooperation with the strike-breaking government unions. Even when millions of Polish workers had repudiated them, the TUC continued to recognise the anti-working-class police-state "unions" as genuine labour organisations.

In the middle of the 10 million strong August 1980 strike movement the TUC stubbornly refused to call off a scheduled visit of its delegates to Poland as guests of the scab unions which were doing their best to help the Government beat down the insurgent workers. In the event the visit was called off by the Poles.

In Russia, the only real trade unions we know of are those in which Vladimir Klebanov is a militant (though there may well exist other underground workers' organisations). The official Russian trade unions are no more trade unions than were the official trade unions in Poland against which the workers revolted. They are a police-state Labour Front apparatus for controlling and policing the working class and for preventing real trade unions and an independent working class movement developing.

It is to preserve the monopoly of these misnamed "trade unions" that working-class militants like Klebanov, and no doubt many others whose names we don't know, are tortured and murdered in the USSR and the other Stalinist states.

But the official British labour movement, from Bill Sirs on the right, who openly defended his "colleagues", the strike-breaking Polish "trade union" leaders, during the strikes of August 1980, to Alex Kitson and Mick McGahey on the left, large sections of the British labour movement indulge in the pretence that the official trade unions in the Stalinist states are real working-class organisations. This endorsement of the Stalinist great lie that they are real unions is scandalous and intolerable.

It says everything about the nature of these unions that their present leader in the USSR was transferred to this post from his previous job as head of the secret political police, which tortures, jails, and kills the militants of the real trade unions, such as Vladimir Klebanov. He moved from the general organisation for controlling and repressing the population to a specialised trade union sub-section, dealing directly with the working class.

During the August 1980 strike movement, the then chairman of the Polish trade unions, Jan Sydlak, was one of the most outspoken and vicious of the bureaucrats in threatening the strikers and their helpers with tanks and slaughter. He called publicly for them to be "taught a lesson they would never forget".

It is not just that many bureaucrats of our trade unions have a real feeling of fellowship with the ruling Stalinist bureaucrats — though obviously they do. Not just that many left wing officials are of a generally Stalinist persuasion — as are Kitson and McGahey.

The reason why they get away with it is that many rank and file militants, too, don't want to come out against the "trade unions" in the Stalinist states and against the British trade union leaders who aid those police-state "unions". Many who consider themselves anti-Stalinist revolutionaries take the same view.

They would feel uncomfortable at having to say on this question something like what Margaret Thatcher and [right-wing electrician's union leader] Frank Chapple say. This is understandable, but it is a really trivial consideration in a situation where the workers of the Stalinist states need our moral and practical support. We have a duty as basic as not crossing a picket line to give it to them.

As people who believe, with Marx and Engels, that the emancipation of the working class can only be achieved by the working class itself, we support any independent workers' movement against the Stalinist police state.

Some in the labour movement believe that contact with the "institutions" of the states in the Stalinist bloc is a force for peace ("peaceful coexistence") and against war. If that view encourages the pretence (and the facts are too well known today to make such an attitude other than pretence) that the Stalinist states are not savagely oppressive; if it leads to ignoring the fact that the "trade unions" there (and most other social institutions as well) have nothing in common with things of the same name in Britain; if it blinds us to the fact that they are "anti-unions" and "counter-unions" rather than working-class organisations — then it amounts to a craven siding with the oppressors against the oppressed in those states.

That a real labour movement should exist is much more important than any social transformations achieved apart from and against the working class.

Yet some militants believe that socialists should refrain from stark denunciation of the Stalinist regimes because they are relatively progressive. They recoil from the demand that the British workers' movement should cut all links with the Stalinist labour fronts. [The Mandelite Fourth International British paper] *Socialist Challenge*, which, in general favours self-governing trade unions in the Stalinist states, nevertheless supported the planned visit of the TUC's delegation to Poland last summer. Earlier it backed a controversial TUC invitation to the Russian political policeman who heads the Stalinist labour front in the USSR to visit them in Britain.

Why? It was probably connected to the bourgeois anti-USSR propaganda outcry in both cases. Yet something fundamental was involved, compared with which all that was unimportant: the attitude we try to get our own labour movement to take to the struggle of our class in the Stalinist states, and to their oppressors.

Our work must be to fight for international working-class solidarity with the real labour movements in the Stalinist states, or with their pioneers, like Klebanov.

To fudge that class issue, worse still, to argue that our movement should have and maintain links with the anti-unions of the Stalinist states, with part of the apparatus that oppresses our people there, is to do the opposite of the work of Trotskyists.

To refuse to call the Stalinists what they are for fear of chiming in with the reactionaries, and to endorse the links our own union bureaucrats maintain with the Stalinist "unions", is to adopt the stance of those Friends of the Soviet Union who called Trotsky a reactionary for speaking out against Stalinist repression in the 30s.

In practice, it leaves the issue of the workers' movement in the Stalinist states to the trade union rightists, like Frank Chapple. It helps keep many good militants entrenched in ignorant Stalinist or semi-Stalinist opposition to what Chapple and Thatcher say they support, because they support it. It amounts to playing Pontius Pilate with the affairs of our own class in the Stalinist states.

Trotsky would turn in his grave at the notion that attitudes such as those of *Socialist Challenge* have anything to do with the politics he fought and died for.

In most respects the USSR is the opposite of the ideal socialists strive for. Its collectivism has more in common with the caricature evoked by enemies of socialism like von Hayek than with what socialists want to achieve.

Trotsky took sides — and tried to get the international labour movement, whatever its given political coloration at that moment, to take sides — squarely with the workers of the USSR (and with the oppressed nations within the USSR, like the Ukrainians) against the totalitarian regime. He never allowed the need to distance himself from the imperialist and pro-imperialist critics of the USSR to determine what he said about conditions in the Stalinist state. The Russian reality and the duty to tell the truth to the labour movement determined that.

He did not hesitate to classify things and name them according to what they were. For the last three years of his life, at least, he insistently repeated his belief that "Stalin's political regime does not differ [from that in fascist countries] save in more unbridled savagery" (*The Death Agony of Capitalism, the Transitional Programme of the Fourth International*, 1938).

Nor is it any different today, 40 years after an agent of that regime struck Trotsky down.

A major psychological reason why there is reluctance to call things like the Russian "trade unions" by their proper names is probably the fear of thereby praising by implication the regime which our movement in the non-Stalinist states exists to fight — that of "liberal" capitalism. There is a subconscious reluctance to face the facts about the Stalinist regimes because those regimes are so terrible compared with the present political regimes in the historically privileged advanced capitalist countries. Of course, horror at the reality of the Stalinist regimes has in the last four or five decades led many one-time revolutionary socialists to a "reconciliation" with "liberal" capitalism.

But the choice is not confined to either Thatcher or Reagan, or Brezhnev and [East German ruler Eric] Honecker: there is also the possibility of a working-class socialist democracy.

Capitalism periodically ravages the lives of working class people with slumps and wars, and is now ravaging the lives of over two million working class families in Britain alone.

In many areas of the world it imposes its own forms of dictatorship. In social crises like Britain's present crisis it has time and again resorted to savage repression. It is now attempting, as yet in a limited way, to tie our own unions to the state. Now less than ever before is there a basis for any labour movement reconciliation with capitalism or its advocates.

Irreconcilable working-class and socialist opposition to our main enemy at home cannot be stable, or politically serious, if it is based on anything other than a clear and independent working-class view of the world, and on the experience of all the struggles of the working class throughout the world.

We must not block out of our consciousness a proper awareness of what our class faces under the Stalinist regimes, or mollify and console ourselves with half-conscious assumptions that the totalitarian Stalinist regimes are really not so bad to those they deprive of civil rights and personal and group autonomy. Or pretend that they are not really dripping with the blood of workers and others who have dared to stand out against them.

They do really drip with workers' blood.

The inspiring rebirth of a labour movement in Poland highlights the situation in the other Stalinist states. It highlights and underlines what our responsibilities are in this situation.

We must actively support the workers in Russia and in the other Stalinist states, and that means opposing their oppressors in every way we can. It means rousing the anger, the hatred, and the active hostility of the labour movement against them.

It is, to repeat, as basic as not crossing a picket line. And as basic as the attitude one takes to those who do.

***Workers' Action*** **(a predecessor of *Socialist Organiser*), March 1981**

# 3. 1983: Arthur Scargill and Solidarnosc

When the press bays at Arthur Scargill the best rule is to support him first and ask questions later. Scargill is not only the best trade union leader in Britain. That is not difficult. He is a consistent advocate of class struggle politics. He was a leader in some of the most important struggles of the 70s.

In Britain right now he advocates policies the labour movement needs if it is not to be beaten into the ground by the Tory offensive. It would be more just to criticise Scargill for reckless wildness and ultra-leftism than for any of the usual vices of the average dim, gutless, time-serving British trade union leader.

The press is now attacking Arthur Scargill for the National Union of Mineworkers' decision to send five miners to Moscow on a trade union course, and for Scargill's attempt to set up a new world mineworkers' federation that will include the police state unions in the Stalinist states.The NUM Conference has endorsed Scargill's initiative for this new world miners' federation.

Questions do need to be asked, in plain and blunt language. And they need to be answered.

Arthur Scargill has denounced Solidarnosc, the only genuine trade union in any Stalinist state. He attacked it at a recent Communist Party rally. He supports its suppression. The NUM has accepted the official Russian explanation of why trade unionist Vladimir Klebanov is imprisoned, like many other dissidents, in a mental hospital — that he is insane!

This attitude to the workers in the Stalinist states is a scandal. It is a betrayal of the interests of the international working class.

International trade union unity is a great good. The problem is that there is no such thing as a real trade union in any of the Stalinist states except Poland. The problem with sending British miners on a trade union course in Moscow is that the last real trade unions in Russia disappeared five or six decades ago. The "unions" there are organs of the state to control and repress the workers. Strikes and all independent working class activity are forbidden.

The real trade unionists, like Vladimir Klebanov, are harassed, jailed, and tortured for trying to create genuine trade unions. After the experience of Solidarnosc there is no good ground for anyone in the British labour movement not to understand this. It is not a matter of capitalist press propaganda but well-attested fact.

In 1980 the Polish workers rose in revolt in a mass strike that lasted a month. The official "union" was pushed aside and a real workers' organisation created. In every one of the known working-class struggles in the Stalinist states, the official "unions" have marched behind the tanks and storm-troopers the workers have had to face.

It was so in the East German uprising of 1953, which was triggered by a mass strike of building workers in Berlin; and it was so in Poland in 1980 — during the mass strike the official "union" leaders threatened the strikers: go back to work or we'll have you shot down.

The British labour movement, whose foreign policy has long mirrored that of the ruling class, does need its own independent foreign policy. It must have as one of its central concerns active support for workers everywhere, in the Stalinist states too, to create and maintain their own independent labour movement and to throw off their oppressors, whether they be capitalists or Stalinist bureaucrats.

Arthur Scargill says he wants to put an end to Cold War divisions. That can't be done by pretending that there is a labour movement in the Stalinist states.

In his "foreign policy", Arthur Scargill adopts the viewpoint of the anti-working-class ruling bureaucracy in Moscow. He accepts their viewpoint where it is most murderously at odds with our interests — where they suppress and systematically destroy independent working class organisations, as in Poland, where striking miners have been shot down.

Working class solidarity is the most basic notion of even the most primitive of labour movements. Even the right wing pays lip service to it for countries like Chile.

It is left to some of the better sections of the left to deny it where, in the Stalinist states, one-third of the world's people, and a working class which is among the most oppressed in the world, are concerned.

Miners shouldn't stand for it. Scargill's militancy and anti-Toryism, yes! Arthur Scargill's Stalinism — no way!

***Socialist Organiser* editorial, 14 July 1983**

# 4. Workers' solidarity and Solidarnosc

"The slave labour of the Polish miner serves to break the resistance of the British miner. British miners!... in the prevailing conditions of terror, the Polish workers' movement is at present not in a position to undertake protest actions. But you may be certain... that we are in solidarity with you."

These words are addressed to striking British miners from members of Solidarnosc, the banned and outlawed underground Polish trade union movement. They come from the inter-factory network of the Mazowsze region, which includes Warsaw and the surrounding towns.

Silesian miners, some of whose comrades were shot down when they struck in protest against the declaration of martial law in December 1981, broadcast this greeting to British miners over the underground radio in Upper Silesia on 17 June:

"The Underground Provisional Co-ordinating Committee of Solidarnosc miners sends you fraternal greetings and our support and solidarity for your struggle for the right to work... we will do everything possible to support your struggle including in action. The protest we have sent to the Polish government and parliament is an initial measure taken in support of your struggle."

The Stalinist rulers of the Polish police state send cheap coal to help Thatcher and MacGregor beat the miners and starve them back to work. The harassed and persecuted Polish workers' movement sends words of encouragement and solidarity.

The workers in the Mazowsze region send their regrets that they can't take action to support the British miners because they live under police state terror, the Silesian miners, who recently faced the bullets of dictator Jaruzelski's soldiers, keep open the possibility of solidarity action, despite the police state terror.

The voice of the underground Polish labour movement is clear and unequivocal: solidarity with British miners on strike and condemnation of the Polish government for helping Thatcher.

The NUM has placed a picket on the Polish embassy in protest against the sending of strike-breaking Polish coal. But the NUM has yet to come out loud and clear in support of Solidarnosc against General Jaruzelski's police state.

An NUM conference rose on Mick McGahey's suggestion to observe two minutes' silence for miners shot down in December 1981.

But Arthur Scargill has at best been equivocal about Solidarnosc, and has often seemed to take the side of the Polish state against Solidarnosc, because he believes the Polish state to be "socialist".

More recently, however, he was reported as saying in Sheffield that he "owes Lech Walesa an apology".

Arthur Scargill is far and away the best trade union leader in Britain. There has been nobody like him for a very long time. He deserves the respect and support of every militant and socialist in the labour movement.

Scargill's basic error lies in the belief — common in the labour movement — that states like Poland and the USSR are socialist. True, there are no capitalists there. But they have been replaced by greedy, grasping, parasitic, anti-working class bureaucrats who suck the workers' blood and run vicious political dictatorships.

These ruling bureaucrats can tolerate neither the real labour movements, nor the liberties we in Britain have won over centuries of struggle with the ruling class and are now defending against Thatcher, not any form of democratic accountability.

In these states it is especially the workers who are ruthlessly kept down. Sometimes, as in Poland, some intellectuals and priests can sometimes have a degree of freedom. But never the workers.

In all the Stalinist states the "unions" are rigidly controlled state agencies for controlling and regimenting the workers and for preventing — with the additional help of police repression — workers organising a real labour movement.

Take the recent experience of Poland, for example.

Solidarnosc was created in a great wave of strikes during the summer of 1980 which culminated in a general strike.

Polish workers rejected the official police state "unions". In Britain, union leaders frequently scab and rat on us: in Poland in 1980 the official police state "union" threatened to have his members shot down. It was no idle threat. An unknown number of workers were shot down in Gdansk shipyards when they went on strike in 1970.

But in 1980 there were too many to shoot down. Poland was paralysed. The working class organised their own "parliament", centred on Gdansk. It was the most democratic parliament ever seen in Poland, and a lot more representative and democratic than what we have now in Britain.

The Polish workers wanted to overthrow the Stalinist dictatorship, but not to replace the bureaucratic parasites with capitalist parasites — that is a lie spread by the Stalinists.

Why didn't they overthrow it? Because of the threat of Russian invasion like the invasion of Hungary in 1956 and of Czechoslovakia in 1968. For Poland, like the other "socialist states" in East Europe, is not really independent but a Russian dependency. So they compromised.

They scaled down the great workers' liberation movement of mid-1980 and tried to turn it into a trade union. The scared and helpless Polish bureaucracy signed "a solemn and binding" agreement to respect and recognise the union — Solidarnosc.

Of course Solidarnosc was always more than a union. In a muted way it played the role of a workers' political party defending the interests of the working class.

But the Polish bureaucrats recovered their nerve, made their preparations and struck back. Martial law was declared in December 1981 and Solidarnosc outlawed. Its leaders and activists were rounded up and interned. Solidarnosc went underground.

As dictatorships go, Poland even now is a great deal less airtight and less repressive than, for example, the USSR.

Some opposition is still tolerated. But they have tried to do to the Polish labour movement what fascist regimes do to the labour movement in capitalist countries. For the Stalinist bureaucrats the workers' movement is the main enemy.

This is not socialism, nor anything like it. Our people in Poland are not the "socialist" bureaucrats but the oppressed workers whose organisation is Solidarnosc.

Any differences we, as trade unionists or socialists, might have with Solidarnosc, or parts of it, or with its leaders, or with some of them, are like differences within the British labour movement. Just as we would defend any part of the labour movement against the ruling class and its state, regardless of our differences with that part of the labour movement, so, too, we should defend Solidarnosc against the Stalinist police state.

Solidarnosc is the Polish labour movement. Its right to exist — and even its right to make what we might think were mistakes — overrides every other consideration in Poland.

In fact the stories that Solidarnosc wants to restore capitalism are Stalinist lies. Its leaders are tremendous working class fighters. The Polish strikes of 1980 are amongst the most important events in the history of the history of the working class of the world. A man like Lech Walesa, in his own way, is the Arthur Scargill of Poland.

Miners owe a debt of solidarity to the persecuted Polish labour movement.

NUM militants must see to it that the union throws its full support behind Solidarnosc and against the bureaucratic dictatorship. The NUM should back the persecuted pioneers of independent labour movements in the USSR and other Stalinist states, like the late Vladimir Klebanov, who recently died in captivity in the USSR.

The message from Warsaw states the principle involved very well:

"We strongly oppose every case where force is used against workers struggling for their rights and interests."

The British labour movement must support other workers against police state oppression wherever it occurs; whether in Chile, South Africa and El Salvador, or in the USSR, Poland and Cuba.

*Socialist Organiser* **191, 9 August 1984**

# 5. Workers' unity, East and West

**Why we should back Solidarnosc despite Fleet Street's effort to use Lech Walesa against the miners**

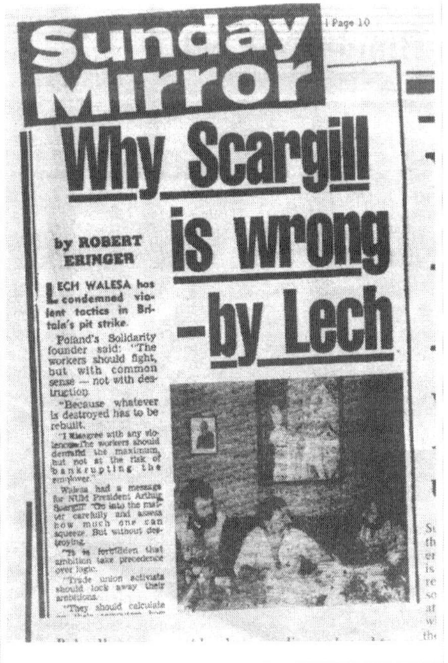

Sunday Mirror

Page 10

**Why Scargill is wrong — by Lech**

by ROBERT ERINGER

LECH WALESA has condemned violent tactics in Britain's pit strike.

Poland's Solidarity founder said: "The workers should fight, but with common sense — not with destruction.

"Because whatever is destroyed has to be rebuilt.

"I disagree with any violence. The workers should demand the maximum, but not at the risk of bankrupting the employer."

Walesa had a message for NUM President Arthur Scargill: "Go into the matter carefully and assess how much one can squeeze. But without destroying.

"It is forbidden that ambition take precedence over logic.

"Trade union activists should lock away their ambitions.

"They should calculate

Poland's government has been sending scab coal to Britain, while Solidarnosc has declared support for the NUM. But some people on the left are using a *Sunday Mirror* report that Lech Walesa attacked Arthur Scargill to justify their hostility to Solidarnosc.

The *Sunday Mirror* some weeks ago printed an account of an interview by Robert Eringer with Solidarnosc leader Lech Walesa in which Walesa appeared to side with Margaret Thatcher against the miners. The *Sunday Mirror* headlined Eringer's piece "Why Scargill is wrong — by Lech".

Quite a lot of Solidarnosc's friends in Britain were shocked and its opponents, semi-opponents and outright enemies, of whom there are a very large number in the British labour movement, seized on the article. It is cited again and again by labour movement activists to condemn Solidarnosc.

What did Walesa say? That is less clear than the *Sunday Mirror*'s headline suggests but I will quote the *Sunday Mirror*.

After an opening sentence by the interviewer (or the sub-editor in the *Sunday Mirror* office), "Lech Walesa has condemned violent tactics in Britain's pit strike", Walesa is quoted as saying:

"The miners should fight, but with common sense, not with destruction. Because whatever is destroyed has to be rebuilt.

"I disagree with any violence. The workers should demand the maximum, but not at the risk of bankrupting the employer."

The interviewer (or sub-editor) introduces another quote like this: "Walesa had a message for Arthur Scargill". This is the "message": "Go into the matter carefully and assess how much one can squeeze. But without destroying.

"It is forbidden that ambition takes precedence over hope.

"Trade union activists should lock away their ambitions.

"They should calculate on their computers how much they can get but, I repeat, not at the sake (sic) of destroying the structure."

Eringer then says that Walesa expressed "much respect" for Margaret Thatcher and quotes him: "With such a wise and brave woman, Britain will find a solution to the strike."

I have cited all the direct quotes attributed to Walesa about the miners' strike and about Thatcher.

Now it is by no means impossible that Walesa would condemn trade union "violence" or produce this rather vapid philosophising on realistic trade unionism. And he may well think Margaret Thatcher is wise and brave because of her strident rhetoric against the USSR, Poland's overlord.

These views would identify him as right wing or soft left if he operated in the British labour movement.

But for many on the left it isn't a matter of disagreeing with Walesa. They question Solidarnosc's right to exist. They adopt a soft, tolerant or even friendly attitude to the Jaruzelski regime which is trying to destroy the Polish independent trade union.

The refusal of the Communist Party's *Morning Star* to print a paid ad or a letter condemning Jaruzelski for sending scab coal to Britain is one measure of the state of the British labour movement on this question: the *Morning Star* was clearly confident that it would not suffer for this implicit solidarising with Jaruzelski against the miners.

In an interview in last week's *Socialist Organiser,* Tony Benn responded to a question about Polish scab coal by asking: "But what about Walesa supporting Thatcher?" And Benn didn't sign the letter to the *Morning Star.*

So Walesa may have made a few Neil Kinnock-like comments to the *Sunday Mirror* criticising miners' violence and Arthur Scargill's ambition. The conclusion does not follow that Jaruzelski, who gives Thatcher scab coal, was therefore justified in banning the Polish trade unions and attempting to destroy them!

Eric Heffer MP was right when he said in *Socialist Organiser* two weeks ago: "The entire movement in this country should have given Solidarnosc total support. Free trade unions [in Poland] would not have allowed coal to come in now."

In any case, whatever Walesa might say against "violence" or against Arthur Scargill is irrelevant to the right of the Polish workers' movement to exist. Our duty to defend its right to exist cannot depend on the opinions of one of its leaders — or of Solidarnosc itself.

There are many in our own unions and in the Labour Party who condemn the miners and would like to cut Arthur Scargill's throat. We denounce them of course and we organise against them. Only a suicidal maniac would conclude that trade unions, because they are led by Eric Hammond or John Lyons or David Basnett, forfeit their right to exist. Yet that is the underlying idea of those who pounce on Walesa's interview and say "We told you so" about Solidarnosc.

Walesa is quoted saying things against a section of the British labour movement — therefore it is right for the Stalinist dictatorship to destroy the Polish labour movement? It is preposterous.

Solidarnosc is a great working class mass movement, which had ten million members when it was outlawed in December 1981, 18 months after coming into being.

It is a unique movement. Never before have independent trade unions emerged in any Stalinist state.

Such a movement will span an immense range of opinions as ours does. The 11 million strong British labour movement has Labour Party right wingers, Liberals, SDPers, Tories, racists, some fascists and... Stalinist supporters of foreign anti-working class dictatorships like Jaruzelski's.

Our movement, unlike Solidarnosc's, is led by a quite distinct caste of materially privileged bureaucrats. We propose to change it politically, reconstruct it, democratise it, not help the "reforming" Tories put it down.

Nor can it make any difference that industry is nationalised in Poland and Jaruzelski can perhaps claim to defend nationalised property.

For socialists, nationalisation is a means to an end, not the end: the end is socialism. The liberation of the working class from capitalist exploitation and from state tyranny.

Nationalisation is necessary for socialism, but it is not socialism, nor the only condition for socialism.

In the Stalinist states nationalised property is controlled by privileged bureaucrats, by means of state tyranny over the people unparalleled in history.

The Polish labour movement was born in conflict with a state tyranny much of whose power over society comes from the state's control of the means of production.

Suppose that movement were, in reaction against Stalinism, to advocate restoring capitalism — though Solidarnosc did not do that — even that could not lead working class socialists to side with a Jaruzelski standing for nationalisation and "socialism" against "counter-revolution".

Real socialism which liberates the working class, and therefore society, from both exploitation and state tyranny, can only be created by the working class itself, acting in freedom.

The Polish labour movement, even were it making terrible errors, is a great deal more important to socialism than is nationalised property under the control of a tyrannical bureaucracy, parasitic on the labour of the workers, and holding them in a police-state vice. The right of the labour movement to live, its ability to grow and to discuss its experience and its programme for society — nothing in Poland, or in any of the Stalinist states, has a greater value than that, for socialists who base themselves on the first letter of the socialist alphabet, formulated by Karl Marx as follows:

"The emancipation of the working class must be the act of the workers themselves".

Many oppositionists in East Europe and the USSR, and probably Walesa, do have a friendly attitude to people like Thatcher and Reagan because they are strident enemies of the Kremlin. Their attitude is: my enemy's enemy is my friend.

For a Walesa that is shortsighted and based on a fundamental misunderstanding.

Thatcher and Reagan may say kind things about Solidarnosc because it is opposed to the Kremlin, but they are hostile to their own "Solidarnoscs" and use the law and the police against them.

Like the Kremlin bureaucrats, in fact, who try to use the labour movements in the West while stamping on the workers in their own domain.

Oppositionists in the East who favour the West are merely a mirror image of those workers in capitalist society who adopt a friendly attitude to the Stalinist dictatorships. Our Stalinists and quasi-Stalinists see only everything negative in the West and think nationalised property is working class socialism in the East. So they favour the East.

The oppositionists in the East see that there is personal freedom in the West, the right of the workers to organise trade unions and political parties and to publish more or less what they like, the rule of law in contrast to the arbitrary state tyranny in the Stalinist states — so they idealise the West,

Both views are one-sided and false: indeed, the easterners' view is probably less one-sided and less false than that of the Stalinist workers in the West.

It is no small difference, after all, that in the advanced capitalist countries we have won the right — through centuries of struggle — to organise freely, while everywhere in the east the workers are subjected to a savage repression which nips in the bud every stirring of independent working class activity and jails or kills its organisers.

It is easy to understand why the eastern oppositionists and especially the fighters for free trade unions in a Stalinist state might idealise the advanced capitalist countries. They shouldn't, of course.

We who live in a country like Britain know how hollowed-out much of the freedom and democracy is, where the multi-millionaires rule, backed by an anti-working class state. We know that the workers are savagely exploited under capitalism and have to fight every inch of the way, as the miners are having to fight now.

If Walesa were really to attack the miners and Scargill, he would only be parallelling the attitude Scargill has adopted to Solidarnosc. In fact it is highly improbable that Walesa would not protest if the Tory government banned the TUC and jailed thousands of militants.

According to the *Sunday Mirror* Walesa attacked miners' "violence". But large sections of the British labour movement, including Scargill, have attacked Solidarnosc's very right to exist. They failed even to protest when it was banned, and they told British workers that Jaruzelski represented socialism in Poland and the Polish labour movement was counter-revolutionary.

Scargill's hostile comments on Solidarnosc will have been used by the Polish media against Solidarnosc just as the *Mirror* used the Walesa interview against the miners.

Scargill said at a meeting in Sheffield a couple of months ago: "I think I owe Lech Walesa an apology".

In any case, he owes Lech Walesa and Solidarnosc basic working class solidarity.

I read somewhere that back in the middle ages, when landlords and priests oppressed peasants and enslaved serfs, lots of peasants worshipped the devil. They reasoned that since the Christian god was the god of their oppressors, and the devil was his enemy, they had better side with the devil.

Rebels and oppositionists in the east and west today too often approach the east-west division of the world into capitalist and Stalinist camps in that spirit.

Instead of such ideas we need independent working-class politics east and west. Workers, east and west, should support each other against the oppression of both the capitalist and Stalinist systems. We need consistent international working class solidarity.

For the British labour movement that must mean:

• Active support for Solidarnosc.

• Support for free trade unions in all the Stalinist states and for those trying to organise them.

• Break off "fraternal" contact between the TUC unions and the police-state fake unions which exist in the Stalinist states.

***Socialist Organiser* 200, 11 October 1984**
**(This article was reprinted in the Polish underground socialist press)**

## True and right

When Scargill said the pits would close,
He said it true and right.
That's when true men like my dad and friends
Stood up to win this fight.

MacGregor came and said that all
Scargill told was lies.
But all MacGregor ever does is
Listen to Maggie's cries.

The working miners of today
Don't seem to understand
That they mustn't whatsoever
Join Maggie's merry band

So strikers whereever you are
Stay out till victory day.
And to you MacGregor and Maggie
You've got a lot of debts to pay.

**Jacqueline Cooper (15)**